THE MIRACLES OF MARY IN
TWELFTH-CENTURY FRANCE

THE MIRACLES
OF MARY IN
TWELFTH-CENTURY
FRANCE

TRANSLATED AND INTRODUCED
BY BRUCE L. VENARDE

CORNELL UNIVERSITY PRESS
Ithaca and London

First published 2024 by Cornell University Press

Library of Congress Cataloging-in-Publication Data

Names: Venarde, Bruce L., 1962– translator, writer of introduction. | Herman, of Tournai, active 12th century. Miracula sanctae Mariae Laudunensis. English. | Hugo Farsitus, approximately 1073-1143. Libellus de miraculis beatae Mariae Virginis in urbe Suessionensi. English. | Haimo, Abbot of Saint-Pierre-sur-Dives, -1148. Litterae ad fratres Totesburiae. English. | John (Son of Peter), active 12th century. Miracula ecclesiae Constantiensis. English. | Gautier, de Compiègne, active 12th century. De miraculis beate virginis Mariae. English. | Hugo Farsitus, approximately 1073-1143. Otium. Selections. English. | Herman, of Tournai, active 12th century. Vita sancti Hildefonsi. English. | Guibert, Abbot of Nogent-sous-Coucy, 1053-approximately 1124. De laude sanctae Mariae. Selections. English. | Guibert, Abbot of Nogent-sous-Coucy, 1053-approximately 1124. De vita sua. Selections. English.
Title: The miracles of Mary in twelfth-century France / translated and introduced by Bruce L. Venarde.
Description: Ithaca : Cornell University Press, 2024. | Includes bibliographical references and index.
Identifiers: LCCN 2024018161 (print) | LCCN 2024018162 (ebook) | ISBN 9781501778421 (hardcover) | ISBN 9781501778438 (paperback) | ISBN 9781501778452 (epub) | ISBN 9781501778445 (pdf)
Subjects: LCSH: Mary, Blessed Virgin, Saint—Apparitions and miracles—France. | Mary, Blessed Virgin, Saint—Devotion to—France—History—To 1500. | Civilization, Medieval—12th century.
Classification: LCC BT652.F8 M57 2024 (print) | LCC BT652.F8 (ebook) | DDC 232.91/7094409021—dc23/eng/20240604
LC record available at https://lccn.loc.gov/2024018161
LC ebook record available at https://lccn.loc.gov/2024018162

For Jack, and still no wonder

Contents

PREFACE

This book offers translations of the first five surviving collections of miracles worked through Mary, the mother of Jesus, written in France. The authors—Herman of Tournai, Hugh Farsit, Haimo of Saint-Pierre-sur-Dives, John, son of Peter, and Gautier of Compiègne—finished these Latin works in the second quarter of the twelfth century. By that time, Mary had become the most important saint in Christian Europe. These stories tell us something about Mary's cult while offering a vivid panorama of life in the twelfth century at its grimmest and most hopeful. After a general survey of saints, relics, pilgrimages, Mary, miracles, medicine, and miracle collections, plus final notes on terminology and my approach to translation, each collection has its own introduction and notes. There are five appendices. The first is the earliest account of the tragic events in the northern French city of Laon in 1112 that Herman sketches as the background for the miracles he narrates. By coincidence it comes from the pen of Hugh Farsit, writing decades before he recounted miracles that took place in Soissons, about eighteen miles from Laon. The second further illuminates Herman's curiosity and storytelling abilities and includes an appearance by Mary. The next two are earlier versions of some miracles that Herman and Gautier recount written by Guibert of Nogent, an abbot whose monastery of Nogent-sur-Coucy was not far from Laon or Hugh's hometown of Soissons. The last appendix is a handlist of emendations, based on five manuscripts of the twelfth and thirteenth centuries, to the printed editions of Hugh's collection.

ACKNOWLEDGMENTS

Most of the stories in this book are about generosity, mercy, and love. As I wrote, I was the recipient of all three. For help and support of various kinds, I thank Steve Biel, Thomas N. Bisson, Renate Blumenfeld-Kosinski, Robert Dyer, Alessandra Foscati, Alison More, Earl Jeffrey Richards, Emily Steiner, William Turpin, Fred Unwalla, and Jan Ziolkowski: teachers and masters all. In an extraordinary display of fraternal affection, David F. Venarde volunteered to read a draft manuscript on which he provided invaluable commentary. Unfortunately, I cannot name the visionary scholars, librarians, archivists, and technical experts who have made so many manuscript reproductions and so much published material available online in the last decade or so. Without their efforts, I quite simply could not have written a book that got its start during the global COVID-19 pandemic. When I began in September 2020, as the plague dragged on and vaccinations were not yet in sight, it was comforting to read about miraculous healings of intractable ailments—even if it took me an embarrassingly long time to make the connection. At first I was only conscious that these fascinating stories reveal much about the lived experience of medieval people, or at least elites' views of it.

It is a real pleasure to return to Cornell University Press after a long absence. Mahinder Kingra generously supported the project from the outset. He furthermore found two splendid peer reviewers, Constance Brittain Bouchard and Nancy Vine Durling, who offered thoughtful and meticulous commentaries that saved me from some embarrassing mistakes. Deborah A. Oosterhouse did me many small favors as copyeditor and Dina Dineva one big favor as indexer. Susan Specter guided the entire production process with patience and good cheer. Gordon Thompson created the handsome maps. I extend my warmest thanks to all of them.

The standard disclaimer about the author's sole responsibility for errors applies.

Trudging through diminished life during a pandemic, I could have had no better companion than my husband, Jack Eckert. Nearly thirty years ago, I dedicated my first book to him "in glad remembrance and joyous prospect." The remembrance is now longer than the prospect, but the joy is undiminished. So, Jack, with all my heart: here's another one for you.

Abbreviations

ca.   circa
d.   died
P   Paris, Bibliothèque nationale de France, MS lat. 12593
P2   Paris, Bibliothèque nationale de France, MS lat. 16565
P3   Paris, Bibliothèque nationale de France, MS lat. 2873
P4   Paris, Bibliothèque nationale de France, MS lat. 17491
P5   Paris, Bibliothèque nationale de France, MS lat. 2333A
PL   *Patrologia cursus completus, Series latina*, ed. J.-P. Migne, 221 vols.
      (Paris: J.-P. Migne, 1844–64)
r.   ruled or reigned
T   Troyes, Médiathèque Jacques Chirac, MS 433

NAMES, DISTANCES, AND PLACE-NAMES

Latin names are generally translated into a modern English equivalent, e.g., "Bartholomew" for *Bartholomeus* (French "Barthélemy"), "Guy" for *Guido* (French "Gui"), and "Ralph" for *Ranulphus* or *Radulphus* (French "Raoul").

Six tables are embedded within the translations. The first two show the distance and trajectory of the relic tours Herman of Tournai describes in Books I and II of *The Miracles of St. Mary of Laon* and a third distances and directions from Laon to the places named in Herman's Book III. For the collections by Hugh Farsit, Abbot Haimo, and John, son of Peter, tables show distances and directions from the churches around which the miracles center. The tables note walking distances derived from Google Maps. Most modern French and English roads overlay very old pathways, so it is likely that the routes were more or less the same as they are today.

Maps show distances as the crow flies, which are shorter than walking itineraries; distances between locations in the introductions and notes follow that system. All distances, whether travel or straight-line, are given in miles, the measure more familiar to most readers. Those better versed in the metric system can multiply miles by 1.6, that is, ten miles is approximately sixteen kilometers. The maps have scales in both miles and kilometers.

To avoid confusion, place-names in the text, tables, and maps reflect modern usage.

THE MIRACLES OF MARY IN
TWELFTH-CENTURY FRANCE

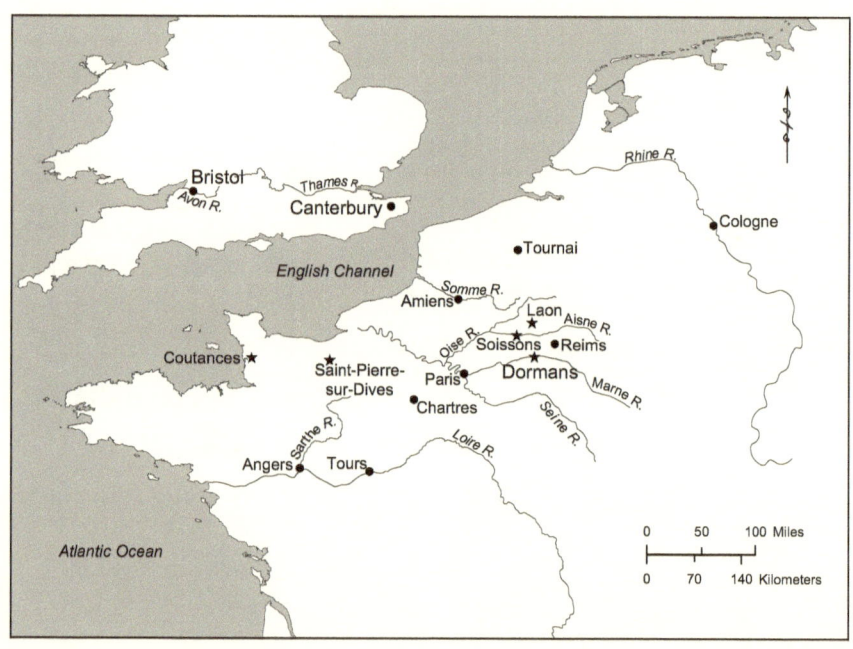

MAP 1. The world of Mary's miracles

General Introduction

Murder in a cathedral, disappearing road-blocks, pirates, a dragon, a brawl about King Arthur, window-shopping clergymen, kleptomania, a footwear ritual, horrifying illnesses and deformities, narrow escapes from injury and death, people dragging carts like draft animals, wondrous lighting effects, an image of the baby Jesus that speaks—the accounts of miracles God worked through the intercession of Jesus's mother Mary gathered in this book provide colorful glimpses into the experiences and beliefs of people from the humble to the mighty. The five collections appeared over approximately two decades, but the authors and, especially, the circumstances that prompted them to write are distinctive.

Herman of Tournai (ca. 1090–ca. 1147) was a monk and former abbot of the monastery of Saint-Martin in his native city of Tournai in what is now southwestern Belgium. He composed *The Miracles of St. Mary of Laon* across several years shortly before he disappears from the historical record in 1146. His collection outlines a long recovery of the northeastern French city of Laon after a violent revolt. Hugh Farsit, about whose biography little is known, lived from the later eleventh to the mid-twelfth century. He spent most of his life in the religious community of Saint-Jean-des-Vignes in Soissons, about eighteen miles from Laon, and wrote *A Little Book of Miracles of the Blessed Virgin Mary in the*

City of Soissons in the mid-1140s. Hugh mostly describes healings by people who suffered from a deadly epidemic in the late 1120s. Haimo (d. 1148) was the abbot of Saint-Pierre-sur-Dives in Normandy, a region of northern France. His letter records miracles that occurred in the year 1145 in and near his monastery. Almost nothing is known about John, son of Peter, who probably lived from the mid- to late eleventh century until the early 1130s. He was a longtime member of the cathedral clergy in Coutances, also in Normandy. He wrote *The Miracles of the Church of Coutances* late in life, probably circa 1130, recalling miraculous events in his city and nearby that went back decades. Lastly, Gautier of Com-piègne (d. ca. 1160), an abbot in the cathedral city of Chartres about fifty miles southwest of Paris, probably wrote his brief *The Miracles of the Blessed Virgin Mary* in the mid-1140s.

All five texts translated here narrate miracles Mary facilitated, but the situations that gave rise to them are varied. Herman of Tournai describes two fund-raising tours. Clergymen who served Laon's cathedral, which had been damaged by fire in the wake of a brutal uprising that included the assassination of Bishop Gaudry in 1112, took relics including some of Mary's hair to western France (in the summer of 1112, Book I) and southern England (in the spring and summer of 1113, Book II). Their purpose was to procure funds necessary for the reconstruction of the church. After describing the rededication of the Laon cathedral in September 1114, eighteen months after the fire, at the start of Book III, Herman proceeds to chronicle a more general religious renewal in the city and diocese of Laon in the decades that followed, carried out under the aegis of his hero Bishop Bartholomew (r. 1113–1151); he seems to consider this one long period of miraculous resurgence. The miracles Hugh Farsit gathers occurred for the most part in the Soissons nunnery dedicated to Mary that housed a Marian relic, her slipper. They occurred amid a public health emergency in northern France during the late 1120s: an outbreak of ergotism, poisoning caused by eating grain or grain products infected with fungus. Hugh seems to have written shortly after the death of the nunnery's abbess Mathilda in 1143, perhaps to commemorate the important events that took place during her time when—although Hugh only alludes to it—the monastery was being rebuilt.

Reconstruction, however, is the central context for Abbot Haimo's account of miracles set during the climactic phase in the decades-long rebuilding of his monastery, destroyed forty years before he wrote in or shortly after 1145; there is no relic involved and there is greater emphasis on nonhealing miracles than in the other four texts. His collection comes in the form of a letter to other monks, meant probably both to inform and to inspire its recipients. John, son of Peter, recounts miracles in a kind of memoir: he describes himself as an old man intent on preserving for posterity a record of miracles in and around his church, many of which he heard about from people now dead. Several of them took place around images of Mary. Strangely, in the middle of his collection John tells us that a Marian relic—another lock of hair, whose authentication is described—was preserved in the cathedral, but he narrates no miracle related to it and it is never mentioned again; the relic was not the focal point of the miracles memorialized. Finally, Gautier of Compiègne provides detailed accounts of four miracles he heard about from the bishop of Chartres, all of them centered on images of Mary.

These five collections are the earliest surviving accounts of Marian miracles written in France. They tell us much about social conditions, religious beliefs and practices, sickness and health, labor, and travel: a panorama of sights, sounds, smells, and human behavior and emotion. I introduce each collection, with more about historical circumstances, the authors, and their writings, in the prefatory commentary to each text. The remainder of this general introduction provides an overview of saints, relics, pilgrimages, Mary, miracles, medicine, and miracle collections, with some bibliographic orientation to these subjects. It aims to give the reader a brief guide to the world in which these miracle collections emerged. The discussion is mostly limited to what is called Roman Christianity, the Western church, or Latin Christendom, the last because its elites' lingua franca was Latin long after it ceased to be anyone's native language in the seventh or eighth century. The remarks here, then, concern primarily western Europe and the western Mediterranean lands with the focus on the central Middle Ages, circa 900 to circa 1200.

Saints, Relics, and Pilgrimages

The first saints in the Christian tradition were the apostles of Jesus, then martyrs, men and women who died for their faith at the hands of Roman officials.[1] From very early in the history of Christianity, the

---

1. Bartlett, *Why Can the Dead Do Such Great Things?* is a massive but very readable survey that synthesizes a vast amount of scholarship and addresses most of the subjects discussed

faithful gathered around martyrs' tombs to commemorate them on the anniversaries of their death, the antecedents of saints' days, also known as feast days. Once Christianity became first a privileged and finally the official religion of the Roman Empire over the course of the fourth century, new sorts of male and female saints emerged, called confessors: ascetics, missionaries (who were sometimes also martyrs), people distinguished for charitable works, ecclesiastical officials, and learned scholars. All were Christian heroes. By the year 400, the Lives (*vitae*) of saints constituted a literary genre. A few such texts became models for later Lives, in particular the *Life of St. Martin* that Sulpicius Severus wrote at the end of the fourth century (when the onetime soldier, hermit, missionary, and finally bishop of Tours in western France was still alive!). The number of people recognized as saints, whether locally, regionally, or by the whole Western church multiplied vastly from the fourth century forward.

Peter Brown describes saints as "the very special dead."[2] They were—and are—considered to have privileged access to God that they use to intercede with him in response to the prayers of the faithful concerning this life and the next. Saints could work to intervene in the natural order, guide events, and help their devotees to attain salvation and eternal life. Christians first worshiped martyrs at simple gravesites but soon built churches to house relics, the visible tokens of invisible power.[3] Relics could be the saint's bodily remains, but also objects associated with them, clothing or other possessions, so-called contact relics, or objects that had touched the relics.

In many cases, shrines sheltered the entire bodies of saints, but from the fourth century, corporeal remains were often divided, so a shrine

---

below. For a brief account of Christian saints from their origins to the modern world, see Yarrow, *The Saints*.

2. Brown, *The Cult of the Saints*, chap. 4, "The Very Special Dead." Despite its focus on the fourth, fifth, and sixth centuries, Brown's book, first published in 1981, remains valuable for its description of the social meaning of saints' cults throughout the Middle Ages and its dismantling of two pervasive ideas: that the cult of saints was merely a new version of ancient Mediterranean polytheism and that it was reluctantly accepted by the intellectuals who led the church.

3. Freeman, *Holy Bones, Holy Dust* is a lively account, although somewhat dismissive of medieval religious beliefs and practices. A more even-handed survey is Bartlett, *Why Can the Dead Do Such Great Things?*, 239–332 (chap. 8, "Relics and Shrines"). On reliquaries, the vessels in which relics were kept, see Hahn, *Strange Beauty*, which covers Christian Europe from the fifth through twelfth centuries. Hahn's *Reliquary Effect* has a longer chronological reach, from the early Middle Ages to the twentieth century, and contains material about non-Christian religious traditions. Both of Hahn's books are gorgeously illustrated.

might have the head, arm, or another piece of a saint's body. This may seem grotesque to many in the twenty-first century, but it was completely ordinary in medieval Europe. The belief was that saints, as living presences on earth as well as in heaven, would not permit any division or transfer of their relics of which they did not approve. Accounts of these transfers, called "translations" (*translationes*), constituted, along with *vitae* and miracle collections, a subgenre within hagiography, writings about saints.[4] Relics and the cult of saints played a vital role in the Christianization of Europe in the early Middle Ages and remained powerful presences, figuratively and literally, thereafter.

The first Christian pilgrimages were travels to holy places, especially Jerusalem, the site of the Crucifixion, and Rome, where there were many martyrs' graves, chief among them those of the apostle Peter, the first pope, and the first-century evangelist Paul, the author of much of the New Testament. But from the fourth century, the faithful traveled to other places where relics resided. Outside Rome, the two most famous pilgrimage sites in medieval Europe were Santiago de Compostela in northwestern Spain and Canterbury in eastern England. Santiago de Compostela, a major pilgrimage site from the tenth century, was thought to be the final resting place of the apostle St. James. Canterbury Cathedral held the grave of St. Thomas Becket, the archbishop assassinated in his cathedral in 1170, which soon began to draw pilgrims from England and beyond. Geoffrey Chaucer's *Canterbury Tales* (1387–1400) narrates stories told by the participants in a fictionalized pilgrimage to Becket's shrine.

Unless the faithful lived nearby, travel to places like Jerusalem, Rome, Compostela, or Canterbury was an expensive, time-consuming, and often dangerous undertaking. Most medieval pilgrims, however, did not need to go far to venerate, pray, or seek healing. The shrines of men and women considered holy dotted the landscape of Latin Christendom; exact figures are impossible to know, but saints numbered in the thousands by the twelfth century.[5] Shrines were far greater in number because saints' bodies were often divided and their noncorporeal relics were also everywhere. For many centuries, saints were homemade, so to speak, canonized by local bishops, frequently spurred by popular

---

4. Geary, *Furta Sacra*.

5. See the synthesis of various attempts to count medieval saints in Bartlett, *Why Can the Dead Do Such Great Things?*, 137–42.

devotion.[6] Most Christians, then, had access to a shrine close at hand. Somewhat unusually for medieval miracle collections, of the five translated here, only Hugh Farsit's concerns pilgrimage to a relic-bearing shrine. Herman of Tournai describes a relic tour, where the relics went to the faithful rather than the other way around. Abbot Haimo describes travel for the benefit of a church, but no relic is involved. Nor are there relic-related miracles in the collections by John of Coutances (known as John, son of Peter) or Gautier of Compiègne, the latter of whom does not mention relics at all.

Mary: A Very Special Saint

As already suggested, not all saints were equal, and many cults had limited, highly localized followings. Some saints, like the archangels Gabriel and Michael and the apostles, were universally recognized. But by the time our five authors were writing, Mary was the most important saint of all.[7] She was everywhere: in prayer, liturgy including several feast days throughout the year, music, painting, sculpture, poetry, biblical commentary, sermons, and miracle collections. Marian relics were housed in churches and cathedrals; the Cistercians, a federation of monks and nuns with origins in the late eleventh century that featured simple, austere living and strict adherence to the Rule of St. Benedict, dedicated all their monastery churches to Mary. As the mother of Jesus, she was considered the greatest intercessor of all, or as an eleventh-century prayer from northern France put it, "Your only begotten son will give you what you want, and you will obtain pardon and glory for whom you want."[8]

But Mary's rise to preeminent status was far from inevitable. First, female saints were a distinct minority in the Middle Ages: men outnumbered women by at least four to one in the ranks of medieval saints.[9] Mary also had to be rescued from obscurity since she is a minor figure

---

6. The first papal declaration of sanctity was not until 993, and bishops continued to canonize saints until the mid-twelfth century. The papal monopoly on canonization coalesced in the early thirteenth century. See Vauchez, *Sainthood in the Later Middle Ages*, 11–57.

7. The literature on the Virgin Mary is vast. An excellent study covering the period from the first decades of Christianity to ca. 1600 is Rubin, *Mother of God*, on which the following paragraphs rely. A vivid feminist account that also considers the modern era is Warner, *Alone of All Her Sex.*

8. Cited in Rubin, *Mother of God*, 132 and n. 45. I have revised Rubin's translation.

9. Bartlett, *Why Can the Dead Do Such Great Things?*, 145–50, summarizes scholarship on sex ratios among medieval and early modern saints. That Mary so dominated the saintly

in the New Testament. Of the four Gospels, only Matthew and Luke provide details of the conception, birth, and infancy of Jesus that feature Mary; Mark mentions her only once. The only gospel that notes Mary's presence at the crucifixion of Jesus is John's. Mary appears one last time as being among the apostles soon after the death of Jesus in Acts of the Apostles 1:14. The letters of St. Paul and the remainder of the New Testament do not mention Mary at all.[10] Not until the mid-second century did writings emerge that discussed her life before the Annunciation, when the angel Gabriel informed Mary that she had been impregnated by the Holy Spirit (Luke 1). Still, she long remained a figure of less interest than martyrs, including women like Perpetua (d. ca. 203), whose mostly autobiographical account of her final days was completed after her brutal public execution in a Roman arena.

Because relics were so central to saints' cults, Mary's presented a problem. Scripture does not discuss her death, but there arose in the early Christian centuries the idea that Mary had not died a human death but was rather bodily assumed into heaven. The Assumption, as it is known, meant that like Jesus, she left no remains on earth. Her relics, then, were few: her clothing, hair, and breast milk were the only ones recognized in late Roman and medieval tradition. Nonetheless, with the rapid rise of Christianity in the fourth century and vigorous debates about the nature of Jesus, Mary became a focus of interest and devotion in the Greek-speaking eastern Mediterranean, as the human mother of one ultimately understood as both fully human and fully divine. In 431, bishops gathered at the Council of Ephesus declared Mary "Mother of God" (*Theotokos*, literally "Bearer of God"). In the East, Mary was imagined as a regal figure. As Christianity made its way into western Europe during the late Roman and early medieval eras, however, Mary was much less revered, again overshadowed by martyr saints everywhere but Britain, where Mary's cult was important from the early Middle Ages.[11]

Only in the tenth century did Mary begin to emerge as a major figure across northwestern Europe. The first accounts of healings at Marian shrines in the French lands are noted in the *Annals* of the historian

---

landscape in the twelfth century is a reminder that statistical analysis can tell only so much about the importance of female sanctity.

10. Mary is named almost twice as often in the Koran as in the Christian gospels: Rubin, *Mother of God*, 83.

11. Clayton, *The Cult of the Virgin Mary in Anglo-Saxon England*.

Flodoard of Reims (893/94–966).[12] Major new Marian pilgrimage shrines arose in Montserrat in Catalonia, Rocamadour in southwestern France, and Soissons in northern France, where Hugh Farsit wrote of her miracles in the nunnery dedicated to Mary there. Specific cults were associated with places: Notre-Dame ("Our Lady") of Laon, Notre-Dame of Soissons, Notre-Dame of Chartres, and Notre-Dame of Paris, to name a few of the best-known shrines in northern France.

From relative obscurity in the early medieval Western church, Mary had risen to primacy. Because her cult became important at different times in different places—later in Iberia than in northwestern Europe and still later in central and eastern Europe—the question of why it emerged where and when it did must have multiple answers.[13] In northwestern Europe, this was not in origin a popular cult but rather monastic and elite. It was an element of "affective piety," a highly emotional and personal religious devotion to Jesus and his mother that emerged in monastic circles, perhaps in part because of the increased presence in northwestern Europe of monks from the Greek East, where Mary had long been central to Christian worship.[14] Mary was likely also appealing as a multivalent figure: virgin and mother, wife of a humble artisan and the queen of heaven, and a powerful intercessor between God and faithful Christians. Around the year 1000 a cross was made for a house of religious women in Essen, about fifteen miles east-northeast of the Rhine River. It featured a woman kneeling before the enthroned Mary, who has her son on her knee. Mary is thus made an object of supplication as well as adoration. The same community also commissioned a gilded statue of Mary, the baby Jesus in her lap, "realized as a patron, but also as an intimate companion."[15]

As northwestern European villages and towns sprang up early in the second millennium amid economic growth, the faithful often dedicated their churches to her at the same time major pilgrimage shrines emerged. A minor figure in the collective imagination of the early

---

12. *The Annals of Flodoard of Reims*, ed. and trans. Fanning and Bachrach, 12 (Notre-Dame in Reims in 924), 43 (Notre-Dame in Paris in 945), and 54 (in two smaller churches in northern France in 949). Flodoard also noted in his *History of the Church of Reims* that he had written a verse collection of Marian miracles occurring in or around Reims, but it has not survived; he included several Marian miracles in his prose history. See Roberts, *Flodoard of Rheims*, 207–8.

13. For this idea I am grateful to Miri Rubin (personal communication, September 11, 2023).

14. See Mancia, *Emotional Monasticism* and Shoemaker, "Mary at the Cross, East and West."

15. Rubin, *Mother of God*, 117–18 (quotation from 118).

Middle Ages, Mary was a towering figure by 1100. In the twelfth century, our authors wrote of miracles effected through the saint of saints. Mary's different aspects get various degrees of emphasis in these accounts. For example, Herman of Tournai stresses Mary's motherhood while Hugh Farsit refers often to her virginity. In any guise, Mary served as example, comforter, healer, and, as is clear in some of the miracles recounted here, a fierce defender of her own cult and the Christian faith.

Miracles

From the beginning, the very special Christian dead worked miracles; many saints had already worked miracles before their deaths.[16] A Christian miracle can be described as an event that transcends the ordinary workings of the natural world through supernatural means, a manifestation of God's omnipotence and ubiquity that his saints acted to bring about through their intercession. The first miracle worker in the Christian tradition was, of course, Jesus. The Gospels tell how he performed miracles of control over nature, like turning water into wine, resurrecting the dead, and casting out evil spirits. The largest group of Jesus's miracles, however, are cures of illness or impairment: blindness, leprosy, paralysis, deafness, muteness, dropsy, withered limbs, and other, sometimes unspecified healings, in two cases for a whole crowd of people. In late Roman and medieval society, many miracles attributed to the intercession of saints involve bodily healing. That is true of the accounts in this book, which also echo the gospel accounts in the types of ailments healed: apart from leprosy, all types of cures attributed to Jesus appear.

Taken collectively, the miracles recounted in this book were quite typical of their time and place. A survey of 4,756 events reported in France from 1000 to 1200 shows that 57 percent were healing miracles and 43 percent nonhealing miracles.[17] Paralysis, blindness and other

---

16. A groundbreaking study, still frequently cited forty years after its original publication, is Ward, *Miracles and the Medieval Mind*. For more recent approaches and updated bibliography, see the essays in Mesley and Wilson, eds., *Contextualizing Miracles* and Katajala-Peltomaa, Kuuliala, and McCleery, eds., *A Companion to Medieval Miracle Collections*. Twelftree, ed., *The Cambridge Companion to Miracles* offers a comparative approach by way of essays on miracles in the Hebrew Bible, the ancient Greek and Roman worlds, Judaism after the biblical era, the Christian gospels, Christianity from its origins to the twentieth century, and early Hinduism, Islam, and Buddhism.

17. The miracles are examined in Sigal, *L'homme et le miracle*; its statistical findings are summarized in two tables in Bartlett, *Why Can the Dead Do Such Great Things?*, 343–44.

eye afflictions, deafness, muteness, tumors, fevers, ergotism, and mental disturbances account for three-quarters of healing miracles. Nonhealing miracles were dominated by visions, punishments, favorable interventions, protection from danger, deliverance from prison, and obtaining children, which together make up 90 percent of nonhealing miracles. An instance of each of these types of miracle appears at least once in the collections translated here, many of them multiple times. To put it another way, the miracles in this book taken as a group are a fair sample of all those recorded in eleventh- and twelfth-century France. In this time and place the proportion of males to females healed was roughly 3:2, and the same holds for other places in the central and later Middle Ages. This is roughly the case among the miracles narrated here.[18]

Because miracle stories usually adhere to the pattern of healings set in the Gospels, a sort of canon, some caution about what they can and cannot tell us is in order. Those cured as well as those who wrote about the events were aware of what kinds of conditions were considered most susceptible to miraculous healing. Collections of miracles do not, therefore, provide a full profile of medieval sickness or describe all ailments. Heart attack and stroke are never called by those names or anything like them, and what is clearly cancer makes only a few appearances, although it is possible to speculate that such diseases may have been the cause of some of the illnesses healed by miracles—paralysis after a stroke, for example. The details of miracle stories can sometimes reveal people's experiences otherwise invisible in the available documentary record, often through background that is incidental to the miracle itself.[19] Those are the "colorful glimpses" with which I began. On the whole, however, it is best to treat miracle stories "as expressions of the social and cultural values and assumptions both of the people who believed they had become involved in the operation of the miraculous and of the writers who recorded their experiences."[20] If there is

---

18. Bartlett, *Why Can the Dead Do Such Great Things?*, 346, synthesizes studies of sex ratios in miracle accounts. Because Herman, Hugo, and Haimo all write of group miracles, a precise statistical analysis of the relatively small sample of individual miracles seems beside the point. But of the individual healing miracles Bartlett considers, men were about 60 percent of those healed. That could reflect reporting bias or "since there were greater inhibitions on women's travel than on men's, it may well be that male pilgrims did predominate slightly" (346).

19. For example, Finucane, *The Rescue of the Innocents* examines six hundred stories in miracle collections from the twelfth and thirteenth centuries to reveal much about the perils of childhood, family relations, and gender in that era.

20. *The Miracles of Our Lady of Rocamadour*, trans. Bull, 16.

some medieval social history in miracle stories, even more so are there medieval perceptions of this world and the next.

But did these extraordinary things really happen? It is clear from the vast number of miracle stories that circulated during the Middle Ages that most people believed they did. Nor was such belief the domain of the illiterate: the educated Christian elite from early times, including towering figures like the prolific theologian St. Augustine of Hippo (354–430), theorized miracles and strove, sometimes even struggled, to believe them.[21] The English theologian Adelard of Bath, a rough contemporary of the authors translated here, thought that miracles were the explanation of last resort after human knowledge failed to account for mysterious phenomena.[22] Accounts of the miraculous were frequently met with disbelief. Around 1013, the learned cleric Bernard of Angers, in western France, made a journey of about 280 miles southeast to Conques, where a church had a gold-plated, gem-encrusted reliquary statue containing the skull of the fourth-century child martyr St. Faith around which many miracles were reported. Bernard originally thought these miracles were "so much worthless fiction." A visit to Conques changed his mind, even though "I was not gullible when I listened and I did not easily believe what I had heard."[23] Convinced, Bernard soon after wrote nearly fifty accounts of St. Faith's miracles.

There are open skeptics in the pages that follow. There is also frequent emphasis that an illness or impairment was congenital or chronic and well known to the associates of the one healed—that is, that the cure was not of a transitory affliction—or that there were multiple witnesses to a healing miracle. Such details were meant to counter doubt. There is direct and indirect evidence, then, of considerable uncertainty about whether these things happened or if so, whether there is an explanation for events that does not require otherworldly interference in this world.

A different approach juxtaposes medieval accounts with the findings of modern biomedical, social, and behavioral sciences to account for the apparently miraculous. For example, modern medicine recognizes that illnesses, even serious ones, often resolve themselves and that changes in diet and daily routine of the sort that pilgrimage entails can improve health. Modern people with chronic illnesses that have more

---

21. Ward, *Miracles and the Medieval Mind*, 3–19 (chap. 1, "The Theory of Miracles"). On the struggle to believe among learned elites, see Justice, "Did the Middle Ages Believe in Their Miracles?"

22. Ward, *Miracles and the Medieval Mind*, 6–7.

23. *The Book of Sainte Foy*, trans. Sheingorn, 39, 40.

and less acute stages are more likely to seek help when symptoms are the worst and to attribute improvement to medical treatment rather than natural ebb and flow. Optimism, social scientists note, is highly correlated to the improvement of health. So perhaps medieval people with severe illness would be most likely to find relief at a shrine to which they travel in high hopes of improvement. Belief in the powers of a saint to bring about physical improvements is perhaps a manifestation of what modern medicine calls the placebo effect.[24] Another possible explanation is that the ailments were often psychosomatic and some combination of changes in mental or physical status could alleviate or cure them.[25] Such studies make some of the healings medieval authors describe seem, from a modern perspective, more plausible. The risk is that such approaches can explain away what sincere medieval observers thought had occurred: miracles.

The best way of accounting for belief in miracles is what Marcia Colish calls the "capacity to live in more than one imaginative universe at the same time" among medieval writers, their patrons, and their audiences.[26] If nearly five thousand recorded miracles from eleventh- and twelfth-century France alone have survived, then miracles, however understood, whether experienced personally or known at second, third, or fourth hand, were an ordinary feature of medieval life. Possibly they were a sort of psychological necessity in a society where the vast majority lived amid great deprivation and uncertainty; many of the people in the pages that follow were poor, some surviving on the streets or the domestic charity of the better-off. As Benedicta Ward puts it in her study of miracles in the central Middle Ages, "For some readers it will seem that I have avoided a direct answer to the question of whether miracles 'really' happen. It seems to me that such a question is beyond the scope of a historical work; it belongs to theology and especially to philosophy"—and, it could be added, psychology, anthropology, and sociology. Ward further remarks that "there is rarely deliberate fraud in the records of miracles in this early period. Those who recorded or acclaimed a 'miracle' believed in it."[27] A contemporary philosopher goes further: "On scientific, philosophical and theological grounds belief

---

24. Scott, *Miracle Cures*. This fascinating study by a sociologist considers medieval and postmedieval miracles and pilgrimages.

25. On this subject, see the work of a practicing neurologist: O'Sullivan, *Is It All in Your Head?*

26. Colish, "When Did the Middle Ages End?," 216.

27. Ward, *Miracles and the Medieval Mind*, 215.

in miracles is entirely rational."[28] Miracles (with or without quotation marks) were simply a fact of life for medieval Christians, part and parcel of their daily existence. "But what really happened?" is a modern question to which there may be modern answers. But about belief in and ubiquity of miracles in medieval Europe there is no doubt.

Medicine

It is easy to underestimate medieval medicine.[29] Contrary to myth, medical theory and practice in medieval Europe did not simply assume physical affliction was the product of sin and thus recourse to religion the only path to healing. Most medicine was based on ancient Mediterranean ideas that attributed illness to natural causes and treated it with natural remedies. Medieval people knew that some diseases were contagious and that some individuals are naturally more prone to illness than others. Medieval medicine was, however, a long way from modern biomedicine. Its theoretical orientation was derived from ancient Greek medicine as fully developed by Galen (129–216). The essential principle was that every human body had four principal fluids, or humors: black bile, yellow bile, phlegm, and blood. The balance of humors varied from individual to individual, and an imbalance of humors owing to poor diet or the malfunction of bodily organs was the cause of illness. Humoral theory remained unchallenged in Europe until the early modern period and was not definitively discarded until the late nineteenth century.

However, medieval medical treatments were often effective. Practitioners often recommended salutary changes in diet and had access to a wide variety of medicines, usually herb-based. The most enduring encyclopedia of pharmacology was (in Latin translation) *De materia medica*. Written by the Greek physician Dioscorides in the first century, it discussed not only herbs but aromatic oils, roots, seeds, fruits, vegetables, grains, and animal products as well as their preparation for medical use—a total of more than five hundred ingredients. In the early Middle Ages, monasteries were the most important centers of medical learning and healing practice, where illness was treated with a combination

---

28. Larmer, "The Meanings of Miracle," 50.

29. For a brief debunking of widespread views and a brief introduction to medieval medicine by an expert in the field, see Black, *The Middle Ages*, 169–89 (chap. 9, "Medieval Medicine Was Nothing but Superstition"), a brief synthesis of important scholarship on which I draw below.

of physical and spiritual remedies. Sin, then, was sometimes linked to disease, but sin was often considered an aspect of the human condition rather than the failings of individuals.[30] Monasteries had herb gardens, sometimes very large ones, and books called herbals were copied, annotated, and revised when new treatments came to light, the result of new information or the availability of different herbs. These medieval herbals usually relied heavily on *De materia medica* but with changes that reflected the climate and hence ingredients available north of the Mediterranean basin.

Medicine, then, was for many centuries a craft learned through observation and practice, almost always in a monastery, rather than a profession studied in schools. The first institution in Latin Christendom that might be called a medical school was in the southern Italian city of Salerno, its origins dating to around 900. Salerno-trained physicians appeared in northern France in the mid-tenth century, and by the twelfth century, the knowledge and skill of those trained in Salerno were known and sought across western Europe. When our authors were writing their miracle collections, there was a relatively new but already important medical school at Montpellier, in southern France; in the twelfth century, medical care was available not just in monasteries but increasingly from secular professionals. But school-learned medicine had hardly overtaken practical monastic medicine by the time our authors wrote. Unlike monks, whose care was a matter of charity, secular physicians charged for their services, so their clientele was mostly affluent. Whatever their training, healers focused on the practical, striving to diagnose and treat the illnesses they encountered.

Medieval medicinal and miracle cures were not mutually exclusive. Miracle accounts, including some translated here, often note that the ill sought both secular and spiritual healing, perhaps simultaneously.[31] Herman of Tournai shows that the canons of Laon, who oversaw miracles around relics, also had at least rudimentary training in emergency first aid. It is important to stress that a high percentage of cures in medieval miracle stories, including many in this book, involved long-standing,

---

30. Metzler, *Disability in Medieval Europe* argues convincingly that the association of sin with illness was loose, not expressed or applied consistently. Metzler was not the first to make this point, and more recent scholarship concurs with her conclusions.

31. For the variety of therapeutic treatments offered by medieval women in the thirteenth-century Low Countries, see Ritchey, *Acts of Care*. What Ritchey describes as a mingling of "physical, social, emotional, and spiritual aspects" (5) of healthcare is far more visible after 1200, when sources available to historians of Europe become much more numerous. But there is every reason to think Ritchey's description applies to medical care before 1200.

often congenital impairments like those cataloged above. These were precisely the sorts of illnesses medieval medicine had very little capacity to treat and about which medical books, based on ancient Mediterranean texts, said little.[32] Nor was it very effective in the face of epidemics like the outbreak of ergotism whose symptoms Hugh Farsit describes in graphic detail. This did not keep the impaired or otherwise ill from consulting doctors or, at times, looking to secular medicine if spiritual medicine failed on first attempt. Medicine and miracle were not poles but elements along a therapeutic continuum.[33]

Miracle Collections

Miracles, medical and otherwise, abound in the accounts of Christianity's first saints, the martyrs, and continued to make frequent appearances in writing about saints after persecution ended in the early fourth century. The earliest free-standing miracle collections, also called miracle books, date to the early fifth century, recounting the miracles worked through Stephen (d. ca. 34), the first Christian martyr, and the quasi-legendary Thecla, a companion of St. Paul, preacher, and ascetic virgin.[34] The *Miracles of St. Stephen* contains about twenty miracle stories, the *Miracles of Thecla* twice that number. St. Augustine encouraged the faithful to write down accounts of healing at the shrines housing St. Stephen's relics and himself wrote about contemporary miracles of his day in his massive theological treatise, *The City of God* (ca. 413–ca. 426). In Book XXII he includes what may be the first miracle collection, appearing at about the same time as the *Miracles of St. Stephen*.

His successor Christians did as Augustine suggested. In the late sixth century, Bishop Gregory of Tours (ca. 538–94) recounted hundreds of miracles in hagiographical works and his lengthy *History of the Franks*.[35]

---

32. Metzler, *Disability in Medieval Europe*, especially 126–90 (chap. 5, "Medieval Miracles and Impairment" and "Conclusion"). A recent study of impaired bodies and miracles is Kuuliala, "Physical Disability and Bodily Difference."

33. For more on this point, see the essays in Bowers and Keyser, eds., *The Sacred and the Secular in Medieval Healing*.

34. See Bartlett, *Why Can the Dead Do Such Great Things?*, 22–26 and 558–70, on which I draw below. Essays on various topics related to miracle collections ca. 1000–ca. 1500 are gathered in Katajala-Peltomaa, Kuuliala, and McCleery, eds., *A Companion to Medieval Miracle Collections*.

35. Bartlett, *Why Can the Dead Do Such Great Things?*, 35–38, with a bibliography of English translations at 660, to which should be added Gregory of Tours, *A History of the Franks*; Gregory's *The Suffering and Miracles of the Martyr St. Julian* and *The Miracles of the Bishop St. Martin* are translated in Van Dam, *Saints and Their Miracles in Late Antique Gaul*, 162–303.

In them, the pattern of miraculous healings noted above was taking shape. Miracle collections continued to appear in great number and were "one of the most popular and widespread—if not the most widespread—literary genres during the Middle Ages."[36] Some were relatively brief, including only a handful of miracles; others, like the collections of miracles around the tomb of St. Thomas Becket that two monks wrote shortly after his martyrdom in 1170, are far longer than all the miracles recounted in this book put together.[37] Some collections were put together by a single author in a relatively short time, others across decades by more than one writer.[38]

These accounts of miraculous events, then, are not direct testimonies of the people who experienced them. They were instead products of what Gabriela Signori memorably calls "the miracle kitchen," carefully concocted to instruct, inspire, and promote the shrines around which they took place.[39] Individuals gave oral accounts—the "raw" miracles—which were sometimes written down by those who oversaw the shrine at which it took place. In the case of *The Miracles of St. Mary of Laon*, we know that Herman of Tournai was working from notes jotted down a generation earlier, which he edited and reshaped. He explicitly says that he excluded some stories so as not to bore his audience. Hugh Farsit, the author of *A Little Book of Miracles of the Blessed Virgin Mary in the City of Soissons*, does not reveal his sources, but living in the city where most of the miracles took place, he probably had access to notes as well. Because the events he describes go back only about fifteen years, he could probably also interview eyewitnesses and those healed; in one case he saw evidence of a miraculous cure himself. Haimo of Saint-Pierre-sur-Dives's "Letter to the Brothers of Tutbury" concerned extremely recent events, so he must have gotten his information largely from eyewitnesses, either the recipients of a miracle or those present

---

36. Katajala-Peltomaa, Kuuliala, and McCleery, "Introduction," 1.

37. On the two long collections by Benedict of Peterborough and William of Canterbury, see Koopmans, *Wonderful to Relate*, 139–200. According to the lists in Koopmans's appendices (215–24), the total number of miracles is about six hundred, with only eighteen narrated by both authors (139).

38. Two twelfth-century collections of Marian miracles that have been translated into English were the work of a single author and, like those translated here, were finished in a short period: William of Malmesbury, *The Miracles of the Blessed Virgin Mary* (completed ca. 1137) and *The Miracles of Our Lady of Rocamadour* (written in the early 1170s). On the other hand, the miracles of St. Faith were written by several authors from ca. 1020 to ca. 1050: *The Book of Sainte Foy*, trans. Sheingorn, 24–25.

39. Signori, "The Miracle Kitchen and Its Ingredients," from which this paragraph derives its inspiration.

when it took place, of whom the abbot was probably one. Like Herman, Hugh, Haimo, and John note that they do not include everything; John specifies that many of the stories he tells had been passed down orally, and because they were not written down and as an old man his memory is imperfect, he chooses to omit material so as not to get things wrong and offend God. Gautier of Compiègne says he got the material for his brief account from a contemporary, Bishop Geoffrey of Chartres, but at least two of the four miracles in his brief account had been recorded before, one of them in the late eleventh century. All authors of miracle collections chose material they thought the most impressive and suitable to record. We have their "cooked" versions of events. The vivid stories told here are part of a genre with its own rules and traditions.

In the eastern Mediterranean, monks began to make collections of Mary's miracles as she became a central figure in Greek-speaking Christendom in the fourth and fifth centuries.[40] But just as Mary remained a relatively minor figure in western Europe until much later, so too do collections devoted solely to miracles effected through her appear only centuries into the Christian era.[41] In the early twelfth century, collections of two types emerge.[42] In England, they were "universal," that is, they recounted events that took place across centuries and in many places. Despite early interest in Mary in England and many churches dedicated to her, there was no specifically Marian shrine until one was built in Walsingham around 1153. Across the English Channel in northern France, authors wrote of miracles closer to their own time and associated with relics and local cults: west-central France (1112), southern England (1113), and the diocese of Laon (ca. 1113–ca. 1146) for Herman, Soissons from 1128 to 1132 for Hugh, and Normandy in 1145 for Haimo. John mostly related miracles associated with the cathedral of Coutances that occurred in the later eleventh century; two of Gautier's miracles are adaptations of older accounts, but the other two are original to him so probably recent.

Our authors, then, were pioneers, among the first in Latin Christendom to gather recent stories of miracles accomplished through Mary's intercession. Some of their narratives had important afterlives. Sermons in Latin and the vernacular often drew on miracle collections

---

40. Rubin, *Mother of God*, 182.

41. That is not to say that Mary's miracles went unrecorded. But they were embedded in larger collections, like those Gregory of Tours assembled.

42. For this paragraph, see Ihnat, *Mother of Mercy, Bane of the Jews*, 100–137 (chap. 4, "Hagiographies of Mary: Miracle Collections").

for edifying material, and some of those recounted here likely made their way into sermons.[43] In at least one case, the retelling of a story was via outright plagiarism. The cathedral in Chartres had a Marian relic, a tunic that, according to legend, King Charles the Bald (d. 877) had procured and donated. After a fire in 1134, the cathedral was rebuilt as a pilgrimage shrine around this relic. In about 1210, an anonymous author collected twenty-seven miracles worked at the shrine, one of which was lifted word for word from Hugh's section 7. The Chartres account reproduced Gundrada's vow to visit the Virgin of Soissons, simply inserting a conversation between Gundrada and Mary in which Mary explains that the miracle should be attributed to Our Lady of Chartres.[44] The Chartres collection, in turn, was translated into French verse in the mid-thirteenth century.[45]

Many of these stories made their way into other vernacular collections as well, often considerably adapted.[46] Adgar, a monk based in London, wrote the first such compilation around 1165. Adgar's Anglo-Norman verse text, the *Gracial*, includes reworkings of Hugh Farsit's final section and Gautier's section 2 and section 4 (in two versions).[47] The monk Gautier de Coinci (1177–1236) spent most of his life in or around Soissons. While serving as prior of the monastery of Vic-sur-Aisne, about ten miles west of Soissons, from circa 1218 to circa 1228, Gautier assembled a collection of nearly sixty Mary miracles from numerous sources and presented them in Old French octosyllables, a total of thirty thousand verses entitled *Les Miracles de Nostre Dame*.[48]

---

43. On sermons and saints, see Bartlett, *Why Can the Dead Do Such Great Things?*, 570–76.

44. As noted in Foscati, *Saint Anthony's Fire*, 80–81.

45. Latin prose version: *Miracula beatae Mariae virginis in Carnotensi ecclesia facta* in Thomas, "Les miracles de Notre-Dame de Chartres," 508–50. French verse version: Jean Le Marchant, *Miracles de Notre-Dame de Chartres*.

46. In what follows, I do not mean to claim that all the vernacular versions were directly derived from the Latin texts translated here. Many of them clearly were, especially in the case of Herman and Hugh, of whose collections multiple twelfth- and thirteenth-century manuscripts have survived. The point is that these stories, most of which originated with the collections translated in this book, had a strong purchase on the medieval imagination.

47. Adgar, *Le Gracial*, ed. and trans. Benoit, 30–35, 134–47 (two versions of Gautier's section 4) and 439–41 (a version of Gautier's section 2), provides the Anglo-Norman texts and modern French prose translations. Since Gautier's section 2 was not original to him (see the introduction to *The Miracles of the Blessed Virgin Mary*), it may well be that Adgar was working from a different text. I have not discovered an earlier version of Gautier's section 4.

48. Gautier de Coinci, *Les Miracles de Nostre Dame*, ed. Koenig. There is no full English version, but for a taste of Gautier's detailed and somewhat diffuse storytelling, see nine miracles translated into prose: Gautier de Coincy, "Miracles of the Virgin Mary," trans. Blumenfeld-Kosinski. For an edition and English translation of Gautier's version of the story of the sixth-century cleric Theophilus, who made a deal with the devil for high position that became the

Gautier included much-embellished adaptations of at least six of Herman's miracle stories (II, 2; II, 4; II, 5; II, 10; II, 11; and III, 27) and four of Hugh's (sections 7, 9, 12, and 31). He also includes the appearance of St. Leocadia and Mary to St. Ildefonsus of Toledo found in Herman's brief Life of the holy bishop translated below.[49] Gautier's collection was widely circulated; more than eighty medieval manuscripts survive, many of them beautifully illustrated.

Even more of the stories in this book were translated into Galician-Portuguese, a literary language of northwestern Iberia. Four hundred and twenty-seven *Cantigas de Santa Maria*, poems with musical notation in some manuscripts, were assembled between 1257 and 1283 at the behest of King Alfonso X ("the Wise") of Castile, León, and Galicia, who had a hand in composing some of them.[50] The collection includes versions of three of Herman's miracle stories (II, 2; II, 5; III, 27) and ten of Hugh's (sections 1, 7, 9, 11, 12, 16, 18, 22, 25, and 26), again often significantly reshaped.[51] About ten manuscripts of *Les Miracles de Nostre Dame* also have musical notation, so the miracles Herman, Hugh, and Gautier recounted were read, recited, and sung for centuries after they wrote. There are numerous recordings based on *Les Miracles de Nostre Dame* and the *Cantigas de Santa Maria*.

A final historical note concerns Mary and the Jews of medieval Europe.[52] Christians sometimes depicted Mary as the gentle vehicle for the conversion of Jews to Christianity. However, harsh anti-Jewish sentiment and anti-Jewish violence were regular features of European life first evident on a wide scale with the Rhineland pogroms of 1095–96 following the preaching of the First Crusade. In a collection of Marian

---

inspiration for the Faust legend, see Gautier de Coinci, *The Miracle of Theophilus*, ed. and trans. Root.

49. The sixth of the set, the story of the woman who could not be burned, is told by more than one author, but its appearance in *Les Miracles de Nostre Dame* immediately after the five miracles for which Herman was certainly the source is suggestive. The stories of the two saints who appeared to Ildefonsus of Toledo were very well known and probably not taken directly from Herman's account.

50. Complete English translation: *Songs of Holy Mary of Alfonso X, the Wise*, trans. Kulp-Hill. An ongoing project is the Oxford Cantigas de Santa Maria Database, which includes the original texts, references to earlier and subsequent versions of the stories in Latin and several vernacular languages, plus bibliography and discography for each song: https://csm.mml.ox.ac.uk.

51. The *Cantigas* also include versions of the stories in sections 2 and 3 in Gautier of Compiègne's short text, but since there are versions of both that predate Gautier's, it is impossible to know their source(s).

52. See in general Rubin, *Mother of God*, 161–68, 228–36. A detailed study of England in the eleventh and twelfth centuries is Ihnat, *Mother of Mercy, Bane of the Jews*.

miracles dating to circa 1137 by the English monk William of Malmesbury, the author, as his translators put it, "gives full vent to what can
only be described as violent anti-Semitism."[53] Such hostility is also on
full display in the three vernacular collections noted above. But no anti-
Jewish sentiment appears in the miracle collections translated here.
Herman of Tournai mentions Jews twice, once in a purely historical
context and once to claim that David wrote the Psalms for Christians
rather than Jews. Hugh sketches an evil moneylender who is possibly
meant to be Jewish, but Herman presents a Christian moneylender.
Haimo, John, and Gautier do not mention Jews at all. Since it would
have been easy to shape any number of the miracle stories translated
in this book to be anti-Jewish, the absence of such bigotry is a pleasant
surprise for which I have no explanation. Readers should simply know
that this absence is atypical.

Terminology

The fundamental distinction among medieval Christians divided the
clergy (or clerics), those whose lives are devoted to religious service,
from the laity, the ordinary faithful. The religious personnel in these
accounts are both secular clergy, those who live in the world (*saeculum*),
and regular clergy, those who live under a rule (*regula*), mostly withdrawn from the world. The most important of the former are priests
and deacons, who had the status immediately below the priesthood.[54]
The latter are monks and nuns, presided over by abbots and abbesses.
Other ecclesiastical officials were bishops, the spiritual leaders of a territory called a diocese and who often had deputies known as archdea-
cons; archbishops, who oversaw a cluster of dioceses; and the pope, the
spiritual head of the Roman church. In honor of St. Peter, the papacy is
also called "the apostolic see." Any of these high officers are "prelates."

A confusing word that frequently appears in this book is "canon."[55]
In general, canons were clergymen who performed liturgies in large

---

53. William of Malmesbury, *The Miracles of the Blessed Virgin Mary*, trans. Thomson and
Winterbottom, xxii.

54. In Latin Christianity there followed, in descending order, the offices of subdeacon,
acolyte, exorcist, reader, and doorkeeper. Medieval clergymen rarely ascended to priesthood
from the bottom up. For example, St. Norbert of Xanten (see Herman of Tournai, *The Miracles
of St. Mary of Laon*, III, 1) held no other office in the list of seven before he was ordained a
priest.

55. On this slippery category, see Constable, *The Reformation of the Twelfth Century*, 11–13,
54–56.

churches, in particular cathedrals, the major churches of a diocese. Some lived like monks under a rule, led a common life, and performed the cycle of eight daily communal prayer services (like monks and nuns: see below). These are known as regular canons. But many canons had their own households and families, did not participate in daily communal prayers, and led fairly worldly lives. These men were secular canons. Some canons were priests, that is, of the highest order of ordinary clergymen, but many were not. The canons of Laon that Herman discusses were members of the cathedral staff but did not follow a rule; most of them were not priests. Herman himself was a monk, if of an unusual sort: see the introduction to *The Miracles of St. Mary of Laon*. Hugh Farsit was a regular canon and wrote of events centered around a community of nuns and their leader, Abbess Mathilda. Haimo and Gautier were abbots. John was a cathedral canon.

The lives of monks, nuns, and most regular canons were structured around eight prayer services, or offices, throughout the day: Matins, Lauds, Prime, Terce, Sext, None, Vespers, and Compline. Matins took place before dawn, sometimes several hours before, with Vespers and Compline in the evening. As per the Rule of St. Benedict, all the psalms were said or chanted each week; there were other, usually shorter, prayers each day that depended on the time of year. Religious men and women sometimes also stayed awake through the night before a major holiday like Easter or the day on which a saint's death was commemorated. These all-nighters are called vigils; some laypeople also kept vigil in shrine churches as a mark of special devotion or as they awaited a miracle. Another strategy to facilitate a miracle was to sleep near relics, a practice known as incubation.

The central sacrament or rite of medieval Christian practice for clergy and laity was the Mass, a re-creation of the Last Supper in the Gospels (a seder), during which the bread and wine were believed to become the actual body and blood of Jesus while retaining their ordinary appearance. Among the various kinds of Christians, attendance at Mass ranged from daily (for some regular clergy) to quite infrequent (for most of the laity).

The stories in this book also refer to two different kinds of medieval lordship. In one sort, landowners delegated property to others in exchange for (often) military service. The landowners could be lay people or clerics. This was a patron–client relationship between legally free people. In the second kind of lordship, propertied lords had dependent, legally unfree serfs, usually agricultural laborers. Serfs were not enslaved, but they were obligated to do their lords' bidding, including working on his or her land and paying various taxes and user fees—for baking bread in communal ovens, for example. In some regions of twelfth-century France, only a minority of peasants were serfs, but *servi* and *ancillae*, the medieval Latin words for male and female serfs, appear occasionally in this book.[56] Both kinds of lordship included mutual obligations of service and protection, but the social and legal distinctions between vassals and serfs were stark.

Translations

What I hope to provide here are accessible translations of texts in Latin, an ancient, inflected language that works very differently from English. The aim is to be faithful rather than literal, meaning there is considerable adaptation of the Latin syntax. Long sentences are often split into two or three. I often translate passive voice constructions, which are much more natural in Latin than English, in the active voice. There are also many cases where participles and gerunds became simple verbs. I almost always dispense with orienting words like *supradictus, praedictus, ipse,* and *idem* ("abovementioned," "aforementioned," "the very same," and "the same") when the antecedent is obvious. In medieval Latin, *quidam* ("a certain"), comes to resemble the article "a" in a language that has no articles; I have often translated it that way. I sometimes substitute names for pronouns (stated or implied) and vice versa. I usually omit words of transition like *autem* ("but," "moreover," or "and"), *deinde* ("next"), *ecce* ("behold!"), *ergo* ("therefore"), *enim* ("for" or "in fact"), *igitur* ("therefore"), *itaque* ("so, "thus," or "accordingly"), *nam* ("for"), *siquidem* ("indeed"), *tamen* ("yet" or "nevertheless"), and *tunc* ("then"), and several words that mean "immediately," for example, *confestim, ilico, protinus,* and *statim,* whose overly literal inclusion would weary readers more than the miracles Herman of Tournai chose not to recount lest he inspire boredom.

In translating, I use terminology for certain medical conditions that offends twenty-first-century sensibilities. But "crippled" is really the only way to translate *contractus.* Herman of Tournai notes without comment that a man with severe bone abnormalities is called Glutinus, meaning "glued together." To rely on modern language like "impairment," or even the increasingly contested "disability," would

---

56. On terminology and status, see Bouchard, *Negotiation and Resistance,* 32–34.

misrepresent a turbulent, often violent world in which casual cruelty directed at the unfortunate people our authors describe was a fact of life.[57] I do, however, sometimes translate the adjective *incolumis*, which refers to healed individuals, as "unimpaired."

Herman of Tournai writes straightforward narrative prose that is relatively easy to translate into idiomatic English. Not so Hugh Farsit, whose Latin is very compact, at times telegraphic. Hugh pens sentences that are a sea of ablatives, Latin's grammatical case that can be variously translated, absent governing prepositions—and with Hugh they are usually absent—as "at," "by," "by means of," "from," "in," "through," and "with." The Latin of Haimo of Saint-Pierre-sur-Dives and John, son of Peter lies somewhere in between, mostly direct but with occasional elliptical moments. With Gautier of Compiègne, we return to simpler Latin (as Gautier says he intends). I have made some attempt to reproduce these styles in the translations and hope the authors, all of whom are excellent storytellers, read at least a bit differently from one another.

Finally, I offer a taste of medieval vocabulary. The best example is the Latin word *feretrum* dear to Herman of Tournai. It can mean either a reliquary, the container in which relics are kept, or a bier on which one or more reliquaries are carried. When it is not clear which meaning is intended, I have simply used the English "feretory," a word more common in the nineteenth century than before or since, and in all times very rare. The overall intention, to repeat, is to make these writings readable without draining them of all their distinctively Latinate and medieval quality.

---

57. Because our authors call some of the afflicted *surdus et mutus*, "deaf and mute," I have opted not to use the now offensive term "deaf-mute." Those who do not hear or speak can communicate in nonverbal ways. Medieval monks pledged to silence had highly developed systems of nonverbal communication: see Bruce, *Silence and Sign Language*. There is no reason not to think lay people who needed to communicate via gestures and signs did so, perhaps in a fairly elaborate fashion.

Herman of Tournai, *The Miracles of St. Mary of Laon*

Introduction

The city of Laon, about seventy-five miles northeast of Paris, sits on a butte—Herman of Tournai calls it a mountain—that rises dramatically three hundred feet from the surrounding plains. It lies in the southern part of the region of Picardy.[1] Settled in pre-Roman times, by the early twelfth century Laon was a prosperous market town, a center of trade in grains, meat, fish, fruits and vegetables, and wine. It was also a center of communication, religion, and learning. The seat of a bishop since the late fifth century, Laon was home to one of the most famous schools in Europe, then directed by Master Anselm, who taught there from about 1090 until he died in 1117.

Laon was also a royal city. In the tenth century, it had been a frequent residence and capital of some of the last of the Carolingians, the dynasty named for its most notable member, Charlemagne (*Carolus Magnus*, r. 768–814). But in the early twelfth century, being a royal city was more important than it may sound. By then, the men who called themselves "kings of the Franks" were in direct control of a very small

---

1. On Laon and its surrounding countryside, I rely primarily on Saint-Denis, *Apogée d'une cité*.

part of their realm.[2] In the times of Kings Philip I (r. 1060–1108) and Louis VI (r. 1108–37), the kingdom was hemmed in on all sides by powerful neighbors in political units that often were larger, better organized, or both. The royal domain, the network of lands over which the kings exercised direct control, was spread out over the region around Paris and then some seventy miles south and southwest as far as the city of Orléans. When Louis VI ascended to the throne, in theory as the overlord of much of present-day France, he was in fact a weak monarch in a small principality. Within the royal lands, petty lords based in (usually quite modest) castles, known as castellans, exercised the powers of justice and taxation, often quite arbitrarily. Castellans acted with casual brutality to enforce their dubiously legitimate authority: they were self-appointed strongmen, akin to modern mobsters.[3] One of Louis VI's advisors was Suger, the abbot of Saint-Denis (r. 1122–51) in what is now a northern suburb of Paris. In the early 1140s, Suger wrote an account of Louis VI that showed him constantly striving to keep order.[4]

The kings of the Franks shared rule with some of the bishops in their realm, including those of Laon. In Laon, kings had urban and suburban properties closely tied to those of the monastery of Saint-Jean and a share in some tax revenues based on a lively market in foodstuffs and, especially, wine.[5] But given that royal presence was rare, the bishops were the most powerful figures in Laon, its de facto lords. Bishop Helinand (r. 1052–96) built and enhanced urban and regional monasteries, enriched his cathedral, Notre-Dame of Laon, and maintained good relations with the most important local families, making the late eleventh century a time of relative peace amid rapid economic growth that continued into the twelfth century.

But this prosperous city was also a powder keg. It suffered a revolt, the assassination of its bishop, and a damaging fire in the spring

---

2. See Hallam and West, *Capetian France*, 33–157, on the organization of the French lands in this period. The political history of France in the eleventh and twelfth centuries is the story of the various principalities. The maps in this book show the putative kingdom in the twelfth century rather than what kings directly controlled.

3. On this theme, see Bisson, *The Crisis of the Twelfth Century*. The analogy to mobsters is mine.

4. Suger, *The Deeds of Louis the Fat*, trans. Cusimano and Moorhead. Suger presents his subject as strong and successful, but even a little reading between the lines suggests the enormous difficulties Louis had in maintaining anything like peace or uniform governance. Cusimano and Moorhead's translation of Suger's biography is the one cited subsequently.

5. Wine production for export was a big business in the Laonnois in the twelfth century. It has largely disappeared since.

of 1112. Our best source for these events is the highly opinionated Guibert of Nogent (r. 1104–ca. 1125), abbot of the small monastery of Nogent-sous-Coucy about fourteen miles west-southwest of Laon that was founded in 1059 with the encouragement of Bishop Helinand. In his autobiographical *Monodies* (ca. 1115)—a monody is a sung lament in ancient Greek drama—Guibert devotes much of the third and final book to events in Laon in the early twelfth century.[6] Guibert begins by saying of Laon's tragic fate that "the origin of all the evil lies, as it seems to me, in the corruption of its bishops."[7] First Guibert offers an unflattering sketch of Bishop Helinand, whom he describes as, if a generous patron of his cathedral and other churches, nonetheless low-class, poorly educated, and overambitious. He then turns to Helinand's successor, Bishop Enguerrand (r. 1098–1104), in Guibert's account an irreligious buffoon who showed excessive and immoral favor to the local family from which he came. The see was vacant for two years after Enguerrand's death—kings did not object to such gaps because they picked up bishops' revenues in the meantime—until the election of Gaudry in 1106.

Guibert and modern scholars agree that the brief reign of Gaudry was a disaster. He had been the chancellor, the chief advisor, to King Henry I of England (r. 1100–1135), but without clerical qualifications; his election was publicly opposed by Master Anselm and privately by others. He was a warrior and courtier rather than a pastor, in character not much different from the violent castellans King Louis VI labored to tame. As bishop, he abused his judicial authority and debased the local coinage, which slowed the booming economy of the town and region. Of his many intrigues, the most significant involved the castellan Gerard of Quierzy. After a rift with Gerard, Gaudry slipped away to Rome after crafting a plot to have his enemy killed. Gerard was assassinated as he prayed in the cathedral on January 13, 1111.

From there things went from bad to worse. The king suspected the bishop's complicity in Gerard's murder and had his residence ransacked. On his return from Rome, Gaudry further inflamed matters by excommunicating (that is, banning from Christian churches and their sacraments) the men who had attacked Gerard's murderers. He then set off for England to raise funds. In his absence, citizens sought

---

6. Guibert of Nogent, *Monodies*, trans. McAlhany and Rubenstein, 107–66. This translation of Guibert's autobiography-cum-chronicle is the one cited subsequently.

7. Guibert of Nogent, *Monodies*, 107.

a commune, a sworn association that allowed individuals to pay a head tax that would free them from the erratic exactions (essentially shake-downs) of regional lords, many of whom had residences in the city. On his return, Gaudry vacillated about accepting an arrangement that, according to Guibert, the king was bribed to accept.

As lords including the bishop found themselves without the power to continue their capricious taxation and as efforts to squelch the commune and continued debasement of coinage began to ruin peasants and merchants, the social fabric unraveled. Some of the wealthier citizens entered into a conspiracy of their own: the assassination of the bishop. A general revolt broke out on April 25, 1112. The bishop was murdered by an angry mob and his body mutilated. A fire broke out in the cathedral and spread to other parts of the city; attempts to restore order by peaceful and violent means failed for some weeks until the uproar was savagely repressed by royal soldiers. Subsequent pacification was accomplished largely by local clergy, led by Master Anselm.

A thriving city and its surroundings had been laid low, and its cathedral needed repair. The murder of the bishop and the fire caused shock waves, first locally, then further afield, appearing in accounts far and wide. By coincidence, what is probably the earliest mention of the events comes from the pen of Hugh Farsit, decades before he wrote the miracle collection translated in this book. The section of Hugh's theological *Otium* that sketches the tragedy of Laon is edited and translated in Appendix 1.

Such details about the uprising, murder, and fire are necessary to contextualize the account of Herman of Tournai. Herman describes the events of 1111 and 1112 and their aftermath in two distinct parts. After briefly outlining the horrors of those years, the first two books of his account narrate journeys undertaken by canons, members of the cathedral clergy of Laon. They took with them relics including those of Jesus, the Virgin Mary, and two early medieval saints, aiming to raise funds to restore the cathedral.[8] The first journey, in 1112, was to west-central France, the regions of Berry, Touraine, Anjou, and Chartrain (Book I), the second, in 1113, to southern England from Canterbury in the east as far as Bodmin in the west (Book II). The third book, as long as the first two combined, recounts the revival of the region, mostly through the establishment of new monastic communities through the offices of Bishop Gaudry's successor, the hero of the piece, Bishop Bartholomew

---

8. On the relics, see the preface to Book II and II, 2.

de Jur (r. 1113–51). Here Herman stresses Bartholomew's close association with St. Norbert of Xanten (ca. 1075–1134) who founded first the monastery of Prémontré, ten miles west-southwest of Laon, then others that followed the same customs, in the decades after 1120.

Relic tours during which miracles took place were not unusual. Monks and canons had traveled with their precious cargos to raise money since at least the mid-eleventh century.[9] They did so after disaster struck, to defend property rights, to seek funds for nonemergency construction projects, or simply to make a saint's cult better known in the hopes of attracting more pilgrims and thus more offerings. The tours of the Laon canons stand out, however, for their sheer scope. Some relic tours were local, while others involved travel of a few hundred miles; they lasted up to about two months. But the itineraries Herman describes were unprecedented in their ambition: the French tour of three and a half months covered almost 650 miles, the English tour of more than five months nearly 1,250 miles. It is difficult not to interpret these extraordinary undertakings as a sign of ambition and perhaps some desperation on the part of the canons, who took a known fund-raising practice and, so to speak, put it on steroids. Such journeys were dangerous, too: petty lords feuded in the countryside, banditry was widespread, and the Laon canons needed Mary's protection when pirates attacked them on the English Channel.

Nor were they welcomed everywhere: they met with a decidedly hostile reception at one stop on each tour. However, the canons succeeded in raising money, especially in England. The proceeds allowed speedy restoration of their cathedral, rededicated in September 1114, a year and a half after the fire and only a year after the canons returned from their lucrative English voyage.[10] Herman describes this joyous event at the beginning of Book III, making it the prelude to decades of renewal in Laon and the surrounding region, most of all in the establishment of new religious communities.

---

9. On early relic tours, see Sigal, "Les voyages de reliques." Craig, *Mobile Saints*, considers relic travel beyond the eight texts Sigal examines but focuses primarily on them.

10. The rapid rebuilding suggests that the cathedral was far from wrecked and that in general Herman's account of the fire, like Guibert of Nogent's, exaggerates the extent of destruction and dislocation. Beyond the cathedral, damage appears to have been limited to the bishop's residence, a few dwellings of clerics and aristocrats, and the abbey of Saint-Jean, none of which was totally destroyed: see Hériman, *Les Miracles*, ed. and trans. Saint-Denis, 133n12, and Saint-Denis, *Apogeé d'une cité*, 103–4. Perhaps in Herman's view, the bishop's shocking murder needed to be matched rhetorically by the apocalyptic ruin that he narrates early in Book I.

Herman came to be the narrator of Laon's disaster and recovery via an indirect route.[11] He was born circa 1090 in Tournai, about seventy miles north of Laon, in the medieval county of Hainaut, now in south-western Belgium near the border with France. He was a member of the local nobility whose parents entered the religious life not long after his birth.[12] From boyhood a monk in the house of Saint-Martin in his native city, he was elected its third abbot in 1127. About a decade later he resigned from his post. There are two different stories about why. One has Herman afflicted with debilitating paralysis, the other that he was an incompetent abbot whose monastery had become disorderly and insufficiently attentive to the Rule of St. Benedict under which its monks performed their duties. The latter seems more likely to be true: Herman was an active traveler and diplomat in the next decade. Perhaps he preferred to research and write rather than supervise a monastery; all his extant literary production comes from after he left Saint-Martin.[13] His way of life after his resignation, however, was a clear violation of the Benedictine Rule, which prized stability and did not allow monks to live independently. Perhaps personal resources or connections allowed Herman to get away with continuing to call himself a monk—although he opens his dedicatory letter here by describing himself as "the scum [*peripsema*] of monks."

Herman's activities are not well documented again until 1142, but it is certain that in the late 1130s he went to Spain, to Zaragoza and

---

11. It must be noted that some scholars have long denied that "Herman the monk," the self-described author of *The Miracles of St. Mary of Laon*, was the same person as the abbot who wrote a history of his own monastery: [Herman of Tournai], *Liber de restauratione ecclesie Sancti Martini Tornacensis*, ed. Huygens; Herman of Tournai, *The Restoration of the Monastery of Saint Martin of Tournai*, trans. Nelson. In the introduction to his edition of Herman of Tournai's miracle collection, Saint-Denis addresses the controversy and, expanding on the work of Gerlinde Niemeyer, argues forcefully that Herman the monk and Herman of Tournai are the same person. To call the author of *The Miracles of St. Mary of Laon* "Herman of Laon" requires inventing a person who otherwise left no traces in the substantial historical record of the city in this era. See Niemeyer, "Die miracula S. Mariae Laudunensis" and Saint-Denis's remarks in Hériman, *Les Miracles*, 37–75. Most recently, R. B. C. Huygens collated some forty identical or near-identical passages from the Latin texts of *The Restoration* and *The Miracles* ("Herman von Tournai—Herman von Laon"). I would add to the historical and philological analyses of Niemeyer, Saint-Denis, and Huygens that the Latin of both *The Restoration* and *The Miracles* features long sentences that begin with two (or more) gerund clauses before arriving at the main verb and both favor the use of the somewhat unusual word *protinus* ("immediately"). Herman the monk was Herman of Tournai.

12. For this biographical sketch, see Hériman, *Les Miracles*, ed. and trans. Saint-Denis, 65–71, on which the next few paragraphs rely.

13. For a full list of Herman's extant writing, some of it still available only in manuscript form, see d'Haenens, "Hériman," 168–70.

probably elsewhere. An account of his visit to Zaragoza appears in a letter to Anselm, abbot of the monastery of Saint-Vincent in Laon.[14] In 1142, Herman was deputized to go to Rome to get papal approval for the reestablishment of his native Tournai as an episcopal city. Tournai was the home of bishops by about 500, but in the seventh century its diocese had been united with Noyon, about seventy-five miles to its south-southwest. Herman successfully presented the case to Pope Innocent II and during a long stay got to know Abbot Anselm of Saint-Vincent in Laon, the eventual bishop of the newly independent see of Tournai. In 1143, Herman returned to Laon. Four years later, he left for Jerusalem to join the Second Crusade, perhaps with the retinue of King Louis VII (r. 1137–80), who departed for the east in June of 1147. Herman then disappears from the historical record. He probably died in the Holy Land.

In the last years of his life, Herman was busily writing both *The Restoration of the Monastery of St. Martin of Tournai*, an account of the house where he served as abbot, and *The Miracles of St. Mary of Laon*. In a dedicatory letter addressed to Bishop Bartholomew, he notes that on a recent visit to Spain the bishop had obtained a promise from his cousin, King Alfonso, that in exchange for a copy of the writings by the early medieval archbishop Ildefonsus of Toledo, Bartholomew would receive the body of the early Christian martyr St. Vincent. That exchange never happened; if the journey to Spain was anything like recent, it was late in the life of Alfonso, who died in 1134. However, as Herman notes, he found a copy of Ildefonsus's tract on the perpetual virginity of Mary and wrote a brief *vita* of the archbishop, translated in Appendix 2. Herman goes on to explain that he proceeded to write about the relic tours as well as the efflorescence of monastic life in Laon and its surroundings in the times of Bishop Bartholomew. He does not mention that at the end of the third book, the one focused on Bartholomew's deeds, he returns to miracles, one of which dates to the time of Bishop Helinand in the late eleventh century. Guibert of Nogent wrote his own account of it, translated in Appendix 3.

The Miracles of St. Mary of Laon, then, is a mixed lot of material: it might have been titled *The Restoration of the Diocese of Laon*. Herman seems to have considered the spiritual renewal of the region in Bartholomew's time, and with his vital participation, one long miracle. At

---

14. See Constable, "Herman of Tournai and the Monastery of Saint Vincent at Valencia," which includes a translation of the letter.

a few junctures in Book III he is explicit that monastic success was a kind of miracle, while also showing how the monasteries of his diocese were nurseries of numerous abbots and bishops in the 1120s, 1130s, and 1140s. It is clear from the dedicatory letter and the (not completely accurate) last sentence of Book III—"These are the things that happened in Laon in the time of the lord bishop Bartholomew"—that Herman's final intention was to provide an admiring account of the bishop. But to do this, the monk has to perform a sleight of hand that has fooled more than one modern scholar. He mentions the election of Bartholomew before he begins his account of the relic tours, suggesting (albeit without claiming) that they went at the bishop's behest. But the French tour began only a few weeks after the disasters of the spring of 1112 while the see was vacant and the English tour only a few weeks after Bartholomew was elected bishop in March 1113. Bartholomew, then, can have done no more than approve the second tour. Both were carefully planned, the primary instigator in each case being Master Anselm of Laon. This is especially obvious for the tour of 1113, where the canons meet a number of people who had studied in Laon. "Although Bartholomew was installed in advance of the second tour, its destination and itinerary [were] clearly planned with reference to Anselm's address book."[15] Guibert of Nogent, writing only a few years after the tours, provided an account of several of their miracles in his *Monodies*, which are translated in Appendix 4. There is no indication that Herman knew of Guibert's versions of the miracles, which appear in a text quite obscure in the Middle Ages and of which no medieval manuscripts survive.

The two books that recount miracles during the relic tours appear to have been completed by 1141, whereas in III, 21, Herman notes the election of Abbot Anselm of Saint-Vincent as bishop of Tournai in early 1146.[16] Herman, then, drafted parts of the text as we have it across the course of several years; what we have represents a version that he did not consider final, as shown by his remark in the dedicatory letter to Bishop Bartholomew that he intends to write more.

Herman does not mention that the failed commune of Laon was reestablished with the approval of King Louis VI in 1128. Nor does he mention that in 1142 Bartholomew, along with the bishops of Senlis and Noyon, was suspended for agreeing to the annulment of the

---

15. Yarrow, *Saints and Their Communities*, 79.

16. See the remarks in Saint-Denis's introduction to the text: Hériman, *Les Miracles*, 71–75.

marriage of the count of Vermandois to a niece of the count of Champagne, a humiliation reversed only in 1148. Herman did not live long enough to know of his hero's rather sad end. In 1151, Bartholomew retired as a monk to the house of Foigny, which he had helped found, had supported for thirty years, and where his nephew was abbot. In 1155, Bartholomew's second successor, Gautier de Mortagne (r. 1155–74) complained that Bartholomew had mishandled his church's properties; Bartholomew wrote a letter in reply pointing out that he had founded nine monasteries and reformed five others.[17]

Bartholomew died in about 1158 as a simple monk. But however Herman manipulated chronology to enhance the bishop's role, modern historians agree that under Bartholomew's stewardship, Laon and its diocese were revitalized. The most striking evidence of renewal is the impressive cathedral of Laon, rebuilt in the new Gothic style across several decades beginning in the late twelfth century. Its towers still dominate the butte of Laon.

Text: Hériman de Tournai [=Herman of Tournai], *Les Miracles de Sainte Marie de Laon*, ed. and trans. Saint-Denis, 126–274. I have made a few emendations to Saint-Denis's excellent edition from three manuscripts: P, P3, and P4. Saint-Denis provides a full translation into French. The material about St. Norbert (III, 1–10) has been previously translated into English: *Norbert and Early Norbertine Spirituality*, trans. Antry and Neel, 69–84; the story of the dragon of Christchurch (II, 11) is translated in *The Penguin Book of Dragons*, ed. Bruce, 96–98.

---

17. *Actes des évêques de Laon*, ed. Dufour-Malbezin, 20.

The Miracles of St. Mary of Laon

Letter of the monk Herman to Bishop Bartholomew of Laon

To his venerable father and lord Bartholomew, by the grace of God bishop of the city of Laon, Brother Herman, the scum of monks: may he be united with the greatest prelates in the heavenly court.

Recently you went to Spain to see the glorious king Alfonso, the son of your maternal aunt Felicia. You received from him the very happy promise that if you went back to see him again, he would give you the body of St. Vincent, deacon and martyr, as well as the most precious chasuble that the holy Mother of God had given to St. Ildefonsus, archbishop of the city of Toledo, as a reward for the three little books on her virginity that Ildefonsus had written.[18] You then asked my humble self if I had seen those little books anywhere and ordered me to look carefully for them everywhere. When I had chanced to find them in the city of Châlons and reported it to you, you immediately gave me prepared parchment and sent me back to copy them.[19]

Therefore, I first wrote a Life of this same Ildefonsus, then joined to it his little books.[20] These written, I added the miracles that the holy Mother of God performed in France and England through her relics that are kept in her church in Laon. In fact, I wrote these miracles at your paternal command, but so that they would have greater authority and not be scorned by anyone for the crudeness of their composition, I did not want the name of my humble self to be attached to them but attributed them instead to the canons of that same church.[21] After

---

18. Alfonso (r. 1104–34), known as "the Battler" for his aggressive wars with Muslims and Christians, was king of the northern Iberian realms of Aragon and Navarre. His mother, Felicia de Roucy, was the sister of Bartholomew's mother Alix, making the bishop and the king first cousins: see below, I, 2. The body of St. Vincent of Zaragoza, martyred in ca. 304, never went to Laon. St. Ildefonsus was the archbishop of Toledo from 660 to 670. Bartholomew's sojourn to Spain is thought to have taken place somewhere from late 1118 to the autumn of 1119, so not "recently" when Herman wrote. Deacon is the clerical office just below priest.

19. Châlons-en-Champagne, known until 1998 as Châlons-sur-Marne, is about fifty-five miles southeast of Laon. For an English version of Ildefonsus's treatise, see [Ildefonsus of Toledo], *A Translation from Latin into English of De virginitate perpetua Sanctae Mariae*, trans. Donalson.

20. See Appendix 2 for the Life.

21. This likely means that Herman based his account on notes made by the canons about miracles during the relic tours recounted in Books I and II of Herman's text, reworking them in his distinctive style, which he denigrates here. He appears to have decided in the end to take credit, although Book I begins with a salutation from the canons and proceeds in the third person plural whereas Book II is in the first person plural. At the end of this introductory

those miracles, I also added material on how in your times and through your efforts, divine mercy caused nine, or rather ten, monasteries to be built through Lord Norbert and Lord Bernard, the abbot of Clairvaux, none of which existed in the time of your forty-three predecessor bishops. You furthermore appointed abbots for each new house and yet you did not refrain from reforming older ones that you found. And if by God's will life remains my companion, I have also resolved to add other things that happened in your times or that I will see happen.

Therefore, I leave this book to your paternity and the church of Laon in memory of my insignificance so that I might share in the good deeds that will have been done there.

Here begins Book I of the miracles of St. Mary of Laon

1. The prosperity and adversity of the church of Laon, the murder of Bishop Gaudry and Gerard of Quierzy, and the burning of twelve churches

To all the sons of the holy mother church scattered throughout the entire world, the canons of the church of St. Mary of Laon: may you see the god of gods in Zion.[22]

Because according to the apostle St. Paul the entire holy church is the one body of Christ and different churches and each of the faithful are the limbs of his body [see Colossians 1:24 and Romans 12:4–5], when one limb suffers all limbs suffer with it, and when one limb is glorified all limbs rejoice together, we make known to your affection in writing about the trouble and anguish our church met with in our times, as well as the consolation that it received through Our Lady, the holy Mother of God, after the affliction of that trouble, so that you, too, rejoicing together with us, may give thanks to God and his holy mother.

It is certain that from ancient times the church of Laon was famed among the distinguished churches of the kingdom of France. St. Remigius, the archbishop of Reims, enriched it with his own properties, as it says in his Life, and consecrated as its first bishop that most

---

letter, Herman mentions his plan to expand his book, so perhaps the peculiarity means he was undecided about first or third person at this stage of drafting. Guibert of Nogent, who wrote about miracles during the relic tours of 1112 and 1113 in his *Monodies* a few decades earlier (see Appendix 4) may have had access to the same notes and also worked in part from interviews with participants. It is unlikely Herman knew of Guibert's earlier narration of the journeys and miracles; he does not mention it. Guibert's accounts are somewhat different from Herman's.

22. Zion refers to the holy city of Jerusalem but also to the kingdom of heaven.

noble and vigorous man, St. Genebald.[23] And although from his times
to our age, for some five hundred years and more, Laon had flourished
in great prosperity, now in the days of Louis, king of the Franks, who
was the son of King Philip and the father of Louis the Younger, it suffered the harsh punishment of the just Judge, the king of kings.[24] Just
as at one time almighty God had excellently glorified the city of Jerusalem through King David and his son Solomon, but afterward allowed
it to be utterly destroyed by the Babylonian king Nebuchadnezzar because of the sins of its inhabitants, so also our church that, as mentioned before, God had lifted up in great glory for a very long time, he
allowed not to be completely destroyed in our days, but plagued with
great trouble to the extent that this prophecy could truly be said of it:
"It suffered twofold at the hand of God for all its sins" [Isaiah 40:2].[25]

Moreover, a certain disturbance preceded the trouble, which seems
to have been, as it were, its seed and root, the harbinger of future ca-
lamity. When a certain prince, indeed a noble one, Gerard of Quierzy
by name, the castellan of Laon, was humbly praying on bended knee
in the church of the holy Mother of God, his enemies—who did not
dare to attack him elsewhere—deceitfully surrounded him. As he rose
from prayer he was murdered on the spot by numerous sword thrusts.[26]
The pavement of the church was spattered with his blood, which could
not be fully washed away after it was mopped several times. Many who
came to look marveled at this to no small degree. The most wise man
Master Anselm, at that time canon and dean of our church, well known

---

23. St. Remigius (d. 533) was best known for converting and baptizing Clovis, the king of
the Franks, in 496. A Life of Remigius, which is probably largely legendary, was not written
until the ninth century. That Remigius founded the diocese of Laon is subject to debate; the
Genebald Herman mentions (d. ca. 550) is reported to have been Remigius's nephew.

24. King Philip I was succeeded by his son Louis VI and grandson Louis VII. Not until the
times of Louis VII's son Philip II (r. 1180–1223) did kings in what was once the western part
of the empire of Charlemagne begin to style themselves "King of France."

25. The biblical kings of Israel David and Solomon, whose deeds are recorded in the
biblical books of Samuel and Kings, and then (from a different interpretive perspective) in
Chronicles, ruled in the tenth century BCE. Solomon is credited with building the sumptu-
ous First Temple. During the capture of Jerusalem in 587 BCE by Nebuchadnezzar II, king of
Babylon, the temple was looted and destroyed as punishment for a series of wicked kings (2
Kings 19–25; 2 Chronicles 36).

26. Gerard of Quierzy was the royal castellan, or master of the king's castle, in Laon, as
well as lord of his own domain west of the city. He was also the advocate, a layman charged
with carrying out secular business for an ecclesiastical lord or a religious institution, of Laon's
ancient abbey of Saint-Jean. He was thus one of the most important people in the city. For a
colorful account of his life and death, and the part played in it by Bishop Gaudry, see Guibert
of Nogent, *Monodies*, 117–20. Gerard's murder took place on Friday, January 13, 1111.

throughout almost the whole Latin world for his learning and eloquence, is said to have pronounced during private conversations with a number of people that this bloodshed could not be washed away except by the burning of the church: so great a crime would be expiated not by water but fire.[27]

The wise man was not deceived in his opinion. After a short time, with the permission of God and at the goading of the devil, Lord Gaudry, the city's bishop, was cruelly slain in his house along with several of his knights amid a sudden insurrection incited by townspeople.[28] The church of St. Mary, with some ten other neighboring churches, houses adjacent to the bishop's residence, the canons' houses, and those of numerous townspeople were burned through arson. Furthermore, the entire city of Laon, its people dispersed to various places, seemed wrecked nearly to the point of obliteration, so damaged that many who passed through it, seeing its ruins and ashes, poured out tears in great compassion and reflected fittingly on the lamentation of Jeremiah over such things: "How lonely she sits, the city once filled with people, the lady of nations made to be like a widow" [Lamentations 1:1].[29] Furthermore, just as once upon a time God allowed the city of Jerusalem to be destroyed and the sons of Israel to be taken captive, yet left the prophet Jeremiah with them as consolation for the few who remained, he mercifully preserved for us, likewise thrust into grave misfortune, two most wise men, namely the aforementioned Master Anselm and his brother Master Ralph, who sweetly consoled both clergy and laity, refreshed them with various sentences from scripture, and encouraged them not to fail in the face of adversity.[30]

2. On the election of the lord bishop Bartholomew and his nobility

Amid such consoling conversations, the brothers carefully and attentively discussed with wise religious men whether they could find

---

27. Herman does not exaggerate the celebrity and importance of Anselm of Laon (ca. 1050–1117) and his school. Born of humble parents in the city, he was educated elsewhere and returned to Laon by around 1090 to lead its cathedral school while serving as an officer of the cathedral clergy. Cathedral and monastery schools were the chief institutions of higher learning in Europe before the rise of the universities that began in the twelfth century. Anselm was a noted theologian whose teaching drew students from across western Europe, bringing on a housing shortage in Laon. In Herman's hands, Anselm was also a prophet.

28. Gaudry was assassinated on Thursday, April 25, 1112. As noted in the introduction, the uprising was hardly spontaneous.

29. The subject of the biblical book of Lamentations, attributed to the prophet Jeremiah, is the ruin of Jerusalem after its capture by Nebuchadnezzar in 587 BCE.

30. Anselm's brother Ralph (d. ca. 1133) succeeded him as master of the Laon cathedral school on Anselm's death in 1117.

anyone able to repair such wretched and dreadful loss. At last, with God's inspiration, they reached a sound decision: they should choose as the city's bishop Lord Bartholomew, canon and treasurer of the church of St. Mary of Reims, very well known in the lands of Reims and Laon as much for the nobility of his family as for the uprightness of his ways.[31] In fact, the excellence of his kindred was proclaimed not only in France but also in Spain, Burgundy, and Lotharingia.[32]

His grandfather, Count Hilduin of Roucy, married Adelaide, the sister of Archbishop Manasses of Reims.[33] Their children were Ebles, count of Roucy; André, count of Ramerupt and the father of Bishop Ebles of Châlons; and seven daughters.

King Sancho of Aragon married one of the daughters, named Felicia, and fathered with her the mighty king Alfonso, who upon succeeding his father took strong cities and castles from the pagans in violent battles—namely Zaragoza, famed for the archidiaconate of the martyr St. Vincent, Tarragona as well as Tudela, Barbastro, Burgos, and many others—and handed them over to Christians. When he had subjugated nearly all of Spain, his reputation grew to the extent that some called him another Julius [Caesar], others a second Charles, in memory of that renowned Charles, king of the Franks, who was once the victorious conqueror of Spain.[34]

---

31. That is, before his election as bishop of Laon, Bartholomew was a member of the cathedral staff serving as the superintendent of the treasury of the archiepiscopal cathedral of Reims, about thirty miles southeast of Laon.

32. In the twelfth century, Burgundy, in what is now southeastern France and western Switzerland, was a duchy within the Holy Roman Empire. To its north lay Lotharingia (also known as Lorraine), another part of the empire that included most of present-day Belgium and the Netherlands plus parts of northeastern France, western Germany, and all of Luxembourg. The point is that the bishop's reputation was widespread across western Europe.

33. As Herman shows in this section, Bartholomew's relations married into royal and other noble families and some of its other members had distinguished careers in the church. The common ancestor of all of those mentioned here was Count Hilduin III (d. 1063), a nobleman from the Champagne region south of Laon. He was count of Ramerupt by inheritance and count of Roucy by marriage to the heiress Adele. The genealogy of this family is complicated, but Herman—one of whose sources was surely Bartholomew himself—makes, according to modern scholarship, few manifest errors. This sentence contains one of them: Manasses II, archbishop of Reims (r. 1096–1106) was not Adele's brother but Hilduin's nephew. I will comment on only a few of the three dozen or so people in Herman's genealogical excursus. For women in this family Herman calls *Adela, Adelada,* and *Adelaidis,* I anglicize the appellations in Bur, *La formation du comté de Champagne.*

34. On Alfonso, see Herman's dedicatory letter above. He conquered Zaragoza from the Muslims Herman calls "pagans" in 1118, then Tarragona and Tudela in 1119. Barbastro had been conquered by Alfonso's half brother Peter in 1100; Burgos remained, as it had been since the eleventh century, a city in the Christian kingdom of Castile. It is an enormous exaggeration to say Alfonso conquered most of Spain and unlikely that he was thought of as a new

Rotrou, count of Perche, married Count Hilduin's second daughter, who bore Count Rotrou and Juliana, the mother of Queen Marguerite of Navarre.[35]

The third daughter, Margaret, married Hugh, count of Clermont, who was the father of Renaud, who in turn was the father, by Countess Adelaide of Vermandois, of Marguerite, wife of the renowned Count Charles of Flanders.[36]

The fourth daughter, Ermentrude, married Thibaut, count of Reynel, the father of Hildiarde, who in turn was the mother of Count Bertrand who died in Spain. Her sister Beatrice bore Bartholomew, archdeacon and treasurer of Laon, by Hughes of Montcornet.[37]

The fifth daughter, Ada, married Godfrey of Guise, the father of Guy, the father of Bouchard. After Godfrey's death, Ada took as her husband Gautier d'Ath. After his death, she took as her third husband Thierry of Avesnes and with him founded the monastery called Liessies with her own property. After Thierry's death, Ada gave herself entirely to that same monastery where, after many years of religious life, she died and was buried.[38]

Ernulf, count of Warcq, married the sixth daughter, who bore Otho, count of Chiny; Otho was the father of Aubert who was the father of Count Aubert.

A very noble prince in Burgundy called Fulk of Jur (or of la Sarraz) ascertained the nobility and excellence of Count Hilduin and sought the hand of one of his daughters in marriage. When he got nowhere—Hilduin

---

Julius Caesar or Charlemagne (who ruled only a small part of northeastern Spain). But Herman is not wrong that Alfonso was a highly successful warrior who conquered many cities, most of them under Muslim rule.

35. This daughter, Beatrice, married not Rotrou but Geoffrey of Perche.

36. The count of Clermont Margaret married was actually named Renaud. Charles "the Good" was count of Flanders from 1119 until his assassination in 1127. For a detailed account of the brutal murder and its aftermath, see Galbert of Bruges, *The Murder, Betrayal, and Slaughter of the Glorious Charles*, trans. Rider. Oddly, Herman says nothing of the murder and its aftermath, although he participated in the final burial of the count's body: Herman, *The Restoration*, 51–52.

37. Bertrand of Reynel entered the service of his cousin by marriage, King Alfonso, in 1112. He died fighting alongside Alfonso at the Battle of Fraga in 1134. Bertrand's nephew Bartholomew was not the bishop of Laon but his first cousin once removed. This Bartholomew was archdeacon, treasurer, and chancellor of the cathedral of Laon before serving as bishop of Beauvais from 1162 until his death in 1175.

38. This was actually a refoundation, in 1095, of a house first founded in the eighth century. It was not unusual for highborn women to retire to the precincts of a male monastery in this era. Liessies is a little more than forty miles north-northeast of Laon. By "gave herself entirely," Herman may mean that she turned over all her property to the monastery; it appears she was childless.

swore he would never give a daughter to a Burgundian—it happened that Philip, king of the Franks, sent off Count Hilduin with Lord Helinand, the bishop of Laon, and some other nobles to the lord pope in Rome concerning the affairs of his kingdom.[39] When this was announced to Prince Fulk, he set ambushes in many places for them as they returned. He did not want to release these men, captured on their journey and stripped of all their possessions, until the count promised under oath that he would give Fulk his daughter. Once the pledge was accepted, Fulk freed them all, generously conferred many gifts on them, and sent them home with great honor. Therefore, once returned to France, Count Hilduin joined his daughter Alix in marriage with that prince, sending her off to Burgundy with great riches.[40] With her, Fulk fathered the lord bishop Bartholomew as well as other sons and daughters. One of them was Ermentrude, whom Count Henry of Grandpré married after she returned to France from Burgundy. With her, he fathered Count Henry, with whom he shared a name, and his sister Adele, who was the mother of Richard, archdeacon of Verdun and Laon.

Therefore, while still a little boy, this Bartholomew was sent to France to his uncle Ebles, the count of Roucy, then handed over to be educated by the lord archbishop Manasses of Reims, his mother's uncle. He was made first a canon of the church of Notre-Dame of Reims, then its treasurer. But later on, when he was already canon of the church of Laon, Countess Adelaide, of Vermandois, wife of Hugh the Great whose brother was Philip, king of the Franks, after the death of the said Hugh (with whom she had Ralph, count of Vermandois, and Simon, bishop of Noyon) had married Renaud, the count of Clermont. And knowing that this same Bartholomew was her husband's first cousin, for love of Renaud the countess made him treasurer of the church of Saint-Quentin in Vermandois.[41]

---

39. Helinand (r. 1052–96) was a man of modest origins from the Paris region. Scorned by Guibert of Nogent as poorly educated, he became the chaplain of the English king (later St.) Edward the Confessor (r. 1042–66) and Edward's representative to the French king Henry I (r. 1031–60). According to Guibert, after amassing great wealth in England, Helinand bribed Henry to name him bishop of Laon. In any case, surviving documents and Guibert's grudging praise show he was a sincere pastor, patron, and defender of his diocese. See *Actes des évêques de Laon*, ed. Dufour-Malbezin, 15–16 and 97–123, and Guibert of Nogent, *Monodies*, 89 and 108–9.

40. The hostage-taking and subsequent marriage of Alix and Fulk took place in 1074: see *Actes des évêques de Laon*, ed. Dufour-Malbezin, 18.

41. Bartholomew was born around 1080, sent to be educated by his cousin Archbishop Manasses around 1095, and became treasurer of the cathedral chapter of Reims in about

And so, as was said earlier, Bartholomew was renowned for the nobility of his family, the uprightness of his ways, and the abundance of his riches. Thus, elected with the unanimous assent of all the clergy and people to be the bishop of Laon, he was presented to the lord archbishop Ralph of Reims, who had succeeded the aforementioned Manasses, his mother's uncle. Once consecrated amid a distinguished crowd by Ralph and many other bishops in the time of Pope Pascal and Louis, king of the Franks, in the year of the Lord's incarnation 1113, he was sent as the new shepherd to a forsaken flock.[42]

But arriving in Laon and finding no church, no episcopal residence, indeed nearly nothing but cinders and ashes, it is impossible to say how much he grieved, how much he sighed, for he lamented that he had not been lifted up with an honor but weighed down with a burden. This line of scripture could rightly seem to have suited him at the time: "Man is born to trouble" [Job 5:7]. What the Lord says of himself in the gospel was also suitable—"The Son of Man has no place to rest his head" [Luke 9:58]—as well as what the apostle St. Paul wrote: "If someone desires the office of bishop, he desires a good work" [1 Timothy 3:1]—work, Paul says, not honor.

And so Bartholomew came from great leisure and riches and all sorts of bodily pleasure to a desolate place. He did not boast that he had been promoted to the preeminence of high office but said he had been called to perform a task and if he perhaps desired the office of bishop, he desired a good work.[43] Immediately, therefore, as if he had passed into some wasteland, he began to restore the church and the episcopal houses at the same time and rebuild them, as it were, from their foundations.

3. The miracles of St. Mary throughout France

But because, as was said before, not only had the cathedral of Our Lady been burned, but also about twelve other churches along with many houses of clergy and laity, most of the citizens had been scattered around the region and everyone who had stayed in the city was so busy

---

1103. He was named treasurer of the basilica of Saint-Quentin a few years later thanks to the influence of Adelaide, the second wife of his cousin Count Renaud of Clermont.

42. The consecration took place in March 1113; for more details, see III, 1, below. The date is not in the printed edition but appears in P3 and P4: *anno dominicae incarnationis m.° c.° xiii°*.

43. That is, Bartholomew could have continued the easy life as a cathedral canon and official, permitted to live in the style that befitted his wealth. The remark about bodily pleasure suggested that like many secular canons of his day, he lived the high life and perhaps even had a family. The general point, though, is clear: Bartholomew's life was going to become more, not less, difficult with his election as bishop when he was in his early thirties.

with repairing their own houses that scarcely anyone could be found who would come to the aid of the mother church.[44] Several wise and religious men advised that we send some clerics of good reputation around France with the relics of Our Lady and other saints to seek alms from the faithful. Following their advice, we chose from among our brothers seven canons, namely Boso, Robert, Anselm, Herbert, [another] Robert, Boniface, the priest Amisard, and Odo, who was later the abbot of the monastery called Bonne-Espérance in the diocese of Cambrai.[45] We joined with them six lay citizens, namely Richard, John Piot, Odo, Lambert, Boso, and Theodoric of Bruyères. We sent them off with the reliquary of Our Lady and other vessels containing relics to receive the donations of the faithful.

The church had been burned on the Thursday of Easter week, and they departed on the Thursday before Pentecost, that is, on the octave of Ascension Day. They were away until about the feast of Matthew the Evangelist.[46] Thus the Lord—to whom it is said through the prophet, "God, you drove us away and destroyed us, you are angry and then took pity on us" [Psalm 59/60:1] and elsewhere "When you are angry, you will remember mercy" [Habakkuk 3:2]—was placated by the prayers of his most loving mother and in his mercy did not delay reviving our church that he had allowed to be harshly whipped. On this journey, God indeed showed many miracles through Our Lady's relics. We have committed to writing only a few of the best known to the notice of posterity, omitting some others.

4. Two cripples healed at the castle of Issoudun

There is a castle called Issoudun in the territory of Bourges.[47] The lord of this castle was a very rich man named Geoffrey who for the benefit of his soul had long housed and fed two cripples whose heels were so stuck to their buttocks that they could not walk at all or even stand up. When

---

44. Herman has increased the count of burned churches by two since the beginning of Book I!

45. Herman actually names eight canons. Bonne-Espérance was founded in 1130; Odo was its first abbot. It is located about sixty miles northeast of Laon in present-day southwestern Belgium.

46. That is, the fire was on Thursday, April 25, 1112. The canons departed six weeks later, on Thursday, June 6, and returned approximately fifteen weeks after that, around Saturday, September 21.

47. Issoudun, the first recorded stop in this tour, is about two hundred miles southwest of Laon. Herman does not specify the route, but the canons probably went via Paris and Orléans before leaving royal territory and entering the region of Berry.

Table 1. The Laon canons' route, 1112

LOCATION	APPROXIMATE WALKING DISTANCE AND DIRECTION	DATE OF ARRIVAL
Issoudun	216 miles southwest of Laon	
Buzançais	30 miles west and slightly south	
Cormery	41 miles northwest	
Tours	13 miles northwest	
Saint-Laurent-de-Lin	24 miles northwest	Saturday, August 10
Angers	41 miles west	
Le Mans	55 miles northeast	
Mont de la Garde	14 miles north and slightly east	
Chartres	63 miles east and slightly north	Saturday, September 7
Laon	138 miles northeast	ca. Saturday, September 21

Total distance traveled: approximately 635 miles

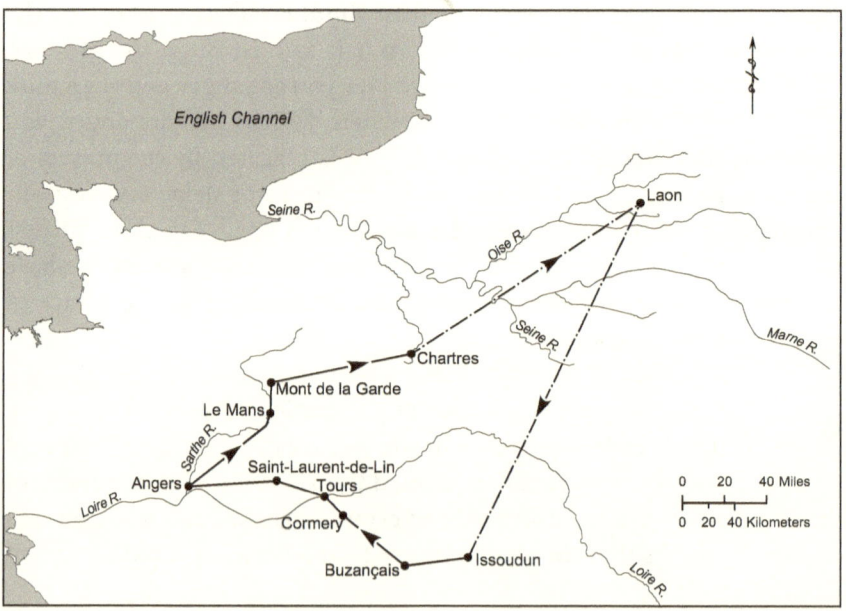

MAP 2. The Laon canons' route, 1112

the feretory of Our Lady had been welcomed in a great procession and placed in the church, the pair asked to be taken there to have their heels and legs washed in water in which the relics had been bathed.[48] Once

---

48. That is, water with which the reliquary had been washed; the fragile items described at the beginning of Book II could not be washed without quickly destroying them. The process is repeated throughout the relic tours.

this was done, in the sight of all the flesh that had stuck to their buttocks began to disintegrate and blood flow abundantly down their legs. Quickly lifted to their feet, they embraced the reliquary. Completely healed, they followed our brothers until they returned to Laon, where every day they urged the people to carry stones, bring water, and prepare cement for work on the church. When the church was finished, one of them returned to his land, that is, to the castle of Issoudun, and the other, named Benedict, stayed in Laon and served in the hospital for the poor for nearly twelve years before dying there.

5. A deaf and mute youth cured at the castle of Buzançais

Leaving Issoudun, they went to another castle, called Buzançais, whose lord was so greedy and savage that many of the inhabitants told our brothers that he had taken away everything they had.[49] He had a son, about fifteen years old, who was deaf and mute from birth. The Mother of Mercy soon came to the aid of our terrified brothers. A certain pious monk who lived there, hearing about the miracles of Our Lady, welcomed the feretory into his church with great honor and then, after putting his liturgical garb back on, washed the relics in wine and water.[50] He poured that water on the head and face of the aforementioned youth and gave him some of it to drink and ordered him to lie down beneath the feretory as he himself, on bended knee, began to pray, beseeching Our Lady. Without delay, the youth fell asleep, and as in his anguish sweat flowed from his entire body, the veins around his ears swelled and blood flowed copiously from them. Soon awakening, he got up and made some noises. The monk, rising from prayer, joyfully ran and spoke to him. The youth, who had never heard before, did not know how to reply, but repeated whatever he heard the monk say.[51] The monk immediately summoned the people by ringing bells, showed them the youth speaking and hearing, and as he wept with joy began the *Te Deum laudamus.*[52] At once a messenger was sent to his father, on his way back from plundering, and reported what had happened to his

---

49. Violent and rapacious castellans were not limited to royal territory.

50. There was no monastery in Buzançais in the twelfth century. There were a few nearby, but the likeliest explanation is that the man was a local hermit living a solitary religious life who had his own small oratory.

51. Here I follow the text of P3. The printed edition, following P, has a crowd around the feretory and then the monk summoning witnesses. The P3 text makes more narrative sense, and its Latin syntax is more straightforward.

52. "We praise you, God," a hymn dating to the fourth century that was part of the monastic liturgy.

son. Removing his boots in haste, he ran barefoot to the church. Throwing himself to the ground before the feretory, he thanked the Mother of Mercy, then offered forty pennies because he did not have much money.

6. Peace made between castles at odds

From here our brothers wanted to go to another castle only two miles off, but because of the savagery and pillaging of the Buzançais brigand, none of the local inhabitants dared to set out with them. However, the brigand, roused by the mercy of the Mother of God, along with his knights and some other inhabitants lifted the feretory and relics on their shoulders. All proceeding barefoot, they headed toward the castle of their enemies, who, upon hearing this and learning about the miracle that the holy Mother of God had worked for the brigand's son, all rushed out, likewise barefoot, to meet their enemies. They joyfully carried into their castle the feretory handed over by the others, praising the mercy of Christ who through his mother had made enemy parties run toward each other in peace.

7. A sick woman cured in Tours

From there they went to Tours via Cormery, and welcomed with the greatest reverence by the archbishop of Tours on a Saturday before Vespers, they rested in the church of Saint-Maurice.[53] For eight years, the wife of a carpenter in this city had been bedridden, so weighed down by great illness that she could not go anywhere unless carried. That night, the Mother of Mercy appeared to her as she slept, telling her that she should have herself brought to her feretory in the church of Saint-Maurice. Waking up, the woman asked her husband that she be taken there at once. Not very rich and having no litter prepared, he had her taken in a lowly apparatus that in the vernacular we call a *vannus*, on which threshed grain is accustomed to be cleaned. Placed under the feretory, she quickly fell asleep. Waking up after a little while she rose, cured. Then in the sight of the people and accompanied by the feretory, she followed it to the church of Saint-Martin.[54]

---

53. Tours was an important pilgrimage site in the Middle Ages because it housed the tomb of St. Martin of Tours, on whom see the general introduction. The cathedral of Saint-Maurice was rebuilt in the early twelfth century, so it may have been under construction when the Laon canons stayed there. The archbishop was Ralph II (r. 1086–1117).

54. It is several hundred yards from the cathedral to the monastery dedicated to St. Martin, an impressive distance for someone who had not walked in eight years.

8. A deaf and mute youth cured in Tours

When they had heard about this, the canons of Saint-Martin, along with the abbot of Saint-Julien, went out to meet them and received the relics of Our Lady with the greatest honor.[55] In that city there was a youth, deaf and mute from his mother's womb, whom a fuller had raised from infancy and trained in his craft. Once brought to the relics of Our Lady, he lay down underneath the feretory and went to sleep. Without delay, he began to suffer anguish and sweat all over his body until, when the veins around his ears had swollen, blood flowed copiously out of them. He got up immediately and heard, yet he did not know how to speak, because he had not learned, but repeated what he heard others say. Because his name was not known, our canons called him Christian. He joined our brothers, went with them to Laon, and stayed about seven years in the house of the lord archdeacon Guy of Laon.[56]

9. The vengeance exacted by St. Mary in Saint-Laurent-de-Lin

Leaving the city of Tours, they came to Saint-Laurent-de-Lin on the feast day of that martyr.[57] A monk who lived there did not want to permit the feretory of Our Lady to be placed on the altar of St. Lawrence but rather put on a lesser altar elsewhere in the church, clearly fearing that he would lose the accustomed offering on this feast day.[58] But when the people of Tours who followed our relics reported the miracles they had seen and encouraged all the pilgrims who arrived to abandon the major altar and make their offerings at the feretory of Our Lady, the monk was stricken with spiteful envy and ordered the feretory and all the relics to be thrown out of the church.

The provost of the castle, reproaching the monk, gave our brothers a roomy pavilion he had readied for himself.[59] Local matrons, bringing many wall hangings, busied themselves with adorning the pavilion

---

55. The monastery of Saint-Julien was near the cathedral.

56. Guibert of Nogent paints an unflattering portrait of Guy of Montaigu, the son of a local castellan and cathedral archdeacon, as one of Bishop Gaudry's allies in the events of 1111 and 1112, complicit in the murder of Gerard de Quierzy (Guibert of Nogent, *Monodies*, 125–27).

57. That is, they arrived on Saturday, August 10, 1112.

58. This monk was apparently also a priest who served the local parish church. Since as in the case of Buzançais there was no monastery in the settlement, he may well have been from a monastery nearby or a solitary religious seeker. For another story of a hostile cleric who feared the diversion of offerings for his church to the Laon canons, see II, 10.

59. A provost was a lord's steward or agent.

most fittingly and furthermore provided enough lamps to make it very bright all night. But the just king Jesus Christ did not want the insult to his mother to go unpunished. At Vespers, the monk, suddenly stricken with falling sickness, sank to the ground in front of all the people and terrified these onlookers.[60] The largest bell fell from its tower and cracked; the tower itself, its upper part split and broken, creaked. At this sight the monk belatedly regretted his bad behavior, and prostrate on the ground, barefoot, he humbly made satisfaction to the queen of heaven before the feretory. He asked that it be placed on the high altar, but our brothers refused to grant his request.

10. A woman in labor healed in Angers

From there they went to Angers and received a splendid welcome from the city's bishop.[61] A woman there, the wife of a very wealthy man, Fulbert Pellicier, had been tormented by great labor pains for some days and now feared that her death was close at hand. Hearing of the miracles of Our Lady, she asked the relics to be brought to her. Once they arrived, she made an offering of a gold spoon and in faith drank water in which the relics had been bathed. The birth was quickly brought; now freed, she gave thanks to God and his kind mother.

11. A sterile woman healed and made fertile

A sterile woman in Le Mans, along with her very wealthy husband, offered hospitality to our brothers. Prostrate before the feretory of Our Lady, she prayed that a child be given to her. She was not disappointed in her faith: after a year passed she bore a son and thereafter went frequently to Laon, giving thanks to Our Lady in her church.

12. A miracle at the castle of Mont de la Garde

Between the city of Le Mans and a castle called Mont de la Garde, the path was extremely perilous, covered over with trees felled by the people of the region because of the current conflict and strife between the king of England and the count of Anjou.[62] Slowly leaving Le Mans, the canons came to this difficult passage. Everyone they met said they could not possibly get through nor reach the castle for which they were

---

60. "Falling sickness" is epilepsy.

61. Angers was the capital city of the counts of Anjou. The bishop was Renaud de Martigné (r. 1102–24), subsequently archbishop of Reims from 1124 to 1139.

62. The conflict was between King Henry I and Count Fulk V (r. 1109–29). Since he was also the duke of Normandy, Henry was frequently at odds with his continental neighbors.

headed. Meanwhile, day turned to night, and the swift arrival of a heavy downpour drove them almost to despair of their safety. "Therefore they called out to the Lord in their affliction and he delivered them from their distress" [Psalm 106/107:28]. Suddenly God took pity on them and they proceeded with such ease that there was no hindrance whatsoever. Knights went out to meet them as they reached the castle and, marveling greatly at how they had gotten through, welcomed them most kindly, saying that truly the mercy of God had been with them. The next day, when on departure they wanted to continue along the same route, they made no headway until the path was cleared with great effort. And thus they gave thanks to the gracious Mother of the Lord, who had shown them great mercy in their hour of great distress.[63]

13. Three miracles St. Mary worked in Chartres

They arrived in Chartres before Vespers on the day before the Nativity of Our Lady and were most honorably welcomed by the lord bishop Ivo of Chartres.[64] Leaving the city, a procession of the city's canons went as far as the vineyards to meet them, and the feretory was placed in the cathedral on the altar of St. Mary. There was a crippled woman in the city whom that same bishop had already supported for five years in the house where his bread was baked. Because of great illness, she lay so bent over that she could not go out for a call of nature unless carried by two people. At the first hour of the night, Our Lady appeared to her as she slept, directing her to get up as soon as possible, go to the cathedral, and seek out her feretory from Laon. Waking at once, she rose, healed, and running to the church through the streets shouted with joy. "Lady St. Mary! Lady St. Mary!" The bishop's household followed her, and the bishop himself was roused from sleep, hearing and rejoicing that the poor woman was healed. She entered the church and asked loudly where the feretory of St. Mary of Laon was. Standing before it, she gave thanks to Mary and told everyone how she had appeared to her.

Right away the bishop ordered all the bells to be rung for a long while, and he himself began the *Te Deum laudamus*. During the hymn, behold! another crippled woman, very well known to the bishop and all

---

63. This story is rather enigmatic. God and Mary miraculously created safe passage only when canons were stalled on a blocked path in a downpour as darkness fell, a mercy seemingly unnecessary in broad daylight.

64. Ivo, bishop of Chartres from 1090 to 1115, was a renowned authority on canon (church) law. Chartres Cathedral was home to another Marian relic, said to be the tunic worn by the Virgin Mary at the birth of Jesus.

the others, entered the church healed. Coming straight to the feretory, she placed on the altar two little hand-trestles that she was accustomed to take with her as she crawled and lifted herself up as she went about begging for alms. Standing before the people, she gave thanks to God and his gentle mother. The bishop instantly ordered all the bells to be rung again, repeating the aforementioned hymn.

Before it was finished, it pleased divine mercy to add a third miracle. A young knight, the son of the vidame of Chartres, who had been held captive in a castle in chains, suddenly and unexpectedly entered the church.[65] As his mother, his knights, and townspeople ran to meet him, in his happiness he went to the altar and on bent knee before the feretory, saying that he had been set free by Our Lady, he straightaway made her an offering of forty silver pennies. At this sight, the bishop ordered that all the bells be rung at length, not only in the cathedral but also in all the other churches, even the smallest, throughout the city, and that praises to God be sung at the direction of his messengers while he began the *Te Deum laudamus* for the third time. How great the clanging and crashing of bells all over the city, what sound of rejoicing, how many rivers of sweet tears of great exultation poured from people of both sexes and different ages the pious reader can easily imagine even if we keep silent.

Thus, our brothers, gladdened by the miracles of St. Mary and enriched by the gifts of the faithful, joyfully returned to us around the feast of St. Matthew the evangelist, causing the entire city of Laon to rejoice greatly at reports of this sort, which brought us new delight after the affliction of trouble. May God, who lives and reigns forever, be blessed in all things.

Here ends Book I concerning the miracles that St. Mary worked in France

Here begins Book II concerning miracles worked throughout England

The church of Our Lady was repaired in considerable part during the fall and winter using the offerings of the faithful collected in France.[66] During the following Lent, since the greater part of the work remained but the money was running out little by little, some wise men advised

---

65. A vidame was a bishop's administrator of secular affairs.
66. That is, the fall of 1112 and the winter of 1112–13.

us that once again, some canons should be chosen who would do honor to the church of Laon as much for their learning as their skill in chanting and that they should be sent, along with the feretory of Our Lady and the relics of the saints, to England, which at that time flourished with a great abundance of riches because of the peace and justice that King Henry, son of King William, made there.[67] So from among the canons the priest Boso and his nephew Robert, the priest Ralph, Matthew and his kinsman Boniface, the English-born Robert, Helinand, John, priest of the parish of Saint-Martin, and the cleric Amisard were chosen.[68] That done, we gave them the feretory of Our Lady and many other saints' relics, among which there stood out for its beauty and worthiness a phylactery on which this inscription is read: "A sponge, the Lord's cross, with a muslin cloth and a face-cloth. May your hair, mother and virgin, also sanctify me."[69]

So we sent off to England our aforementioned companions, supported by such great protection, also praying for their good fortune. We followed them for a little way in a great procession, then we let them go in peace from the city of Laon on the Monday before Palm Sunday. On their return in September of the same year, around the feast of the Nativity of St. Mary, they reported as follows what had happened to them.[70]

---

67. King Henry I was the youngest son of King William I, better known as William the Conqueror (r. 1066–87). The domestic peace Herman refers to was in sharp contrast to a civil war over disputed succession that broke out in England after Henry's death, during the time Herman was writing. On the prosperity of southern England at this time, see Yarrow, *Saints and Their Communities*, 81–84.

68. As many as five of these—Boso, the two Roberts, Boniface, and Amisard—may have been the same men in the party that had set out for west-central France the previous June. "Parish" refers to the area around a local church or the people who attend that church. The parish (in the former sense) of Saint-Martin was just to the west of the cathedral. Herman does not mention laymen, who went on the first tour, but some probably joined the second one as well.

69. A phylactery in Christian tradition is a small reliquary. The exact contents of this one are a little hard to identify. There was a piece of the cross on which Jesus died; a sponge soaked in vinegar or wine is mentioned in the accounts of the Crucifixion by Matthew, Mark, and John. The linens may have been thought to be scraps of Jesus's garb divided among the soldiers standing guard at the cross according to all four Gospels or the shroud in which he was buried, also mentioned in all four accounts. Several churches were said to have some of Mary's hair during the Middle Ages. The inscription is four rhymes in pairs of seven and then nine syllables: *Spongia, crux Domini / cum sindone, cum faciali / Me sacrat atque tui / genitrix et virgo capilli*. On other relics the canons carried, see II, 2, below.

70. The departure was on Monday, March 24, 1113; at the end of this book Herman specifies that the return was two days before the Nativity of Our Lady, that is, Saturday, September 6, 1113. The canons were away for five and a half months.

Table 2.   The Laon canons' route, 1113

LOCATION	APPROXIMATE WALKING DISTANCE AND DIRECTION	DATE OF ARRIVAL
Nesle	38 miles northwest of Laon	
Arras	40 miles north and slightly west	ca. Friday, April 4
Saint-Omer	44 miles northwest	
Wissant	30 miles northwest	
Dover[a]	23 miles northwest via the English Channel	
Canterbury	16 miles northeast (of Dover)	
Winchester	120 miles west and slightly south	by Thursday, May 15
Christchurch	34 miles southwest	Saturday, May 24
Exeter	85 miles west	
Salisbury	88 miles east-northeast	
Wilton	3 miles west and slightly north	
Bodmin	145 miles southwest	
Barnstaple	59 miles northeast	
Totnes	55 miles south-southeast	
Bristol	98 miles northeast	
Bath	12 miles southeast	
Laon	343 miles southeast[b]	Saturday, September 6

Total distance traveled: approximately 1,235 miles

[a] Dover is the likeliest destination from Wissant. Herman does not specify the port of entry.

[b] This calculation assumes the most direct route from Bath back to Dover (180 miles), crossing the English Channel from there to Wissant (23 miles), and finally the most direct route from Wissant to Laon (140 miles).

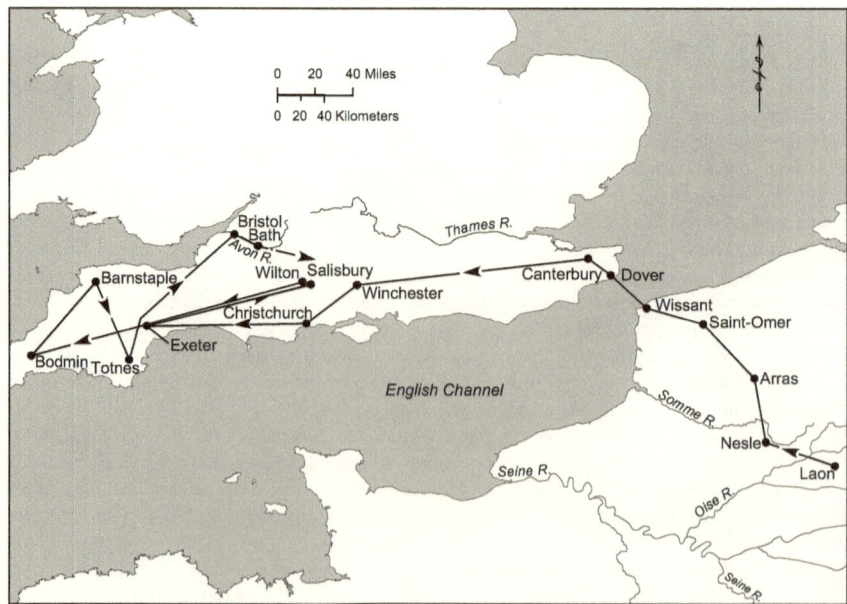

MAP 3.   The Laon canons' route, 1113

1. A deaf and mute man

After leaving you, they said, we came to the castle called Nesle, in the Vermandois region, and were welcomed honorably by the canons and Lord Ralph, prince and master of the castle and father of Lord Ivo.[71] This Ralph had in his house a man named John, deaf and mute from birth, whom he had brought up from infancy to the age of manhood, to the point that by then John had a long beard. Seeing people hasten to the church because of the holy relics, John himself, alerted by his lord through gestures, ran along with the others. Next, after he drank water in which the holy relics had been washed and carefully bathed his mouth and ears in it, he lay down beneath the feretory and went to sleep. Without delay, in the sight of all, he began to sweat all over his body in great anguish. Blood poured copiously out of his ears, nose, and the veins that protruded around his throat and neck as if they had burst. Waking a bit later, he rose and standing before the feretory cried out in a voice of exultation—but not of confession, because he did not know how to speak, never having learned as one who had never heard. Still, hearing what others said and wishing to reply to those who addressed and spoke to him, he repeated what they said. Nobody will be able to report adequately what joy there was among the people and what shouts rang forth. Completely healed, he followed us almost to the sea and would have made the crossing with us had we not asked him to return.[72]

2. A blind goldsmith cured in Arras

From there, coming to the city of Arras around Good Friday, we were no less honorably welcomed. There was an old goldsmith who lived in that city, by then deprived of sight for twelve years. After he heard that the feretory of St. Mary of Laon had arrived, he asked about its form, nature, and dimensions. When he had learned all that, he drew heavy sighs from deep in his chest and wept profusely, saying, "Alas, as a young sinner I made that feretory with my own hands at the order of Lord Helinand, the bishop of Laon. The bishop placed the most precious relics in it, among them the head of the abbot St. Walaric and also the head of St. Montanus who, as I heard it from that bishop, upon

---

71. Ralph (d. ca. 1125) married Ermentrude, heiress to the county of Soissons (on which see the introduction to Hugh Farsit's *A Little Book of Miracles of the Blessed Virgin Mary in the City of Soissons*); their son Ivo later took the title of count of Soissons as well as lord of Nesle.

72. That is, John followed the canons almost to the shore of the English Channel, well over one hundred miles along the route the canons took from Nesle to the port of Wissant via Arras and Saint-Omer.

losing his eyesight foretold the birth of St. Remigius to his mother the blessed Celine and added that some of her milk would restore his sight, which also happened afterward.[73] But, o you, most gentle Mother of God, whom I rejoice has come here today, will you not have mercy on my sinful self, so that having regained my sight like St. Montanus, I might once again see your feretory that I made?" Saying this in tears, he asked that his eyes be touched by water in which the relics had been bathed. This done, he drank some of the same water and thus kept vigil in prayer before the feretory the entire night. In the morning he recovered his sight and gave thanks to God and his kind mother.

3. A girl healed in Saint-Omer

From there we went to Saint-Omer, where a girl with a hand withered from birth drank the relic water and her hand was washed with it and thus she was healed.

4. The delivery of St. Mary's clerics from pirates at sea

Afterward, preparing to cross the sea, we awaited a favorable wind during Eastertide, on the feast of St. Mark. Early in the morning, summoned by sailors, we boarded a ship at the port called Wissant. Many merchants embarked with us; they wanted to go from Flanders to England to buy wool and hoped that they would cross more safely with us, carrying as they were more than three hundred marks of gold in little sacks and purses. The captain of the ship was named Coldistan.[74]

---

73. St. Walaric (French "Valéry") was born in central France. After a career as a monk and preacher, he was finally, by default, made the founder of a monastery: he settled as a hermit at the mouth of the Somme River, but disciples joined him in his solitude. He died in 620. The monastery was in what is now the village of Saint-Valéry-sur-Somme, from which, after a public display of the saint's relics, Duke William II of Normandy set off for his successful invasion of England in 1066. On St. Remigius, see I, 1. The story of the blind hermit Montanus announcing the coming birth of Remigius to his mother Celine and the subsequent restoration of Montanus's sight appears in the ninth-century Life of Remigius with which Bishop Helinand was apparently familiar.

74. The departure date was Friday, April 25, 1113. Wissant is a port on the English Channel, which Herman simply calls "the sea." In the twelfth century, England was a great producer of wool, and Flanders, a region that included much of what is now northern Belgium, was an affluent and urbanized center of cloth manufacture. It is difficult to give modern equivalences for medieval currencies, but the merchants may have carried as much as 150 pounds of gold. In any case, it was a great deal of money. The captain's name shows he was English. The ship was likely a broad, single-masted cargo vessel around fifty feet long, typical of those used to transport goods in northern European waters.

So when we had sailed to about the middle of the sea, one of our companions, looking from afar, saw at a distance a ship that seemed to be in a bay along the shore.[75] When he had pointed this out to Coldistan, the captain ordered a youth to climb to the top of the mast to investigate. From what the youth said, Coldistan knew there was a pirate ship nearby, patrolling the waters for the purpose of plundering.[76] Stricken with great terror, the captain declared to all that death was near at hand. We quickly went white in fear of slaughter and saw the ship approach like a bird in flight. Spears, shields, and swords glittered; breastplates bathed in sunlight gleamed. We confessed our sins to one another and because we now seemed to be at death's door, we did not wait for a priest to hear confession but even the priest, rattled by imminent danger, confessed to a layman.[77]

The merchants, in despair for their lives and put in such a tight corner, offered the little sacks and purses containing all their money to Our Lady and threw them on her feretory, beseeching her mercy amid great lamentation: if she merely snatched their bodies from the hands of the pirates and the ruin of death, they said, she would keep all of their money for the restoration of her church. Meanwhile, the pirates gradually came so much closer that they now seemed to be only an arrow's flight distant.

But when we found ourselves in such dire straits, all of us together despairing entirely of our lives, Coldistan begged the priest Boso, whom he saw as the superior of the others, to pick up the relics of St. Mary and check the pirates' power to kill them. The priest, emboldened by the man's faith, fell to his knees before the feretory and humbly invoked the Mother of the Lord in a flood of tears. Then, rising quickly, he faithfully took up the phylactery with its precious hair in fear and devotion. As Coldistan grasped him with both hands, Boso went to the highest point astern and, with his hand lifted toward the enemies and swearing mightily by the authority of God and his mother St. Mary, prohibited and forbade the pirates to come further or be able to harm them. And,

---

75. P3 specifies this was John, the priest of the parish of Saint-Martin.

76. This was probably a Viking-style warship, smaller, narrower, and faster than a cargo vessel, and thus recognizable as such to Coldistan as something that could overtake his ship. The flash of weapons mentioned just below was another clue.

77. There is some confusion here. Among the canons named at the beginning of Book II, at least three were priests, but now there seems to be only one priest. By "laymen" Herman could mean canons of a lesser clerical status than priest or the laymen who were probably in the Laon party.

o marvelous power of divine strength! As soon as he finished speaking he made the sign of the cross with the phylactery in the direction of the enemies and more rapidly than can be said their ship was driven backward, pushed by a strong headwind. Their ship's mast was shattered, and part of it, falling on one of them, crushed him and hurled him into the sea, dead.

Gentle Jesus, good Jesus, what joy and exultation there was among us when you ripped apart the hairshirt of our agitation and wrapped us in the joy of your mercy! How many praises we, snatched from death, gave to you and your mother, Our Lady! The wind that stymied our enemies was made so favorable and advantageous to us that as we joyfully resumed the Song of Moses, we marveled at how speedily we were carried along.[78] After a short while we reached port happily. We arranged to return to the merchants some of the money that they, in fear of death, gave to Our Lady when they placed it, or rather, in their confusion and distress, flung it on the feretory. But as soon as they saw, on reaching the shore, that they had escaped the danger of death, they forgot their former fear. Without our permission, each of them picked up his little sack and purse and, giving thanks to Our Lady by word alone, left her nothing.

5. The vengeance taken on the merchants

However, let all those who give their goods to God and take them back hear what vengeance her son, the just Judge, took afterward on his mother's behalf. When the merchants, after traveling around almost all of England, had spent their money buying enormous heaps of wool and filled a large warehouse on the seashore with it in a place called Dover, behold! on the night before their crossing, the warehouse and all the wool were burned in a sudden fire. Thus they lost everything and had been rendered paupers; repenting too late, they regretted that they had insulted the queen of heaven.[79]

6. A mother in childbirth delivered

We, as it seemed to us, snatched not from the shadow of death but its very jaws, offered praise and thanksgiving to Our Lady, took up her feretory and relics, and went to Canterbury. The archbishop there at the

---

78. The Song of Moses in Exodus 15:1 celebrates the safe passage of the Hebrews through the Red Sea and the drowning of their enemies, the pharaoh's army, quite apt for the occasion.

79. Herman skips ahead in time here: it would have taken the merchants some weeks, if not months, to traverse England. The implication is that the canons' party disembarked at Dover after crossing from Wissant, but Herman does not say so explicitly.

time was Lord William, very well known to us from long ago. Traveling to Laon to hear the lessons of Master Anselm, he had stayed for many days in the bishop's house and while there taught the sons of Ranulf, the chancellor of the king of the English.[80] So William, coming to meet us with great joy, welcomed us most honorably, as did the monks of St. Augustine, and he kindly provided for us as long as we wanted.[81]

An extremely rich woman of this city, tormented for a week by extreme pain in childbirth, was so entirely despaired of that only her funeral was being discussed. Hearing of our arrival, she sent her husband to us to ask if one of us knew of any medicine for giving birth.[82] Then the priest Boso, to whom care of the relics had been specially entrusted, advised him that his wife be urged to make a truthful confession of her sins to her priest and then faithfully drink some water in which the relics would have been washed. Returning home, the husband reported to his wife what he had learned. But she, who had by now completely lost not only the power of speech but even her memory on account of the enormous pain, with God's help and the very ardor of her faith soon recovered a bit of strength and revived. She took care to confess her sins to the priest when he arrived, then added that on this same night a very beautiful lady coming from France had appeared to her in a vision, instructed her to make a truthful confession, and promised that in that way she would be healed.

When the priest, after hearing the confession, came to us and made a report, we were summoned by the husband. Assured of the woman's future recovery through the priest's account, we went to the confined woman's bedside with the relics. Washing the relics in her presence and giving her the water to drink, we then left. Before we had even returned to the church a messenger ran up behind us and reported that the lady had given birth and was healed. Hence both she and her

---

80. Archbishop Anselm of Canterbury (not the same person as the Laon schoolmaster) died in 1109, and his successor was installed only in 1114, so there was no archbishop of Canterbury when the canons visited. The only English archbishop of this era named William was William of Corbeil (r. 1123–36), who had studied at Laon with Master Anselm and later taught there. It is unlikely the canons on whose notes Herman based his account would have written of a nonexistent archbishop, so the error is Herman's. Ranulf was chancellor, the head of the office that oversaw the production of official royal documents, from ca. 1107 until his death in 1123.

81. The abbey of St. Augustine in Canterbury was founded in ca. 598 by missionary monks sent from Rome by Pope Gregory I (r. 590–604).

82. The canons, then, had at least some training in secular medicine, also apparent in the story set in Bath at the end of Book II.

husband, exulting, granted many gifts and jewels to Our Lady. After we had returned home, she sent precious priestly vestments to the church of Laon.

Furthermore, it seemed utterly undeniable to us that anyone can be healed in the slightest unless they are from the diocese in which we were. As we believe, Our Lady sees to it that no sick stranger, coming from afar, should be said to have been bribed by us in our quest for gain or to have come to us to receive payment, and thus all concerned be made contemptible in the discussions of the ignorant crowd.[83] Even among those who were in their own diocese, nobody was cured unless they first confessed their sins to their priest, assuming they were of appropriate age to do so. In the case of a small child, parents should be admonished to confess in the place of their children.[84]

7. A blind man receives sight in Winchester

Afterward, coming to the city of Winchester and honorably welcomed by the bishop of that place, we remained there for a week, during which we saw many miracles worked.[85] In that city was an honorable knight named Ralph, surnamed Butler, cupbearer of the king of the English, who had lost his eyesight eight years earlier and because of his blindness had asked the king that his office be granted to his sons.[86] On Ascension Day, after learning of the miracles that were being performed, he

---

83. Herman appears to mean the sick person should be a known local so the canons cannot be accused of bribing a stranger to fake a cure, word of which would attract more sick people and more donations.

84. These two conditions—that nobody can be healed except in the bounds of his home diocese and only after a private confession—are surprising. Tens of thousands of medieval miracle cures were effected when the ill had traveled far from home to a shrine, or even through prayer to a saint whose shrine was far distant. Such instances are regularly found in accounts of miracles in this book. Perhaps Herman refers only to miracles during relic tours, but fakery could just as easily be staged at an immobile shrine. See Murray, "Confession Before 1215." Murray finds very little evidence of lay confession in this era, Herman's account being one of the rare instances. As Murray notes, there is no mention of confession in Herman's Book I. He posits that England was a precocious site of lay confession encouraged by churchmen who included the students of Anselm of Laon, several of whom held important offices in the English church and some of whom Herman mentions below. The two conditions are linked by the insistence on the sick person confessing to his or her priest (*suo presbitero*) here and further along in Book II.

85. The bishop was William Giffard (r. 1100–1129).

86. See Tatlock, "The English Journey," 458–61. The *picerna*, cupbearer, was one of the most important offices of the royal household. Tatlock posits that this was Ralph de Mortimer, who as a young man had been in the entourage of William the Conqueror, served William and his sons, Kings William Rufus and Henry I, disappears from the historical record in 1104, and then turns up in Herman's narration nine years later, having been blind for eight years.

had himself brought to the feretory and, after confessing his sins to his priest, faithfully drank water from the washed relics and had his eyes bathed in it.[87] The bishop was celebrating a High Mass in the church for this solemn feast and when, after the gospel reading, he finished his sermon, by popular request we left the church with the relics lest we cause the bishop any trouble.[88] When the sermon was given again in the square in front of the church doors and the bishop was beginning the Mass, suddenly Ralph, who was near the relics placed in front of the doors, recovered his sight and praised God and his mother with a great cry. This miracle was held in such veneration that the people came back five times that day to hear the divine word, honor the relics, and renew their offerings.

8. Another sick man cured there

In that same city there was an extremely rich man named Walter, sur-named Kiburs, who had by then been oppressed for six years with an ill-ness so very grave that he could never get out of bed.[89] On hearing about the miracles of Our Lady, he asked for our help through intermediaries. Along with his other illness, he also so suffered from diarrhea that he could not even be carried in a litter decorously. The priest Boso com-manded that he should make a truthful confession to his priest. Be-cause not only previously, but even during his illness Walter was said to have frequently accepted interest payments from his debtors, he should promise God he would never take them again and make fitting satis-faction to the debtors for what he had accepted.[90] Walter obeyed, then humbly asked that we come to him with the relics because he could not be brought to us. Three of us were sent: the priest Boso, Robert, and Boniface. They went to him, washed the relics in water in his presence, gave him some to drink, and sprinkled some on him. Wonderful to say!

---

87. From at least the fourth century, the feast of the Ascension celebrated the bodily as-sumption of Jesus to heaven forty days after his resurrection.

88. That is, so the excitement engendered by the presence of the relics would not distract people from the service and perhaps lead them to redirect offerings from the bishop's church to the Laon canons.

89. On Walter Kiburs, see Tatlock, "The English Journey," 461.

90. Lending at interest was discouraged by the medieval church and widely condemned by the eleventh century. Archbishop Anselm of Canterbury, who died a few years before the canons' visit, equated usury, by which he meant any interest paid on a debt, with robbery. A general council of the church held in Rome in 1179 noted that the practice of lending at interest was widespread and declared that notorious usurers should be denied the sacraments of communion and Christian burial.

He who had been confined to bed for six years rose from it, healed. He jumped up and ran to Our Lady's feretory in thanksgiving. He gave the three clerics who had come to him three gold rings and offered three silver goblets, a great deal of money, and other precious goods before the feretory.

Some people, seeing all this brought forth in the public square, complained that given his immense wealth Walter had offered too little, for it was reported that he had more than three thousand pounds of English money stored in his treasury.[91] He replied that he did not want to give more until he had returned the interest he had accepted from his debtors, as he had promised God. So he had it cried all over town that anyone who had given him interest payments should come to him and take what belonged to them. How great was the shout of joy and devotion there as everyone said that through Our Lady, St. Mary, a second Zacchaeus had been presented to Winchester; they praised God more for the return of interest paid and the salvation of Walter's soul than his bodily healing.[92] Not even Cicero himself, had he been present, could have worthily related it all.[93]

9. Twelve sick people cured in the same place

During the week we stayed in Winchester, many other sick people were cured as well. We have omitted reporting them all one by one lest we bore those who hear it.[94] We will only declare this: twelve people were cured openly and in public, some deaf, some lame, certain of them blind, certain of them mute. All were from Winchester or its surroundings and therefore known to all.

10. A sick little girl cured in Christchurch

From the city of Winchester we proceeded to a town called *Christikerca*, that is, Christ's Church, where in the annual feast of the octave of

---

91. Again, it is hard to know what the modern equivalent would be, but it is safe to say Walter had amassed a small fortune.

92. Zacchaeus was a wealthy tax collector, hence a loathed figure, in Jericho. A short man, he climbed a tree to catch sight of Jesus, who was passing through the town. Jesus told him to come down because he wanted to visit his house. The crowd complained that Jesus accepted the hospitality of a sinner, to which Zacchaeus replied that he would give half his money to the poor, and if he had cheated anyone, he would pay back four times the ill-gotten gain (Luke 19:1–10).

93. Marcus Tullius Cicero (106–43 BCE) was a famously eloquent lawyer, statesman, and philosopher during the late Roman Republic.

94. Herman hopes—assumes?—that the miracles he recounts will reach elite Latin readers but also be heard by a wider audience, perhaps in sermons given in the vernacular.

Pentecost a very large gathering of merchants was accustomed to take place.[95] Approaching that town, we were overwhelmed by a sudden and violent flood of rain the likes of which we did not remember ever seeing before. A dean occupied the town church along with twelve canons. When we asked to be admitted, he replied that the church was not yet fully constructed and therefore they would not receive us for fear of losing the customary offering of the merchants. Yet he reluctantly conceded that the feretory of Our Lady could be placed on a small altar in a remote corner of the church until the worst of the rain had passed.[96] But when he saw that some merchants who had heard of the miracles worked at Winchester were seeking the feretory of Our Lady with offerings and abandoning the high altar, he was stirred by the poison of wrath and ordered the feretory cast out of the church.

Once the feretory had been cast out, it is not easy to say how much anxiety we suffered, because the downpour had now violently overwhelmed both us and our horses; the entire town being full of merchants, there was no place for us to lodge. But the mercy of Our Lady soon turned its attention to us in our great misery. A lady, taking pity on our misfortune, appealed to her husband: a new house he had built and already rented to some merchants for two marks could, for the day, accommodate the queen of heaven, whom the church's dean had expelled. She further asked her husband to allow both Our Lady and ourselves to stay there overnight and tell the merchants to make other arrangements for themselves in the meantime.

The husband did what his wife asked and welcomed us, by now soaked and disheartened by the violence of the rainstorm, into his new house, had our mud-spattered clothing washed and dried, and set the feretory and relics of Our Lady in a suitable place becomingly decorated with wall hangings. Then he took care to show us every hospitable kindness. One of the merchants hung from the house's paneled ceiling three bells that he had brought to sell and summoned his companions by ringing them.[97] He climbed up to a higher perch and reported how the dean had thrown the feretory out of his church, urging that none

---

95. Christchurch was a busy port and market center in the twelfth century. The "octave of Pentecost" is an eight-day celebration of the descent of the Holy Spirit on the earliest followers of Jesus Christ (Acts 2:1–4). It begins on the seventh Sunday after Easter.

96. The dean, the head of the chapter of canons, was afraid that if the relics from Laon were prominently displayed in his church, the merchants would donate to the visiting canons instead of those of Christchurch (see I, 9 and II, 7, above). His fears were justified.

97. The presence of a coffered ceiling shows this was the house of wealthy people.

of them should attend that church but all instead come together to hear the divine office in our lodging. Ultimately, all gathered together resolved unanimously that if any of the merchants entered that church, he would pay a fine of five pennies to his colleagues. It was then the Saturday before the octave of Pentecost.[98]

Our Lady soon showed that she had welcomed our host's favor with joy. He had a house near the town in which his cattle and sheep were kept in which there was a poor peasant charged with guarding the livestock. His daughter, a little girl, had from birth a twisted foot: the heel was at its front and the toes at its back. Asked by our host that the little girl's crippled foot be touched by water that had washed the relics, we had her brought to us. She drank some of the water and her foot was bathed in it. She kept vigil before the feretory that night. In the morning, while as in usual fashion we were solemnly chanting Mass before the feretory in that house—we carried with us a portable altar and everything needed for Mass—the healed girl showed everyone her straightened foot and greatly delighted the lord and lady who had kindly welcomed us.

11. The extraordinary vengeance wreaked there

That same Sunday, after the midday meal, with the permission of its inhabitants and after thanking them for their kindness, we left Christchurch. But the just Judge did not put off avenging the insult to his mother. We had hardly gotten three hundred feet away when horsemen came up behind us, shouting and asking us to come to the aid of the burning town. We looked back and saw the whole place on fire, burning up. When we asked how this had happened, they told us that a dragon emerged from the nearby sea, flew into the town as we were leaving, and set fire first to the church and then to some houses with the flame that it shot from its nostrils.

Hearing this and thirsting with human curiosity to see such a monster, we put the feretory in the hands of suitable guardians and quickly rode back on our horses. We saw a five-headed dragon of incredible length, shooting sulfurous flames through its nostrils, flying from place to place, and setting fire to houses one by one. Going back to the church we found that it had already been burned up so unbelievably that not only the wood but also the very heavy stone walls and the altar had been so completely reduced to ashes and cinders that all

---

98. Saturday, May 24, 1113.

onlookers were stricken with wondrous stupor at the sight. When the dean saw his house and church had burned down, he hastily gathered his clothes and furnishings, bundled them up, and had them taken to a ship anchored on the nearby shore in the hopes that there they could be saved from the fire. But immediately the dragon, as if it had come only for this reason, flew to the ship, set fire to everything in it, and then—wonderful to say and incredible to hear—at the same time also burned the ship.

Coming to the house of our host, we wanted to know how he was faring. We found him rejoicing that his house and all his possessions were spared and attributing his safety to his good guest, the queen of heaven. Not only the house in which we had lodged remained unharmed, but also the other one, further away, in which his livestock was kept, meaning that he lost none of his property whatsoever. Furthermore, heavenly grace so favored the merchants who had shown us such great kindness that they lost little or nothing of their goods. Because it was the custom that the fair lasted only one day, after the midday meal the merchants had gathered all their wares and laid them aside, packed up, before the dragon came. Still, the sight of the dragon struck such enormous terror in them that we saw them scamper away in different directions.

The dean who had thrown the feretory of Our Lady out of his church was moved to overdue penitence and followed it barefoot. Prostrate before it, he bore witness that the judgments of God were just, and he pleaded to be pardoned for acting badly.

12. Seventeen sick people cured

From there we went to the city called Exeter, whose archdeacon was Robert, who had stayed a long while in Laon to hear the lessons of Master Anselm.[99] Welcomed by him with the greatest joy, we stayed there ten days. During that time many miracles occurred, of which the principal and most excellent concerned seventeen sick people cured, some blind, others deaf, mute, or lame. The citizens argued to an extraordinary degree over which of them would offer us lodgings and who would provide necessities once we were welcomed.

In this city there was a sick man who by then had been taken in a litter to the church door continually for twenty-four years. He could not

---

99. After studying with Anselm in Laon, Robert Warelwast was appointed archdeacon by his uncle, Bishop William Warelwast (r. 1107–38). Robert succeeded his uncle as bishop of Exeter.

go anywhere unless carried by two people. On the seventh day after our arrival, asking our advice, he confessed his sins, drank water from the washed relics, and after bathing in it fell asleep. Immediately, wonderful to say, he was completely healed and jumped up from the pallet on which he had lain for so long. Running to the feretory in the sight of all, he stood before it and gave thanks to God and his kind mother in a voice of rejoicing and acknowledgment.

13. A cripple cured

Another cripple there, named Glutinus, was called that for good reason: he was so glued together that his heels stuck to his buttocks and his legs to his back. He was thus reduced to the shape of a ball and always had his face by his knees. After he confessed his sins and bathed in water in which the relics had been washed, he was not cured in the ten days we stayed there. We were puzzled and when we asked where he was from, he acknowledged that he was not from that diocese but Salisbury. At once we harshly scolded him for having tried to obtain a cure that it was sure and proven nobody could obtain outside his own diocese. With tears and great lamentation, he in his wretchedness begged us that we go to Salisbury for the love of God and his holy mother.

To satisfy not only his prayers but that of the entire populace asking the same thing, after ten days we left Exeter and, reversing course, set out for Salisbury. And he, who knew the way, had gone ahead of us, sitting in a cart and lying in wait at the boundary of the dioceses.[100] We had scarcely gotten six hundred feet into the diocese of Salisbury when behold! he who had gone before us came to meet us in his cart and immediately, as if Our Lady did not want him to be wearied further, jumped up from the cart completely healed. In the sight of a crowd that had flocked from all directions, he ran to the feretory, giving thanks in the middle of the road. This incident truly proved what we said above, that nobody could be cured outside their own diocese.

So from there, as had been decided, we arrived in Salisbury, where we were honorably welcomed by the city's bishop in light of the renown of Master Anselm since the bishop's kinsmen Alexander and Nigel had stayed a long while in Laon at Anselm's school.[101]

---

100. The canons had apparently intended to continue westward but made a detour that added a total of about 180 miles to their journey.

101. Roger of Salisbury (d. 1139) was, before and while bishop, one of King Henry I's most trusted advisors. He ruled England while the king was in Normandy. Roger's nephew Alexander (d. 1148) was named bishop of Lincoln in 1123 after serving as an archdeacon in

14. A man ill with fever cured

Afterward, we came to an abbey of nuns called Wilton, where they showed us the tomb of the venerable Bede, priest and outstanding teacher.[102] Nearby a famous poetess, whose name is Muriel, is buried. A man who had long suffered from fever lay at the tomb of the venerable priest Bede, where many people were accustomed to be healed. On the night we arrived, Muriel appeared to him in a dream, saying, "You cannot be healed here and now through Bede, because the blessed Mother of the Lord has come down to us."[103] When he reported this to us the next day and drank water in which relics had been bathed, he was healed on the spot. We went back via Exeter, yet we did not enter the city—although asked by many to do so—because we had already stayed there ten days.[104]

15. A blind girl healed

From there we went to the province called *Danavexeria* where they showed us the throne and the oven—so they say—of the most celebrated Arthur, king of the Britons, and they told us this was Arthur's land.[105]

---

the diocese of Salisbury under his uncle. Another nephew, Nigel (d. 1169), served as the king's treasurer before becoming, also through Roger's influence, bishop of Ely in 1133. The canons are among the highest ranks of royal and ecclesiastical officials of early twelfth-century England.

102. Wilton, founded in the early tenth century, was one of the wealthiest and most socially prestigious monasteries for women in medieval England. Bede (ca. 672–735) was a monk at Jarrow in northern England, famed as a teacher, historian, theologian, and chronographer. However, his body was never at Wilton. Perhaps the nuns had a small relic.

103. P3, which I follow here, has *Muriel* twice, the first time to name the poet, the second to say who appeared in the dream, whereas the printed edition names her *Murier* and says the figure in the dream was simply *mulier*, "a woman." Sadly, Muriel's writings have disappeared, but she was admired by other major Latin poets of her time including Baudry, the abbot of Bourgueil in the Loire valley and bishop of Dol from 1107 to 1130, and Hildebert of Lavardin, the archbishop of Tours from 1125 to his death in 1133, both of whom wrote epistolary poems to Muriel that have survived. She seems to have been an aristocrat born and educated in France before becoming a nun in southern England; her burial next to the (alleged) grave of so revered a figure as Bede also indicates that her reputation was considerable. See Tatlock, "Muriel."

104. The canons feared criticism of greed if they went back to the same place to raise more money. As the story in II, 20 shows, accusation of crass acquisition of funds was a real concern.

105. *Danavexeria* is a vague geographical term that refers to the southwest of England. The mentions of King Arthur (famed in legend but likely fictional) here and in the next section are highly suspect: see Berard, "King Arthur and the Canons of Laon." Berard argues persuasively that the mentions of Arthur are not reliable evidence of local beliefs in 1113. Rather, they reflect the interest in Arthurian tales that surfaced in the 1120s but rapidly accelerated from the late 1130s with the appearance of Geoffrey of Monmouth's widely circulated *History of the Kings of Britain*. Which Arthurian sites Herman claims the canons visited is impossible to know.

There a cleric named Algare, who had stayed a long time in Laon, honored us greatly. He was afterward made bishop of the city of Coutances in Normandy.[106] While we were there, in a village called Bodmin, a girl of about ten named Kenehelis, blind from birth, came to the feretory, and when her eyes were bathed in the reliquary water she received sight.

16. A deaf man cured in the same place

A young man of the same village, deaf from birth, came to the feretory, and when his ears were bathed in relic water, at once he could hear. A man with a withered hand kept vigils before the feretory to recover his health. But as Britons are accustomed to quarrel with Franks about King Arthur, this same man began an argument with one of our servants, named Haganello, from the household of Lord Guy, the archdeacon of Laon, saying that King Arthur was still alive.[107] As a result, a great brawl broke out: a number of armed men forced their way into the church and unless the cleric Algare had stood in the way, it would have nearly come to bloodshed. We believe that this quarrel before her feretory had displeased Our Lady, for the man with the withered hand who had caused the brawl about Arthur did not recover his health.

17. A crippled girl healed

After that we came to the castle called Barnstaple where a prince by the name of Juhel de Totnes lived; his wife was the sister of Guermond of Picquigny. Partly through our acquaintance with his wife, who was from the region of Amiens and hence seemed to belong to our province, but more for the miracles he had learned were worked through Our Lady, Juhel welcomed us with the greatest delight and kept us with him for three days.[108] He gave us a silver cup, a precious chalice, wall hangings, and other ornaments that are still kept in Laon's cathedral. He also donated a horse to carry it all. He added many other items

---

106. Algare, yet another former student in Laon, was bishop of Coutances from 1132 to 1151.

107. On Archdeacon Guy, see above, note 56. The argument about Arthur is Herman's invention: see above, note 105.

108. Barnstaple was a port city at the narrowest crossing point before the Taw River empties into Bristol Channel. Juhel de Totnes (d. 1123/30), a native of northwestern France, assisted Duke William of Normandy in the conquest of England. Juhel possessed numerous properties in southwestern England, including the barony of Barnstaple, when the canons visited. Guermond of Picquigny (near Amiens, in the northwestern region of Picardy of which Laon was near the southern border) was a member of the family that served as the vidames of the bishop of Amiens.

worth fifteen pounds of Laon money. As if wishing to be prompt to re-
pay his devotion, Our Lady revealed a manifest miracle there. In Juhel's
house there was a twelve-year-old girl whose entire body was so bent
over that she could go nowhere unless she dragged herself along as best
she could, crawling on the ground with little hand-trestles. Brought to
the feretory, after confessing her sins she was bathed in the relic water.
As long as we were there she was not healed, but just as we were leaving,
in great lamentation she cried out, "Alas, most gentle Lady St. Mary, do
not go this way, leaving me unhealed!"[109] Swiftly healed as all looked
on, she threw aside her hand-trestles. Jumping up, she stood straight
and ran to the feretory in thanksgiving.

18. A lame monk cured

A pious monk also lived there on charity in a cell that the aforementioned prince Juhel had built. Already for two years he had so labored
with the incurable illness that the physicians call sciatica that he could
go nowhere except limping along propped up with a staff. He served us
most pleasantly, as far as he was able, the entire three days we stayed in
that same church, and we bathed the site of his illness, above the thigh,
with water in which the relics had been washed. As long as we stayed
there he was not cured. But when we, on leaving the castle, sought the
people's leave as we thanked them, the monk followed us, limping
along with his staff. Suddenly cured, he threw aside the staff, and coming quickly to the feretory as all looked on, he embraced and kissed it
gladly and cheerfully, then hoisted it onto his shoulder and carried one
side of it along with us for quite some distance.

19. A lame man cured

After that, we came to a castle of the aforementioned prince Juhel called
Totnes, with some of his men as our escort. We were honorably welcomed by some monks and stayed there for three days.[110] An old man
lived there, lame from birth and known to all as the brother of the
provost of the castle. After hearing about the miracles being performed,
he came to the feretory in great faith and devotion. Drinking and bathing in relic water, he stood up before the people. This miracle was held
in such great veneration that without delay his brother, the castle's

---

109. The Latin syntax here is a bit scrambled, perhaps meant to reflect the girl's agitated
state.

110. Juhel founded the monastery at Totnes in about 1087.

provost, offered forty pennies of English money, and an infinite number of people added a great deal in turn.

20. The dreadful vengeance exacted on a man who hanged himself

But now a dreadful miracle followed, one that we read had happened only rarely from the time of the betrayer Judas. On seeing so much money brought to the feretory, three young kinsmen from that region disparaged us, saying that we performed such miracles through magic to make a profit. One of them encouraged the other two to go to the feretory and, pretending to kiss it, fill their mouths with coins placed on the altar by licking them up. They refused to commit such a crime and offend the holy Mother of the Lord, but the faithless one carried on with the wickedness he had begun. He left the horse he rode outside, entered the church, went to the feretory, and pretending to kiss it in veneration, slurped up as much of the heap of coins as he could and departed. Mounting his horse, he looked for the companions who waited for him, showed them the coins he had stolen, and invited them to go drinking with him in a nearby tavern. They replied that they would go with him but would not drink from the proceeds of such a theft. The wretch went into the tavern, drank as much as he wanted, and then left sated.

After that, the two lost themselves in the crowd, but the wretch, mounting his horse, set out for a nearby forest hardly half a mile away while heavenly vengeance followed him. He tied a linen rope around his neck and hanged himself from a tree branch.[111] The horse he had ridden wandered back to the crowd, riderless, to the great astonishment of those who saw it. The two aforementioned youths immediately recognized their comrade's horse. Wondering but not knowing what had happened to him, they searched out the horse's tracks, followed them along, and soon reached the forest and found him hanging from the rope, already dead. Cutting him down and loosening the purse that hung from his belt, they found the coins he had stolen, still stained with fresh saliva. Carrying the money to the feretory in great sorrow, they put it back on the altar and, prostrate on the ground and begging for the mercy of the holy Mother of God on the soul of their dead relative, they reported before all the crime the wretched man had committed. You would have seen crowds of people stunned on hearing of such

---

111. The story is much like that of the betrayal of Jesus by his apostle Judas reported in all four Gospels. Chief rabbis in Jerusalem paid Judas to signal to them which man was Jesus by kissing him—a false kiss like the one Herman describes. Matthew 27:5 adds that Judas subsequently hanged himself.

a crime, burst into tears, and beat their breasts in the face of such swift vengeance.[112]

21. St. Mary's warning to her clerics at Bristol Castle

From there we went to a mighty castle called Bristol, which is surrounded by a wide river along which, at that time, many merchants docked seagoing ships from the island of Ireland laden with various merchandise.[113] Welcomed with joy by the castle's clerics, on hearing that many ships had arrived and delighted to have found an opportunity to buy new clothes, we went down to the port. Boarding the ships, we carefully and eagerly looked through a great array of different merchandise, curious as we were to see new things. When he saw this, our host informed us that it was the custom of Irish merchants to seize, abruptly and without warning, strangers who carelessly got on their ships, and then, pushing the ships away from the shore, carry them off to foreign lands and sell them to barbarians. He warned us to beware of their ambushes.

But thinking little of his warnings we did not refrain from frequenting the ships. Lo! by the kind foresight of the Mother of God, on the following night our host, not asleep but keeping vigil, was advised to tell us that we should not board the ships again because should anybody do so that day, there was no doubt he would be promptly kidnapped to be sold to barbarians.[114] When he had informed us of this in the morning and swore an oath, we, believing it was true and that surely we had been warned through the mercy of Our Lady, did not reboard the ships but left after buying what we needed.

22. A boy healed in the city of Bath

From there we went to the city called Bath and were honorably welcomed by the bishop, clerics, and monks.[115] In that city there are hot

---

112. Reading, with P4, *celeri* ("swift") for the printed edition's *sceleri*.

113. Bristol lies along the Avon River about ten miles by water from the head of Bristol Channel. Founded around 1000, it soon became a busy port and trading center through which most goods from Ireland passed. By the time the canons visited, Bristol had one of the best-fortified castles in southern England.

114. Reading *parvipendentes* ("thinking little") with P3 and P4 for the printed edition's *participendentes*.

115. The Romans built a temple and spa on the site of naturally heated springs; some of the Roman bath structures survive. The bishop of Bath when the canons visited was John of Tours (r. 1090–1122), a native of western France who had served as physician to William the Conqueror and soon after William's death became bishop of Wells. He subsequently moved the administrative center of the diocese to Bath.

baths that some call thermal baths. On the day we arrived, a boy of twelve entered the thermal baths to wash along with his friends, but carelessly failing to look out for himself and overwhelmed by the force of the hot water, he sank to the very bottom. He was dragged out by his parents and brought home amid grief: he was said by many to have already taken his last breath. But after hearing about the miracles of Our Lady, his parents brought the boy to her feretory in great faith and devotion. Seeing that the body was already almost cold, we had two fires lit and the body hung between them to absorb heat, with the head hanging below, the feet above. Then we had the mouth opened and a twig placed between the upper and lower jaws. Once this was done, the boy vomited up a great abundance of water, and his body, now sufficiently warmed, was taken down, carried to the feretory, and bathed in relic water, a very little of which was dripped into the boy's mouth. Without delay, by the mercy of God, the boy not only recovered his breath but also had his health completely restored and happily went home with his parents.[116]

There are many other miracles Our Lady worked in England as we looked on that nobody's eloquence could easily set forth one by one. But it should suffice to have recounted a few of the many that, with God and his son as witnesses, we have reported without falsehood in a most truthful narrative. But now we ask you—as brothers, lords, and our fellow canons at whose command we crossed the sea and endured many hardships on the journey—that you commend to the Lord and his gentle mother the souls of those who sent their offerings to you through us, and that you allow them to be sharers in all good things that are accomplished or may be accomplished hereafter in the church of Laon.

Indeed, we brought you 120 marks from England, not to mention wall hangings and other ecclesiastical ornaments. We who left you on the Monday before Palm Sunday are now returned to you with joy two days before the Nativity of Our Lady, praising alongside you the king of kings and lord of lords and his son Our Lord Jesus Christ, who lives and reigns with the Father and the Holy Spirit forever and ever.

---

116. The canons serve as emergency medical technicians before they seek Mary's intercession. This is quite typical of medieval miracle accounts: many of the afflicted seek secular medicine before, and sometimes along with, recourse to the saints.

Here ends Book II of the miracles of St. Mary of Laon

**Here begins Book III concerning events that happened after-
ward in the diocese of Laon**

1. The crowd of people at the dedication of the church of Laon
With the aid of divine clemency, the work on our church from the
offerings of the faithful collected all over France and England so prospered that the next year, its restoration complete, it was dedicated.
The church had been burned on the Thursday of Easter week in the
year from the Lord's incarnation 1112, on the day when the lord
Gaudry, bishop of Laon, was cruelly killed in his house with some of
his men. Lord Hugh succeeded him as bishop but survived scarcely
eight months; after he died, Lord Bartholomew was elected bishop,
as was written above.[117] Once consecrated, Bishop Bartholomew took
such pains to speed up work on God's church that two and a half
years after the fire, its solemn rededication could take place, that is, in
the year from the Lord's incarnation 1114. It pleased the bishop and
canons that the church be consecrated the very day on which its famed
dedication was accustomed to be observed, that is, the octave of the
Ides of September, namely three days before the feast of the Nativity
of St. Mary.[118]

The lord bishop Bartholomew invited Archbishop Ralph of Reims
and the bishops William of Châlons, Lisiard of Soissons, Godfrey
of Amiens, and Hubert of Senlis.[119] But such a crowd flocked to the
dedication that two hundred thousand people of different sexes and

---

117. Hugh was the dean of the cathedral chapter in Orléans, about 140 miles southwest
of Laon. Just as Laon is in the northeastern reaches of early twelfth-century royal control,
so Orléans represented its southern extent. Hugh was consecrated on August 4, 1112, and
probably died during the winter of 1112/13. Herman does not give a date for Bartholomew's
election or consecration, possibly to strengthen his implication that Bartholomew planned
the relic tours.

118. The cathedral was rededicated on Sunday, September 6, 1114, exactly one year after
the canons' return from England.

119. For his grand celebration, Bartholomew invited some very distinguished guests: the
archbishop of Reims; William of Champeaux, a noted theologian and onetime student of
Anselm of Laon who served as bishop of Châlons from 1113 to 1121; the hagiographer Lisiard, bishop of Soissons (r. 1108–26), who lived long enough to see his predecessor Arnulf
(r. 1081–87), whose Life he wrote, be canonized; Godfrey, Guibert of Nogent's predecessor as
abbot of Nogent-sous-Coucy and bishop of Amiens from 1108 to 1115, later canonized; and
Hubert, a former royal official who served as bishop of Senlis from 1099 to 1115. On these
men, see Ott, *Bishops, Authority and Community*, ad loc.

ages are said to have been present.[120] There was great joy in the hearts of all because after such desolation of their church, indeed of the whole city of Laon, that in so short a time (namely, within two and a half years), emerging from a deep chasm of shadows and misfortune, they saw such glistening brightness shine forth through the mercy of God's mother. It seemed to the crowd that a statement of the prophet Haggai—in which he once prophesied the restoration of the temple in Jerusalem after the Babylonian captivity—could be ascribed justly to our church: "The glory of this second house will be great, greater than the first" [Haggai 2:10].[121] If a careful reader wants to look more carefully, truly he will quite easily be able to adduce that after the affliction of desolation, greater glory than the previous one ensued in the church of Laon. For who could worthily recount how great a splendor of religion and new light gleamed afterward in the diocese of Laon, and from there through almost the entire world?

Indeed, after a few years a new inventor and initiator of new light and new conversion both interior and exterior, namely Lord Norbert, came from Lotharingia to France.[122] As divine grace preceded and accompanied him, he sowed in the diocese of Laon the first vine that "planted in love and once established" [Ephesians 3:17] filled the

---

120. The figure must be a considerable exaggeration—which is usually also the case for other figures given below—but the presence of an archbishop and five bishops from other dioceses meant that the rededication of Laon's cathedral was an important and likely well-attended ceremony.

121. The Babylonian captivity, or exile, refers to the deportation of Jews from the kingdom of Judah after the Neo-Babylonian king Nebuchadnezzar destroyed Jerusalem in the early sixth century BCE. After the Persian king Cyrus conquered Babylon in 539 BCE, he ended the exile and some Jews returned to Jerusalem. The prophet Haggai urged the rebuilding of the temple in Jerusalem starting in about 520 BCE.

122. Norbert was born ca. 1075/80 to a wealthy family in the lower Rhine town of Xanten in what is now northwestern Germany. First a canon in his native city, he served as a cathedral canon and chaplain to Archbishop Frederick of Cologne (r. 1100–1131), then in the court of King (later Emperor) Henry V (r. 1099–1125). This very worldly cleric changed his life radically after falling from his horse during a thunderstorm in 1115. By then at least thirty-five, Norbert embarked on intensive study and prayer before ordination as a priest. After failing to reform the canons of Xanten to a life more resembling that of monks, he took up the life of a wandering preacher. An ecclesiastical council in Fritzlar, east of Cologne, in 1118, accused him of lacking the authority to preach in this manner and of hypocrisy as a wealthy man who dressed in ragged attire. Stung, Norbert gave away his worldly goods to the poor and the church and again took to the road, this time in abject poverty. Herman takes up the story from there. There is no recent scholarly study of Norbert in English. The author of a recent brief, unfootnoted account says that he has not written "an academic treatise," but the book serves as a good introduction: Kunkel, *Man on Fire* (quotation on 3). "Conversion" in medieval parlance meant commitment to a formal religious life in a community set apart away from the world (rather than a change of religious adherence, its usual meaning today).

earth. "Extending its vine-sprouts to the sea and its shoots as far as the river" [Psalm 79/80:12] in the "wine of its strength that gladdens the heart of man" [Psalm 103/104:15] it now so abundantly intoxicated many "princes and judges of the earth, youths and virgins, the old with the young" [Psalm 148:11–12], who now, powerfully intoxicated, sought nothing other than to "praise the Lord's name" [Sirach 47:12] and "to sing him a new song" [Psalm 32/33:3]. "Casting off the old man with his deeds and putting on the new one created in the image of God" [Colossians 3:9–10], they tossed all carnal enticements aside, and like the water turned into wine by the Lord at the wedding feast [see John 2:9], "they forgot the past and reached for the future" [Philippians 3:13]. And thus although they were on earth in the body, "they taste what is above, not what is on the earth" [Colossians 3:2], saying with the Apostle, "Our way of life is in heaven" [Philippians 3:20] where Christ sits "at the right hand of God" [Romans 8:34]. United in spirit with the heavenly seraphim, they burn perpetually for the love of Christ alone, to whom they also "show their bodies as a living sacrifice, holy, and acceptable to God" [Romans 12:1], presenting the splendor of the virtues with which they shine inside and also present in their outward garb.[123]

It will be easily understood from what follows that the lord bishop Bartholomew was a partner with and sharer in this so sublime and glorious creation.

2. How the lord bishop Bartholomew met Lord Norbert

After Pope Pascal died in Rome, Cardinal John succeeded him under the name of Gelasius. Wanting to come to France, he ended his life at Cluny.[124] The cardinals who had come with Gelasius saw that they would not be able to return to Rome for a new election. Compelled by necessity, they elected to the apostolic seat the lord archbishop Guy of the nearby city of Vienne, a noble and zealous man, uncle to the queen of the Franks, that is, the wife of King Louis.[125] Consecrating him pope

---

123. Seraphim are the highest order of Christian angels. In Herman's Latin, this paragraph, stuffed with biblical quotations and allusions, is one sentence.

124. Pascal II's successor Gelasius II was pope for only a year and a few days, 1118–19. The abbey of Cluny in Burgundy was founded in the early tenth century on the terms that it was subject to no authority except the pope. It was a fabulously wealthy monastery in the early twelfth century, undertaking a reconstruction of its abbey church that was the largest church in Christendom until the new papal basilica of St. Peter's in Rome was built four hundred years later.

125. It is not clear whether Herman means that a new pope had to be elected in short order or that Henry V, who was continually at odds with the papacy, would block their entry

in the same province, the cardinals called him Calixtus.[126] Before he went to Rome, the new pope wanted to hold a general council and commanded the bishops and archbishops of nearly the whole West, with abbots and other clerics, to assemble in Reims, at which council Louis, king of the Franks, was also present.[127]

To attend this council, the lord bishop Bartholomew reached the city of Reims with his clerics and retinue. They had already passed the monastery of Saint-Thierry when the bishop saw the abovementioned Norbert sitting by the road with two clerics.[128] As he was accustomed to recount afterward, a little while before Norbert had heard two voices, one of which had cried out, "Here are Norbert and his companions," and the second adding, "Here is Norbert and his companion." What this meant will be explained later on. After hearing these two voices from the sky, the stunned Norbert turned off the road, sat in astonishment on the ground with his two companions, and looked around.

Without delay, as the bishop approached, he did not, like the priest and the Levite, pass by after they saw a man wounded by thieves, but stopped along the roadside, kindly greeted the three men, and asked who they were.[129] Norbert replied that he was from Lotharingia and that after leaving his parents and the vanities of this world, he had resolved to follow a religious life. Wanting to begin this rule of living with the authority and council of the apostolic see, he had already been in Reims for three days, but because of the crowd of rich people gathered together, no access to the pope had been granted and he had left the city in sadness and despair, not knowing where he was headed. At this point, moved by great compassion, the bishop urged them to come back to Reims with him, promising that he would take them to the pope. Because they were on foot, Bartholomew ordered his men to

---

to Rome to have an election there. Guy's father was Count William I of Burgundy, one of the wealthiest men in Europe; Guy had been archbishop of Vienne since 1088. He was elected by only nine cardinals—most of the others were still in Rome—at Cluny on February 1, 1119. Guy's niece was Adelaide of Maurienne (1092–1154), who married King Louis VI in 1115.

126. Calixtus II was pope from 1119 to 1124.

127. This council, attended by hundreds of bishops, abbots, and others, took place in October 1119. Its primary purpose was to make peace with Henry V, by now the emperor.

128. Saint-Thierry is about five miles northwest of Reims Cathedral.

129. Herman refers to Jesus's parable of the good Samaritan recounted in Luke 10:30–37. A man traveling from Jericho to Jerusalem was attacked by bandits, robbed, beaten, and left half dead. Both a Jewish priest and a Levite (that is, one who claims descent from the tribe of Levi and hence has important religious and political duties) saw the man but kept going. A passing Samaritan, a member of a group traditionally hostile to Jews, tended to the man's wounds, took him to an inn, and paid his expenses.

dismount, help the three onto their horses, and ride along with him. Along the way, he questioned them attentively and heard that Norbert was of noble birth and had possessed great wealth in the church of Cologne, but abandoned it completely, choosing poverty.

Then, reaching Reims, the bishop went to the pope and modestly suggested that it was not good that he, the father of the universal church, speak only to the rich while the poor were driven away from an audience with him. The pope agreed on the spot. Norbert and his comrades were taken in by the bishop and refreshed with an apostolic audience, but because he was so busy, the pope was unable to complete the conversation with them as they desired. He promised the bishop that once the council was adjourned, he would go to Laon straightaway, rest there a few days, and speak with the three men satisfactorily. The pope further asked the bishop to send them ahead and tell them to stay in Laon. As long as they remained in Reims, the bishop always kept the three by his side; on his return to Laon, he never let them be parted from his company. He welcomed the pope most obligingly—as was right—when Calixtus arrived in Laon as promised and most abundantly sated the thirst of Norbert and his companions for a papal audience.

3. How Bishop Bartholomew took Norbert to many places

At that time there was a little church built in honor of St. Martin outside Laon's city walls in which this same bishop had already placed religious clerics to serve God, but since none were able to succeed there, the little church had been returned to him.[130] The bishop, seeing that Norbert wanted to follow a religious life in poverty, urged him to live in this little church of Saint-Martin and even asked the pope to suggest this to Norbert. Learning of his efforts, Norbert said, "I did not leave behind great riches in Cologne to seek small ones in Laon now. I do not want to live in cities, but rather in deserted and untilled places." The bishop replied, "I will show you plenty of deserted and untilled places suitable for religious life in this diocese and I will give you what you have seen."

So he said, and after the departure of the lord pope the bishop took Norbert and showed him not all the realms of the world and their glory, but a large forest in his diocese called Thiérache.[131] Bartholomew

---

130. Saint-Martin was about nine hundred yards west of the cathedral. There was a clerical community there from the ninth century, apparently vanished by 1119.

131. With "all the realms of the world and their glory," Herman recalls Luke 4, in which the devil unsuccessfully tempts Jesus with great power in exchange for fealty. The forest of

took him to a place called Foigny and showed him that it offered a suitable site for religious life with its water, meadows, forest, and land. After a prayer, Norbert said, "Indeed, it is a completely suitable place for religious life but not destined for me by God." From there, the bishop took him to Thenailles, another place in the same forest.[132] When he had seen it and after a prayer, Norbert repeated what he had said before: indeed the place was suitable for religious life but not destined for him by God. Then the bishop, returning to Laon, took him to the forest of Saint-Gobain and showed him a place in it called *Pratum Monstratum*, or Prémontré.[133] Whoever reads this will see how devout this bishop was in that setting episcopal business aside, he took an unknown man around so many forested and roadless places, not without great labor. Even today, when these locales are tilled by many people, they seem to inspire dread; then they were a great deal harsher and more frightful, far removed from any human habitation, suited only to wolves and wild boar.[134]

4. How the church of Prémontré was begun

Thus, coming to the site of Prémontré, they entered a little church built there in honor of St. John the Baptist to pray. The church belonged to the monastery of Saint-Vincent in Laon, and a monk from that house was sometimes sent there to celebrate the divine office, but once the Mass was said, no food was found there unless it was brought from elsewhere, for the place with its little church remained almost deserted. When the bishop had finished a prayer and was leaving, he urged the man of God to rise from prayer since night was falling, there was no place to stay there, and his settlement called Anizy, where necessity required that they be lodged, was still a mile away.[135] Leaving the church, the man of God asked the bishop to depart along with his men and permit him to keep vigil there for the entire night. The horses were mounted hastily because it was getting dark. The bishop hastened to

---

Thiérache is northeast of Laon.

132. Thenailles is a little closer to Laon than Foigny.

133. Prémontré is about ten miles west-southwest of Laon.

134. Herman does not exaggerate Bartholomew's commitment. Assuming he and Norbert first went to Foigny and returned to Laon via Thenailles, they made a trek of close to seventy miles through thinly inhabited territory, at the mercy of the weather and the ever-present threat of bandits. Now at Prémontré, they were another twelve miles travel distance from Laon in another direction.

135. Anizy-le-Château was a castle under the control of the bishops of Laon. It is actually about four miles walking distance from Prémontré.

Anizy, yet he did not forget about Lord Norbert, sending a messenger back with food and other necessities.

Returning to him in the morning, the bishop asked Norbert what he wanted to do. Norbert said in great delight, "Lord Father, I will remain here because I know this place was destined for me by God. Here I will have rest and a home and here many will be saved through the grace of God. This little church, though, will not be their main house, but they will build themselves one on the other side of the mountain where they will live.[136] Last night I saw as if in a vision a great crowd of men in white carrying silver crosses, candelabras, and censers going around that place chanting." The bishop greatly rejoiced, yet not wanting to do any injury to the monastery of Saint-Vincent, to which the place belonged, he summoned its abbot and made an exchange with him for something that at the time was more useful. And thus by the authority of his privilege, he gave the site with the church to Lord Norbert outright. Thus God's servant Norbert remained there.[137] The bishop returned to Laon but did not cease to take good care of Norbert and his companions.

A few days later the man of God came to Laon and entered the school of Master Ralph, who had succeeded his late brother Master Anselm. He gave a sermon to Ralph's students and on the spot converted the seven richest of them, recent arrivals from Lotharingia. Norbert took them, with a great deal of money, to his church. But the ancient enemy, whose ceaseless way is to envy the successes of the servants of God, tried to throw this one into disorder at the very beginning. Just as he seduced Eve in paradise and perverted Judas among the apostles, now he also corrupted one of the two companions who had come to Laon with Norbert. In the middle of the night, this man stole the money offered by the students and entrusted to him by the master. Fleeing the church, he slipped off secretly and left the students in great poverty and want.

---

136. Apparently Prémontré was some distance from the little church where Norbert spent the night. Prémontré sits in a small valley surrounded on three sides by hills.

137. Prémontré was founded in 1120. Its inhabitants often left to preach, following in Norbert's footsteps. Within Prémontré and the houses that were subsequently founded on its model, the emphasis was on prayer and penance performed in austere circumstances. In keeping with Norbert's vision of men in white, Premonstratensians wore undyed habits. *The Cartulary of Prémontré*, ed. Seale and Wacha, is an outstanding edition of charters, generally speaking the administrative records of a religious institution, for the most part concerned with properties and rights. The vast majority of the 509 documents in the cartulary (which simply means a collection of charters) date to the first 130 years of the history of Prémontré and its order.

And then the man of God, remembering the voices that we said above he had heard near Reims, understood and told the lord bishop who was consoling him on the matter that the second voice, the one that had cried out, "This is Norbert and his companion," meant that of the two companions who had come with him, only one would remain and the other depart like Judas—or so he understood it. Lord Leonius, the abbot of Saint-Bertin, an extremely pious man and most learned in both pagan and divine writings, recently read this little book. He soon interpreted the voice another way and directed me to put his opinion here: depending on time and person it can be plainly understood that the voice bore witness that Bishop Bartholomew was the companion of Norbert. "When he had stayed three days in Reims," the abbot said, "and was unable to speak to the pope, he left the city in sadness and despair, not knowing what he would do or where he would go. It seemed to him that he had no comfort other than God except in the two companions he was sure would stick by him inseparably wherever he went. Then the voice sounded from above: 'This is Norbert and his companion,' as if it had quite clearly said to him, 'Do not despair, nor trust only in your two companions, for the bishop God gave you as a companion is nearby. He will take you back with him, he will see to it that you speak to the pope, and he will be the sweetest consoler in your troubles who will give you a home and church in which to rest and bear fruit.'" The lord abbot Leonius of Saint-Bertin directed me to write this and believing that he in fact had understood well and faithfully, I gladly obeyed him.[138]

5. How Walter was made abbot of the little church
of Saint-Martin in Laon

Later, when the bishop saw that already a not-small number of brothers leading a religious life had gathered at Prémontré, he asked Norbert to place some of them in the little church of Saint-Martin (where, when asked, Norbert had not wanted to stay) and for them to take pains to build and expand it in God's honor. Assenting to the bishop's prayers, Norbert sent a few of his brothers there and put at their head the religious man Lord Walter.[139] God, through the prayers of St. Martin, as we believe, quickly conferred on Walter such grace that it seems it can be

---

138. Herman, then, shared drafts of his work with others. Leonius was elected abbot of Saint-Bertin, located in Saint-Omer, in 1138.

139. Walter of Saint-Maurice was the first abbot of Saint-Martin from its foundation in 1124. In 1151 he was elected to succeed Bartholomew as bishop of Laon.

said about him what the angel said to her father Raguel about Sarah: "No man could have her before because your daughter should be wife to a God-fearing man" [Tobit 7:12]. Likewise, although the bishop had given many men rule over the little church of Saint-Martin and none had been able to succeed there, by divine grace such good fortune followed Abbot Walter as his companion that within twelve years a convent of more than five hundred brothers serving God was found there. Hence I might say justly that the church was destined for him by God.

Yet in the beginning, the church endured such poverty there that the canons possessed nearly nothing besides a donkey named Burdinus. Leading him to the nearby forest of Saint-Gobain in the morning and putting cut wood on his back, they returned to Laon and bought bread for themselves from the sale of the wood. Many times they fasted for a while until bread bought after the ninth hour was brought to them.[140] Yet with the consolation of Abbot Walter, they did not fail amid such poverty but served God incessantly. Progressing little by little in manual labor, through God's gift they were brought to such great plenty that they often have three thousand measures of wine from their vineyards. In farmland, mills, and livestock, they surpass almost all the monasteries in the diocese of Laon. Furthermore, the abundance of charity and hospitality found there is so great that in the interests of constant reception of guests and daily poor relief, God seems to have multiplied and expanded everything to the point that it is numbered among the outstanding and excellent monasteries in France.[141]

6. How Lord Hugh was put in charge of the abbey of Prémontré
Afterward, Lord Norbert did not want to be abbot of even the church at Prémontré but appointed one of the two companions who had remained with him, Hugh by name, as its abbot.[142] Norbert was devoted

---

140. This likely means bread purchased in the afternoon as it was going stale, sold at a discount.

141. A charter issued by Bartholomew in 1131, only seven years after the (re)foundation of Saint-Martin, shows it possessed several dozen holdings: farmland, meadow, pasture, mills, and vineyards (*Actes des évêques de Laon*, ed. Dufour-Malbezin, 228–30). Herman refers to the great prosperity in the wine trade attained by the time he wrote his account. Shortly after Herman made these remarks, Saint-Martin had nearly two hundred rural properties. See Saint-Denis, *Apogée d'une cité*, 158, with a map on the next page showing the type and distribution of holdings by the middle of the twelfth century.

142. Hugh of Fosses (ca. 1093–1164) was born and educated in what is now Fosses-la-Ville in south-central Belgium. He was in the household of Bishop Burchard of Cambrai (see III, 8, below) when he became a disciple of Norbert of Xanten in 1119 and traveled with him on his preaching tours, first appearing in Herman's narrative as one of the two unnamed

to converting to God not only multitudes of men but also women, to the point that today in the various places of this church we may see more than one thousand sisters serving in such rigor and silence that one can scarcely find a similar religious life in the strictest houses of monks.[143] Nor was he content to confine the crowds of his brothers to the diocese of Laon, but like bees that leave the hives in which they made honey fly off to make honey elsewhere, he sought various deserted places and sent brothers to them to build new monasteries. But he decided that the abbot from each monastery that followed the precept and plan of his teaching and rule, either during his lifetime or after his death, would gather every year on the feast of Saint-Denis at the first mother church from which they had come forth, that is, the church of Prémontré, as if to drink from a spring, and that once gathered they would hold a general council; if anything needed to be corrected, generally or in a specific case, it would be corrected there.

Although is it still less than thirty years since Lord Norbert was taken there by Bishop Bartholomew, now, through the manifestation of divine grace, so many monasteries have sprouted from it that nearly one hundred abbots may be found gathered at Prémontré on the aforementioned feast, not only from France and Burgundy but also from Alemannia, Saxony, and Gascony.[144] To remain silent about the others, from the church of Saint-Martin alone, over which the first abbot, Lord Walter, still presides, twelve monasteries have already emerged. And not only are neighboring provinces illuminated by such light, but a ray from this new sun has already crossed the sea and splendidly lit up the city of Jerusalem after some of the brightest stars were sent there.[145]

I do not know what others think, but I believe in my heart and faithfully proclaim with my mouth that Lord Bartholomew is the sharer, partner, and fellow laborer in all good things that take place or

---

companions of Norbert that Bishop Bartholomew met outside of Reims in October 1119 (see III, 2, above).

143. Women were members of Prémontré and other houses of what soon became the Premonstratensian Order (which Herman calls a "church") from the beginning. But shortly after Norbert's death in 1134, the leadership began to physically separate men's and women's compounds, with varying results: the sisters of Prémontré were relocated in short order, but men and women stayed together in other houses until the late twelfth century and beyond. The two *vitae* of Norbert, written shortly after *The Miracles of St. Mary of Laon*, do not mention Premonstratensian sisters.

144. Alemannia and Saxony are regions of what is now western Germany; Gascony is in the southwest of modern France. Unusually for Herman, the figure of nearly one hundred abbots, thus one hundred houses of the Premonstratensian Order, is not inflated.

145. A Premonstratensian house was founded near Jerusalem in 1141.

will take place hereafter in these many monasteries. Since the Truth says in the gospel, "He who receives a prophet as a prophet will receive a prophet's reward" [Matthew 10:41], it is perfectly clear that this bishop—who not only received the aforementioned servant of God but also, as noted above, interrupted episcopal business to take him around so many pathless forests and dreadful places, in the end planted him firmly in the solitude of Prémontré and took pains to water him once planted—surely will not lack the sweet reward of his fruit. The blessed Gregory in his homily on the gospel reading "In the fourteenth year" [Luke 3:1], explains the aforementioned passage more precisely. "It should be noted," he says, "that the Lord did not say 'he will receive a reward from the prophet' but 'a prophet's reward' because he knows the one who aids a prophet by welcoming him will earn exactly the same reward the prophet receives from God for his good work."[146] To show more clearly the certainty of the matter, the same St. Gregory also adds the testimony of the prophet Isaiah that also mentions, among cedar, olive, fir, and other very precious trees, the elm that although it does not bear fruit of itself nevertheless is counted among the fruit-bearing trees by God because it supports a vine with grapes [see Isaiah 41:19].[147]

If someone wants to consider this judgment of St. Gregory more carefully, I think he will not mock me for having written this, but will also state confidently that Bishop Bartholomew, although seemingly busy with ecclesiastical duties and involved in secular business, still always took great pains to help the servants of God who fled worldly life and through God's grace was a partner with sweet desire in their pious way of life and hence will not want for future reward. In any case, I acknowledge that the opinion of Lord Leonius, the abbot of Saint-Bertin named above, namely that the heavenly voice proclaimed that the bishop himself was the companion of Norbert, deserves to be praised.[148]

7. Many commendations of Lord Norbert

But now to conclude briefly about the aforementioned Norbert: many testify that nobody's conversion to religious life has borne so much fruit in the holy church in such a short time since the times of the apostles. For although some say that Lord Bernard, the abbot of Clairvaux,

---

146. Herman paraphrases one of Pope Gregory I's sermons.

147. The list of trees here refers to Isaiah 41:19 but differs considerably from it: the vine-supporting elm is not mentioned there.

148. See above, III, 4.

bore no less fruit during the same time, if one pays very close attention, I think he will not deny that Norbert surpasses him.[149]

Bernard, you see, was not the founder of his order, which already flourished in the monastery of Cîteaux, where the cleric Bernard took the monastic habit under Abbot Stephen after hearing of the reputation of the order.[150] From that monastery came Clairvaux, of which Bernard was named the first abbot because of his holiness.[151] He converted many through his preaching and through God's grace brought forth many monasteries from Clairvaux, yet although a great propagator and irrigator of his order, he was not its first planter. On the other hand, Norbert was the first planter of his order and by God's gift its founder because, although his disciples say that they follow the Rule of St. Augustine, we would say, with St. Augustine's permission, that the teaching of Norbert is much stricter, much more severe and austere, than that of Augustine.[152]

Furthermore, only men are received as Cistercians, but Norbert decided that women were to be received for conversion along with the men, with the result that we may see women's religious practice in his monasteries is more severe and strict than men's.[153] The men, going out in public after their conversion for necessary work and other business, are frequently involved in ecclesiastical and even secular advising and diplomacy. Many times those whom we know were either peasants or poor men in their prior life we now see riding proudly, so to speak, in their religious habit.[154] For the women, however, as soon as

---

149. This is a considerable claim. Bernard of Clairvaux (1090–1153), abbot of an influential Burgundian abbey, was a monastic founder, theologian, preacher who inspired many to enter monasteries or go on crusade, and advisor to popes and kings—and probably the most famous saint of twelfth-century Europe. An excellent recent study is McGuire, *Bernard of Clairvaux*.

150. Cîteaux, near Dijon in the region of Burgundy, was founded in 1098 by monks who desired to adhere strictly to the Rule of St. Benedict. It became head of the Cistercian Order, which in the next half century grew to include hundreds of monasteries. Bernard, who entered Cîteaux in 1112 under its third abbot, Stephen Harding (ca. 1060–1134), was instrumental in the order's rapid spread across western and central Europe.

151. Clairvaux was founded in 1115, with the twenty-five-year-old Bernard as its first abbot.

152. From 1121, Premonstratensians followed a rule the extremely influential theologian St. Augustine of Hippo (354–430) wrote around 400. Norbert adapted it to include even more demanding religious practices.

153. That there were no Cistercian nunneries in the twelfth century is a tenacious myth. Women's communities closely associated with Bernard and Cîteaux and following Cistercian practice began to appear quite early in the order's history. See Berman, *The White Nuns*, 1–46.

154. Religious garb, then, served as a metaphorical mount for people who in their former lives could not afford a horse. Entry into religious life was one of the few paths to social advancement for the poor who made up the vast majority of medieval European society.

they have converted, the principle of life is thereafter permanent: they are enclosed within the confines of their house and never again leave it, speaking to no man, whether stranger, brother, or relative, except at a window in the church, two lay brothers with the man outside and two lay sisters who live with them on the inside, all of whom hear everything said.[155] As soon as they are received at the beginning of their conversion, their hair is shorn to their ears to cut away all pride and carnal desire so they will be more pleasing to Christ, their heavenly spouse. Their weak and enticing flesh is completely disfigured for the love of him. Thereafter none of them is allowed to have expensive clothing, only wool or sheepskin, nor to wear a silk veil on their heads like some nuns, but a rather cheap bit of black cloth. Since they are known to be enclosed in such austerity, lowliness, and silence, every day, through Christ's power, we see not only peasant or poor women but even the most noble and wealthy, both young widows and young girls, hasten as if rushing to mortify their tender flesh to the monasteries of the order after rejecting the pleasures of the world for the sake of conversion. We believe there are now ten thousand women in those monasteries today.

Therefore, if Lord Norbert had done nothing else, leaving aside the conversion of men, except draw so many women to divine service through his exhortation, would he not have been worthy of the highest praise? But now, because so many thousands of men and women serve Christ through Norbert's teaching and so many monasteries of his order gleam throughout the world, well, I do not know what others think, but what many say seems true to me: since the time of the apostles there had been nobody who acquired for Christ so many imitators of the perfect life in so short a time.

Had he stayed longer in the monastery of Prémontré, perhaps he would have accomplished much else. But it pleased divine providence that he pursue (in religious habit) the honor that he declined through his flight from secular life, and he who before conversion did not want to be a bishop was an archbishop after it.

8. How he refused to be bishop of Cambrai

Lord Hugh, the abbot of Prémontré, recently told me that when Norbert had left the church of Cologne and his parents at the beginning

---

155. Lay brothers and lay sisters were members of religious houses who did not take formal vows but served the practical needs of the community. Usually of lower social class than professed religious men and women, they were very common in medieval monasticism.

of his conversion, he went barefoot to Valenciennes and there found Lord Burchard, the bishop of Cambrai.[156] When he had heard that the bishop was going to say a morning Mass, he went to the church and asked Hugh, then the bishop's chaplain, to get him an opportunity to speak to the bishop. Hugh, not knowing who he was, went in and told the bishop that some foreign cleric was outside and wanted to speak with him. Led in at Burchard's command, the bishop had recognized Norbert: he had often seen him, then a rich and powerful man, frequenting the imperial court. The bishop was immediately struck with wonder and shed many tears. "O Lord Norbert," he said, "who would have believed you left such wealth to go voluntarily into such poverty? Lord God, what is it I see in Lord Norbert, whom I once saw so splendidly dressed, accustomed to going about with pompous haughtiness?" When the bishop's chaplain Hugh saw Burchard weeping so astonishingly, barely able to speak through his tears, he asked him who was this Norbert for whom he wept so copiously. The bishop replied, "If you knew who he was, you would marvel at the sort of man he is now. When the emperor gave me the diocese of Cambrai, he offered it first to this Norbert, who did not want to receive it or hold it. Among the canons of Cologne, he was honorable and very rich, but now, as you see, he has left everything for God and busies himself with seeking God barefoot."

Hearing this from the bishop's mouth, the chaplain Hugh, immediately lit on fire with love for Norbert because he himself had already been pondering renunciation of the world, gave thanks to God in his heart for choosing such a companion for him. Just as long ago Andrew, upon hearing the Lord praised by his master John the Baptist [see John 1:40–42] left John to follow the Lord, so too Hugh, hearing Norbert praised by his lord, Bishop Burchard, whose chaplain he had been for a long while, left the bishop and joined Norbert. After disposing of his property on Norbert's advice, Hugh became his inseparable companion in travel and preaching, and went with him everywhere barefoot until, coming to Reims for the council of Pope Calixtus, he was made known to Lord Bartholomew, the bishop of Laon, as we related above.

---

156. The events described in this section took place in 1119, shortly after Pope Gelasius II granted Norbert permission to preach, and also refer back to when Burchard became bishop in 1113.

9. How Norbert was made archbishop of Magdeburg

Because I have reported that Norbert could have been bishop of Cambrai, but refused, I now add how he was made an archbishop.[157] When he had converted many people of both sexes, who left the emptiness of the world, to God's service, and built many monasteries far and wide, his renown extended everywhere. He was sent by Thibaut, the respected count of Champagne—who was the son of the sister of the English king Henry—to a most excellent prince of Lotharingia, whose daughter this count had married.[158] It happened meanwhile that on the death of the archbishop of Magdeburg, the clerics of that city gathered to elect another. In the same year, Norbert spoke privately with his friend Lord Geoffrey, the bishop of Chartres.[159] He told Geoffrey that he knew from a vision that he would be a bishop that year, but of which city or province he did not know. Therefore, when the Magdeburg clerics had found several candidates but were unable to agree unanimously to anyone's election, it was announced to them that two legates of the apostolic see, religious men, had come to Mainz from Rome. One was named Peter, the other Gerard, who was afterward pope, succeeding Celestine and preceding Eugenius.[160] The aforementioned clerics, fearful that the disputed election might be harmful and dissent would arise among them, after taking counsel went to the legates of the apostolic see, put the election in their hands, and promised that they would accept whomever the legates chose. Seeing how great their devotion was, the legates decided they would accept no money, which was offered to

---

157. The polemical account that follows is largely Herman's invention. Choosing a new archbishop of Magdeburg, some four hundred miles northeast of Prémontré in what is now central Germany, was indeed a long process: Archbishop Rudigar died in late 1124, more than eighteen months before Norbert succeeded him. However, Norbert was elected not in the Rhineland town of Mainz but in Speyer, about fifty miles south, and with the cooperation of King (later Emperor) Lothair III. Furthermore, Norbert's election seems to have been encouraged by Pope Honorius III (r. 1124–30) for some months. See Kunkel, *Man on Fire*, 125–30. Norbert's elevation was hardly the accidental and spontaneous event free from lay participation that Herman makes it.

158. Thibaut II of Champagne (r. 1125–52) was the son of Adela, sister of King Henry I of England. Thibaut's wife was Mahaut, daughter of Duke Engelbert of Carinthia (r. 1123–35). Carinthia, in what is now southern Austria, is a long way from Lotharingia, another error on Herman's part. Norbert's reputation was now international.

159. Geoffrey of Lèves, bishop of Chartres (1116–48).

160. Legates were papal ambassadors, frequently sent from Rome to carry out papal business; some bishops served as legates while remaining in their dioceses. Pope Celestine II (r. 1143–44) was succeeded by the former legate Gerard as Lucius II (r. 1144–45). The next pope, Eugenius III (r. 1145–53), was a Cistercian monk, a protégé of Bernard of Clairvaux.

them by some people through intermediaries, lest it happen that the apostolic see, and especially they themselves, be disgraced thereby.[161]

While, therefore, the legates sought the Lord's mercy to finish this important business decently and praiseworthily, without any whiff of simony, and while they carefully consulted with wise men in the church on the matter, behold, Norbert, unhoped for and unforeseen, arrived from France and entered the church to pray, completely unaware of the business being conducted there.[162] When they saw him, the legates were astonished and amazed. Rejoicing that God had heard their prayers, they called together the Magdeburg clerics and asked them if they would keep their word and accept the one they chose. Together and unanimously they answered that they would accept whomever the legates named without objection. The legates hastened to agree. "In the name of the Father, and of the Son, and of the Holy Spirit, we name and elect you, Lord Norbert, a proven religious man sent to us and to you by the Lord God, as we believe, to conclude the present business."

Stunned by a deed so incredible and hurried, Norbert was struck senseless: he did not know whether he was awake or asleep, where he was or where he had come from, and he marveled as he asked himself. He was seized and dragged by the clerics, not taken to the altar but violently carried. The *Te Deum* was sung in a lofty voice and then, forced by the bond of obedience, Norbert was consecrated bishop. So although he fled the diocese of Cambrai, by God's will he obtained the archdiocese of Magdeburg. Living in it religiously for some years, at last he rested from his labors in a holy death.[163]

10. Change and improvement in the church of Prémontré
His companion Lord Hugh, chosen as abbot of the monastery of Prémontré by Norbert and confirmed by the lord bishop Bartholomew,

---

161. In Herman's telling the legates were being offered bribes by some of the candidates for the archbishopric or their supporters. Since the mid-eleventh century, the popes had done their best to assure that all elections to high office were made by clerics and without money changing hands, but cash payments and powerful laypeople still often influenced the election of abbots, abbesses, bishops, and archbishops in the twelfth century (see Burchard's description in the previous section of how he became bishop of Cambrai: the emperor offered it to him after Norbert turned it down). In reality, Norbert's election as archbishop was the outcome of negotiations among lay and ecclesiastical authorities quite standard at the time.

162. Simony is the purchase of church offices. It is so called after Simon Magus, who offered two of Jesus's disciples cash in exchange for the power of the Holy Spirit (Acts 8).

163. Norbert was consecrated in late July 1126 in a solemn ceremony in Speyer. He died on January 26, 1134, having survived, according to his Lives, at least two assassination attempts after garnering resentment for his vigorous reforming efforts.

zealously applied himself, in labor and exhortation, to watering the vineyard that Lord Norbert had planted along with him as God mercifully granted it growth in all matters. He saw that the little church did not suffice for the great crowd of brothers who had gathered and increased daily through God's grace and knew as well that Lord Norbert, as was said above, had foreseen in his spirit that a large church would have to be built on the other side of the mountain. After consulting with his brothers, he asked the lord bishop Bartholomew, as the founder and father of the place, to come and place the first stone in the foundation of the church once all the other buildings had been properly arranged.

On the bishop's arrival, the entire army of God went out to meet him joyfully in a great procession, praising God in words of exultation and acknowledgment. The bishop soon recalled a vision that Norbert had reported to have seen on the first night of his arrival at the place: a crowd of men in white carrying silver crosses with candelabras and censers, going around the place chanting. Bartholomew greatly rejoiced and thanked God because he now saw before his very eyes as a reality what Norbert had seen in a vision. Hugh had seen to a church, dormitory, refectory, other buildings, and a kind of wall around the monastery, the likes of which any visitor may clearly see are scarcely to be found in the richest and most ancient monasteries in Gaul, to the extent that all who come and survey it blurt out, "Because in truth this was done neither by man nor through man, but by God, it is also a miracle in our eyes."[164] Good Jesus, with what joy Bishop Bartholomew is filled every time he goes there to visit as he gazes on such a splendid monastery built, in his own times and with his counsel and initiative, by God. It seems to me that Bartholomew can say with the apostle Paul, "I have done more than my predecessor bishops of Laon, although it was not I but the grace of God that is with me."[165]

11. The construction of the monastery of Foigny

This same bishop offered his help not only to Lord Norbert and his followers who serve God as clerics, but also he strove to have monasteries

---

164. Herman here justifies his title despite Book III being quite different in character from Books I and II. "Gaul" is the ancient Roman name for what is now roughly France. The refectory is where religious communities gather to eat, the dormitory where they sleep.

165. 1 Corinthians 15:10 reads in part "I worked more than all others, although it was not I, but the grace of God that is with me."

of Cistercian monks in his diocese. He gave them a place called Foigny in the forest of Thiérache that, as was mentioned above, he showed to Lord Norbert, who had said it was indeed suitable for religious life but not destined for him by God. Therefore the Lord—who places his servants here and there and directs them where he likes and how he likes—destined Prémontré for Norbert, Foigny for Cistercian monks. The bishop, staying with the monks there sometimes for an entire week, sometimes for two weeks, supported their work and poverty most kindly, comforted them sweetly and without ceasing, and took pains to construct and complete the church with necessary buildings as well as mills and farmlands.

12. The construction of the monastery of Épinois

Nor did he stop until, when Lord Gossuin was abbot there and a great multitude of brothers had gathered, he saw another monastery proceed from it in his diocese, near Guise, that was called Épinois. He named as its abbot Odo, who had fled the city of Laon in his youth and had been made a monk at Foigny.[166]

13. The construction of the monastery of Vauclair

The bishop also built a third monastery of the Cistercian Order in a place that is improperly called "Vauclair" by its inhabitants.[167]

14. The construction of the church of Thenailles

Moreover, the bishop did not want to leave empty the place called Thenailles, which Lord Norbert had said was indeed suitable for religious life but not destined for him by God. He placed some clerics from the church of Saint-Martin of Laon there and gave them the pious man Lord Walfrid as their abbot. As he had done at Foigny, Bartholomew also stayed there with the monks a week or two at a time and began to construct a stone church and other buildings.

---

166. Abbot Gossuin, abbot of Foigny from 1131 to 1148, and Bishop Bartholomew collaborated in the foundation of Épinois, about thirty miles north of Laon, in 1140 or 1141. In 1143, the new community moved a few miles further north and became the permanent monastery of Bohéries. Monks from existing Cistercian abbeys were usually the first monks of a new house, as in this case.

167. The first abbot of Vauclair was Henry Murdac, subsequently the abbot of Fountains Abbey in his native Yorkshire, and finally, from 1147 to his death in 1153, the archbishop of York. Why Herman thinks the name of the place improper is unclear. Perhaps because it inverts the syllables of "Clairvaux"?

Table 3. Monastic foundations, refoundations, and reforms linked to Bishop Bartholomew

MONASTERY	DATE	APPROXIMATE WALKING DISTANCE AND DIRECTION FROM LAON
Clairfontaine	1131	37 miles northeast
Cuissy	1122	13 miles south-southeast
Épinois/Bohéries	1140–41	28 miles north and slightly west
Foigny	1121	30 miles northeast
Montreuil-les-Dames	1136	39 miles northeast
Prémontré	1120	11 miles west and slightly south
Saint-Jean	1128[a]	Inside the medieval city walls
Saint-Martin	1124[b]	900 yards west of the medieval city walls
Saint-Michel-en-Thiérache	1124[c]	38 miles northeast
Saint-Nicolas-aux-Bois	1115[d]	11 miles west and slightly north
Thenailles	1130	25 miles northeast
Vauclair	1134	10 miles southeast

[a] Originally founded ca. 640.

[b] Originally founded in the ninth century.

[c] Originally founded in the tenth century.

[d] Originally founded in the 1080s.

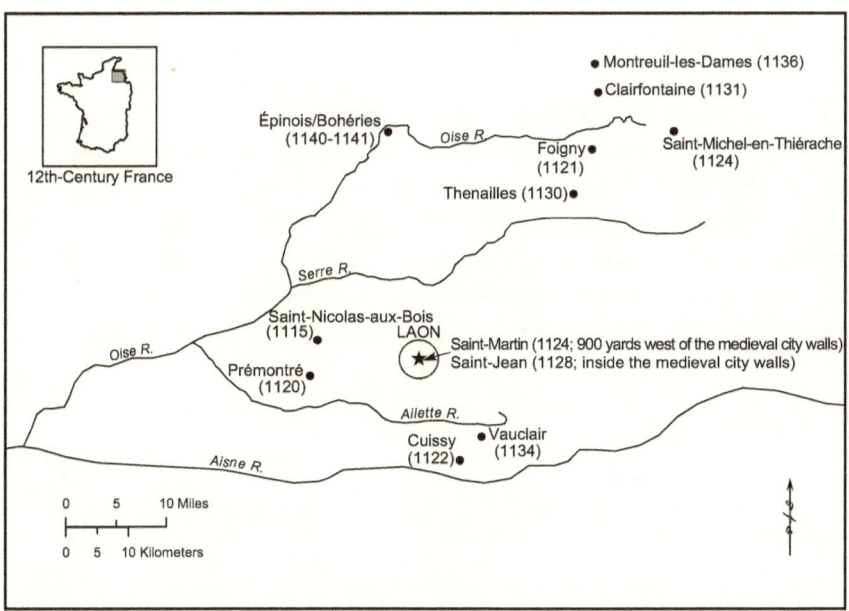

MAP 4. Monastic foundations, refoundations, and reforms linked to Bishop Bartholomew

15. The construction of a church called Clairfontaine

He also built another monastery of the Premonstratensian Order in a place called Clairfontaine and named as its abbot the pious Gerard.

16. The construction of the church of Cuissy

He also built another monastery of clerics in a place called Cuissy and named as its abbot the pious Lord Luke.[168] But when he saw the monks of Vauclair, who lived nearby, quarreling with the neighboring canons of Cuissy over a local forest, with each side saying that it had first been given to them by the lay people who had owned it and each defending their rights, it got to the point that Lord Samson, archbishop of Reims, and Lord Josselin, bishop of Soissons, along with the lord bishop Bartholomew, who frequently met at nearby abbeys, could not end this quarrel between the two houses.[169] Bartholomew took it badly that such discord had arisen between religious men in his diocese and regretted the bad example it presented to brigands and other lay people. He thought that he could restrain this kind of strife with his own money. So he gave fifteen pounds to some knights, buying another forest from them that he gave to the canons of Cuissy in exchange for the one they claimed and with this donation finally settled a lengthy dispute.[170] Thus we believe that he deserved to be counted in the number of those of whom the Lord said, "Blessed are the peacemakers, for they shall be called the children of God" [Matthew 5:9].

17. The construction of the nunnery called Montreuil

So on the model of the eight gospel beatitudes, the lord bishop Bartholomew built eight monasteries in his diocese, three of the order of Cistercian monks and five of Premonstratensian canons, and named an abbot for each.[171] In the end, to complete the number of the nine angelic virtues, he added a ninth, a monastery for women in a place called Montreuil near Clairfontaine. He named as its abbess a very

---

168. Cuissy was settled in 1118 by Luke of Roucy, a former canon of Laon, and a few disciples. It joined the Premonstratensian Order in 1122.

169. Samson, archbishop of Reims (r. 1140–61), Josselin, bishop of Soissons (r. 1126–52), and Bartholomew were frequent collaborators. See Ott, *Bishops, Authority, and Community*, 302–8.

170. Bartholomew settled the dispute in 1143. See *Actes des évêques de Laon*, ed. Dufour-Malbezin, 350, for the details.

171. These are the eight blessings of Jesus in the Sermon on the Mount (Matthew 5:3–10), one of which Herman has just quoted at the end of the previous section.

pious girl named Guiberge.[172] I might justly say that because of this one monastery, the church of Laon should be preferred to all others, for it is neither read in books nor heard with ears that there ever was an abbey of women with this kind of religious devotion anywhere in the world. They carried out, as it were, the word of the Lord—"The kingdom of heaven suffers violence and the violent ravage it" [Matthew 11:12]—and they labored with every effort to ascend to that kingdom.[173] They utterly scorn earthly matters and delight in defeating not only the world but their very sex: they passionately, indeed freely and voluntarily, took up the Cistercian practice that many men and hardy youths fear to approach. They put aside all linen clothing and fur coats, wearing only wool tunics. They labor incessantly not only in spinning and weaving, which it is agreed is women's work, but also in digging the fields, clearing felled forest with axes and hoes, and rooting out thorns and brambles. Working constantly with their own hands, they seek their food in silence. Imitating in every regard the life of Cistercian monks, they showed through themselves the truth of the Lord's word, that "all things are possible for one who believes" [Mark 9:22].

Therefore this ninth monastery that Bartholomew built for women, as I rightly said before, was made in the likeness of the ninth order of angels, called the seraphim, that is, burning or blazing, for truly these women, unless they had burned with the wondrous fire of divine love, would have been absolutely unable to sustain so many great labors previously untried and unpracticed by women.[174] But while they burn brightly inside, they both work these miracles and by their example set others on fire to despise the world. They are like live coals that, mixed with dead ones, soon kindle them and set them aflame.

---

172. According to tradition dating back to the early Middle Ages, there are nine orders of angels: seraphim, cherubim, thrones, lordships, virtues, powers, rulers, archangels, and angels. The first abbess was certainly not a girl (*puella*), but Herman wanted to stress her relative youthfulness.

173. Herman appears to use the quotation to assert that the women are storming heaven in the best way possible. The full sentence of Matthew 11:12, however, means that with the arrival of John the Baptist, attacks on the kingdom of heaven have ended.

174. Herman makes an important point. Elite women, who would have constituted the majority of the nuns of Montreuil, did not ordinarily perform outdoor manual labor. Among the rural peasant majority, however, there was a gendered division of labor. Women working outside the house participated in weeding, haymaking, and harvesting, but it was men who did almost all of the plowing and back-breaking tasks of clearing forests to create farmland. The nuns of Montreuil took all this on themselves. Many of them, then, did work that was not typical of their class or gender.

The bishop built these nine monasteries in his time, and yet he did not refrain from reforming older ones that he found already built.

18. Lord Simon, abbot of Saint-Nicolas

Seeing that religious practice in the monastery of Saint-Nicolas in the Saint-Gobain forest had become a little lukewarm, Bartholomew chose a very vigorous monk from Saint-Nicaise of Reims, Simon by name, to be its abbot.[175] Thanks to Simon's efforts, through God's gift, in a short time the church was so improved that it flourished inwardly in religious practice and outwardly in various properties. Hence Count Thibaut of Champagne, at the advice of Lord Norbert, named a monk of Saint-Nicolas whom Simon had received, Ralph by name, to be the abbot of the very rich abbey of Lagny.[176] Furthermore, Lord Simon, bishop of Noyon, a most noble man and the brother of Count Ralph of Vermandois, asked Bishop Bartholomew to have two monks from the monastery of Saint-Nicolas sent to him. Simon made one of these, Thierry by name, abbot of the monastery of Saint-Éloi in Noyon and the other, called Absalom, he put at the head of the monastery of Saint-Amand d'Elnone in the diocese of Tournai.[177] How these men reformed and rendered excellent the churches entrusted to them, both internally and externally, can be shown today more by seeing than hearing.

19. Lord Gilbert, abbot of Saint-Michel

Bishop Bartholomew made Lord Gilbert the abbot of Saint-Michel-en-Thiérache.[178] He was the prior of that same monastery of Saint-Nicolas who, before he entered religious life, was called Plato for the knowledge of letters he possessed in great abundance. In a short time, through God's gift, he made Saint-Michel a monastery blooming in both religious practice and wealth to a much greater extent than before and as he found it. But when after a few years Abbot Simon of Saint-Nicolas died, the lord

---

175. Simon became abbot of Saint-Nicolas-aux-Bois between 1115 and 1120.

176. Count Thibaut named Ralph abbot of Lagny around 1124. The house, located in what are now the eastern suburbs of Paris, was founded in the seventh century.

177. Simon became bishop of Noyon in 1123. He was Bartholomew's cousin by marriage: see I, 2, above. Thierry was abbot of Saint-Éloi in Noyon, about thirty miles west of Laon, from about the beginning of Simon's episcopate, then elected bishop of Amiens in 1144: see below, III, 26. Also in about 1123, Absalom became abbot of Saint-Amand, about fifty-five miles north of Laon, which like Saint-Éloi was founded in the seventh century. Absalom spent his final years as bishop of Tournai.

178. Saint-Michel-en-Thiérache was founded in the middle of the tenth century. Gilbert was named abbot to reform the house in 1124.

bishop Bartholomew, on the advice of abbots and religious men, transferred Gilbert from the monastery of Saint-Michel, naming him, given his reputation for honesty, abbot of the church of Saint-Nicolas where he had been a monk and prior. To this day he has accomplished many labors, for he went to Rome for the good of his church several times.

20. Lord Anselm, abbot of Saint-Vincent

In addition, Bishop Bartholomew ordained Lord Anselm, whom he summoned from the monastery of Saint-Médard in Soissons to be the abbot of Saint-Vincent, which lies outside the walls of the city of Laon and is called the second episcopal seat.[179] The goodness of this Anselm can be clearly observed in this one matter: today there flourish as abbots in different churches nine most honorable men who came from Saint-Vincent. They are Lord Baldwin in the monastery of Orbais, William at Morimond, Robert at Vertus, John at Saint-Michel-en-Thiérache, William at Saint-Nicolas-de-Ribemont, Gerard at Fesmy, Parvin at Saint-Sépulcre in Cambrai, Adam at Saint-André du Câteau, and Fulk at Hasnon.[180] These venerable abbots, all of whom call the church of Laon their mother and Bishop Bartholomew their father and pastor, remain today.

21. How Anselm was elected bishop of Tournai in Rome

When Anselm had presided over the monastery of Saint-Vincent for almost seventeen years, he went to Rome for the benefit of his monastery in the company of a fellow monk, his brother Lord Walter. There he was found by some clerics from Tournai, who by then had lacked their own bishop for four hundred years, and in a wondrous turn of events, through God's arrangement Anselm was elected bishop. Unwilling and reluctant but constrained by the bonds of obedience, he was consecrated by the lord pope Eugenius. Thus through Anselm, the ancient dignity of the church of Tournai was restored in the year from the incarnation of the Lord 1146, on Laetare Sunday.[181] Returning from Rome, he was welcomed in Laon with a grand procession. Not wanting

---

179. Anselm arrived at Saint-Vincent in 1129 from the prestigious abbey of Saint-Médard just outside Soissons.

180. These monasteries, founded from the seventh to the early twelfth century, lie in all directions from Laon, as close as twenty miles and as far away as two hundred. It is indeed impressive that in sixteen or seventeen years, from 1130 to 1146 or 1147, nine monks from Saint-Vincent became abbots elsewhere.

181. Sunday, March 24, 1146. Tournai was its own diocese for about a hundred years in the early Middle Ages, then folded into the new diocese of Noyon-Tournai in the early seventh century, so it had actually been five hundred years since Tournai was an independent diocese.

to leave his former sons, the monks of Saint-Vincent, as orphans, he gave them as abbot in his place one of their own, Lord Baldwin, young in years but venerable in habits, and had him ordained by the lord bishop Bartholomew.[182] And so Anselm set out for Tournai to tend the flock entrusted to him.

22. The monastery of Saint-Jean in Laon

After seeing to these monasteries, Bartholomew took care to reform the abbey of Saint-Jean, which of all the other houses mentioned above is said to have been the oldest, wealthiest, and most noble. It was built by St. Salaberge, as it reads in her Life; she placed nuns there and was their first abbess.[183] As tradition reports, she strove to raise up the monastery with great authority in the way we read in the Apocalypse of John: "Write the seven churches in Asia" [see Revelation 1:11]. Wanting this abbey to be like another Asia, she built seven churches in it. At first she wanted the principal church founded in honor of the holy Mother of God to be called Sainte-Marie-la-Profonde, perhaps to distinguish it from the cathedral of St. Mary, in which the bishop's chair sat. The second was dedicated to St. Michael and all the angels, the third to St. John the Baptist and all the patriarchs and prophets, and the fourth to St. Peter the apostle and all the apostles. After these four she built a fifth at the entrance to the abbey in honor of the Holy Cross, that is, so that through the power of that cross, every attack of diabolical deceit would be repelled at the very entrance, a sixth in honor of the martyr St. Aprus, and a seventh in honor of St. Mary Magdalene.[184] Of these seven churches, five remain; two, those of the Holy Cross and St. Aprus, have disappeared because they were so old.

This abbey was held in such regard that whenever the king of the Franks was to be coronated on ceremonial days, he made a point to

---

182. Baldwin of Rethel was abbot of Saint-Vincent from 1145 until his death in 1156.

183. St. Salaberge (ca. 605–ca. 670) was the daughter of the duke of Alsace in what is now eastern France. While young she was drawn to religious life, but her parents forced her to marry. Her first husband died soon thereafter, and she was remarried to Blandinus, a close associate of King Dagobert. They had five children together, two of whom, Anstrude and Baldwin, were also saints. Salaberge and Blandinus, yet another saint, eventually separated so each could pursue monastic life. Salaberge founded her abbey around 640.

184. St. Aprus was the seventh bishop of Toul, a city some 120 miles southeast of Laon, from 500 to 507. Although he preached vigorously against paganism, there is no record that he was martyred.

carry his gold crown into it.[185] No four-footed animal was able to come inside the walls or the gate of the abbey because it would instantly turn rabid and mad, so when a king, bishop, or other prince arrived at the abbey, all their horses had to be left outside the gate and they went into the compound on foot. On the death of St. Salaberge, her daughter St. Anstrude succeeded her as abbess. For more than three hundred years there were nuns there, and for a long time, they owned many lands given to them by kings and princes.[186]

But in the days of the lord bishop Bartholomew, ancient devotion had grown quite cold in that monastery, and its possessions had gradually diminished. Furthermore, ugly rumors about the virgins were spreading. The bishop was greatly saddened: he saw that when he frequently admonished them, they gave their word that they would improve but did not carry out their promise. With the advice and by the authority of the lord pope Innocent and Lord Renaud, the archbishop of Reims, as well as Louis, king of the Franks, to whom, it was said, the church property belonged, all of them together expelled the nuns from the abbey.[187]

Also receiving the pious Lord Drogo, prior of the monastery of Saint-Nicaise in Reims, Bartholomew ordained him the first abbot of Saint-Jean and settled there a sufficient number of monks from other monasteries. But since through God's gift, Drogo had already had considerable success, and the good odor of his wisdom and honesty had

---

185. Monarchs did not (and still do not) wear a crown at all times, donning them—being "coronated," in Herman's parlance—only for important occasions. The arrival of the king in Laon was one such occasion.

186. In fact, there had been nuns in the abbey for nearly five hundred years when Bartholomew reformed it.

187. On this incident, see Schulze, "Eliminating a 'Cause of Ruin'?" Schulze emphasizes that Bartholomew and Archbishop Renaud of Reims were the instigators of the removal of nuns from Saint-Jean, to which the king agreed and a papal legate confirmed. The house had suffered numerous challenges in recent years. Gerard of Quierzy, murdered in January 1111, was its advocate. The monastery was damaged in the fire following the uprising in April 1112, and then its abbess was murdered only a few months later (see Appendix 4). The nuns had also worked to recover property taken out of their hands. Schulze concludes that the surviving evidence "points not to moral laxity, but toward difficulty managing the possessions of their monastery as well as plain bad luck" (170). Herman's long, defensive justification of the expulsion below shows that it still rankled, at least locally, more than fifteen years later. His comments on Premonstratensian sisters and the nuns of Montreuil (above, III, 7 and 17) are an implied contrast to what he claims were a lack of spiritual fervor and poor property management at Saint-Jean (Schulze, "Eliminating a 'Cause of Ruin'?," 171–72).

spread far and wide, Pope Innocent forced him, constrained by the bonds of obedience, to go to Rome and consecrated him bishop of Ostia.[188]

23. The election of Abbot Baldwin

The monks of Saint-Jean, made fatherless orphans, unanimously chose as the abbot of the place Lord Baldwin, the son of Drogo's sister, who had made Baldwin a monk there. They presented Baldwin—although young in years, an old man in habits and piety—to the bishop for confirmation. Many men came to him from different provinces seeking the monastic habit, among them one from the region of Toul named Hugh. Baldwin, seeing that Hugh was not only mighty in religious fervor but also superior in knowledge of letters, made him prior of his monastery, rejoicing and thanking God for having given him such a helper. When the aforementioned Pope Innocent, at the advice of Bishop Drogo of Ostia, summoned the lord abbot Hugh of Homblières to Rome and consecrated him, bound as he was by the bonds of obedience, as bishop of the city of Alba, he also suggested by letter that the monks of Homblières choose as their abbot Hugh, the prior of Saint-Jean, so they took him from Lord Baldwin.[189] So you see how the abbot of another monastery came from the new church of monks at Saint-Jean, a development that clearly pertains to the honor of its founder, Bishop Bartholomew.

But I have heard some nonexperts disparage him in this matter, saying that such a change should not have been made, that innocent nuns should not have been expelled for the sins of a few of them and the entire church handed over to monks, especially because the noble lady St. Salaberge with her daughter St. Anstrude had built it with their own possessions and placed nuns in it and made it bright with the manifestation of many miracles.

To curb and check the foolishness and ignorance of these people, it is pleasing to recall a few examples from divine scripture concerning similar or even greater changes. Is what God plants not greater than what man plants? And surely it was said of the Jews by David, king and prophet, "You brought a vineyard from Egypt, you expelled the gentiles, and you planted it. You were the leader in its sight and you planted its roots and it filled the land and the rest" [Psalm 79/80:8–9] added as

---

188. Drogo became bishop of Ostia, near Rome, in 1136.

189. Homblières is about twenty-three miles northeast of Laon. Alba is a city in the eastern Piedmont region, today the Italian province of Coni. Hugh became its bishop in 1143.

confirmation. When the law was given to them by Moses, they received
the promised land, they fathered kings and prophets who performed
many miracles, and the Lord promised them a permanent dwelling
place in that land. Yet the tenants threw the patriarch's son out of the
vineyard and killed him, saying, "Here is the heir. Come, let us kill him
and it will be our inheritance" [Matthew 21:38]. They immediately elic-
ited the judgment of God, who ruled against them as follows: "He will
lose those wretches wretchedly and he will lease his vineyard to other
farmers" [Matthew 21:41]. Immediately they heard him add that "the
kingdom of God will be taken from you and given to a people who will
produce its fruit" [Matthew 21:43].

In another place the Lord related the parable of the fig tree. Coming
to it three years in a row and finding it bore no fruit, he ordered it to
be cut down, but through the intervention of the vineyard's planter, he
allowed a delay to the fourth year [Luke 13:6-9]. In the same way, the
lord bishop Bartholomew, personally and then through religious men,
admonishing those nuns to reform in one year, a second, third, fourth,
and even a fifth and a sixth and seeing that he made no headway, cut
down the barren tree as he should have according to the Lord's teaching
and handed over the Lord's vineyard to others "who may produce its
fruit in their times" [Matthew 21:41].

Bartholomew did this not only according to his sense of the situation
but also on the advice of the pope and religious men so that it would
be worthy not of blame but praise. It should not be feared that on this
account he had incurred the wrath of Sts. Salaberge and Anstrude, who
in building this church made it a community of nuns. We should rather
believe that such a desire had come to him from above through their
prayers and that abbots of the sort who took unending care to pursue
God's service and the rebuilding of the church were destined to do so
by God. Indeed, in no other monastery in the kingdom of the Franks,
at least among those who follow the same rule, does there blaze greater
piety and charitable hospitality than we see in Saint-Jean today. Despite Abbot Baldwin's great effort to seek out and reclaim the church's
properties that the nuns had carelessly allowed to be taken away and his
exhaustion from daily endeavor, he complains about nothing except his
inability to be always present at the assembly of brothers or offer the
courtesy of kindness to guests as he would like.

Therefore—since the two saints whose bodies are kept in that same
church see that perpetually, day and night, the divine office is carried out so devoutly, that silence and piety are fervently maintained,

that the sacrifice of Christ's body and blood is celebrated a hundred times more devotedly and frequently than before, and that pious guests who arrive daily are welcomed with the sweetness of charity—should we not believe that they delight in such sweet service to God and that when they see the monks pass before the altar and bow humbly, heads cast down, before their relics, these saints often say to them, "May the blessing of the Lord be on you" [Psalm 128/129:8] and "May you be blessed by the Lord, who made heaven and earth" [Psalm 113/114–15:23]?

I do not know what others think, but I believe in my heart and in my belief faithfully proclaim with my mouth that these saints delight more in the divine prayers of such monks than of the nuns who were there in Lord Bartholomew's time and that they beseech the Lord's mercy for the salvation of the monks and the bishop. As he composed the psalms King David said, "Let them write these things for the next generation and the people he creates will praise the Lord" [Psalm 101/102:19], clearly showing that he composed them not for Jews but Christians. Thus I believe these saints rejoice that the church they built came into the hands of monks of this sort and that the Lord agreed to grant their properties for their sustenance.

Since as was noted above, Lord Bartholomew built nine abbeys where he had found none, if someone considers the matter carefully, he will proclaim that this one was actually the tenth. It was built more than three hundred years before Bartholomew's time, but by then had grown lukewarm in religious fervor; it is recognized to have been refounded and renewed by introducing monks with the aid of divine grace. This renewal took place in the year of the incarnation of the Lord 1127.[190]

24. The cathedral of St. Mary

Moreover, since the aforementioned bishop took such pains in the construction of other monasteries, it can easily be believed that he labored mightily for the cathedral of St. Mary, where his episcopal seat was located, to increase its income. And although he was unable to bring about a different religious observance there—the cathedral's canons could not easily be forced to change their old ways—still he took the trouble to increase their income, just as he established that they would

---

190. The transfer of the abbey to monks was in fact approved at Arras on May 10, 1128. See Schulze, "Eliminating a 'Cause of Ruin'?," 165–67.

eat together in the refectory for most of the year and provided their daily bread fully and richly, so that, as the canons themselves bear witness, he nearly doubled their allowances over what they had before, as can be seen in his charters that are kept in the church.[191]

25. Lord Guy, the bishop of Châlons

In addition, it is to the praise and honor of the church of Laon and Lord Bartholomew that Lord Guy—a man of the high nobility, who for his piety and devotion and since he was reputed to be a lover of chastity and incessant attender of church services the bishop had made canon and dean of the cathedral of St. Mary when he was still quite young—was elected bishop of the city of Châlons and consecrated by Lord Samson, the archbishop of Reims.[192] Coming to his episcopal see, he named a young cleric from the church in Laon who had gone with him, Haimo by name, archdeacon in the very year of his consecration. Thus in the course of one year, the city of Châlons got both a bishop and an archdeacon from the church of Laon.[193]

26. Bishop Thierry of Amiens

The next year, Thierry, who was first a monk in the monastery of Saint-Nicolas in the diocese of Laon and later, as noted above, abbot of Saint-Éloi in Noyon, was consecrated bishop of Amiens by the aforementioned Archbishop Samson.[194] Thus, within two years two cities, Châlons and Amiens, took as their bishops sons reared in the church of Laon.

Therefore I might have rightly said above that in the church of Laon the statement of the prophet Haggai, "The glory of this second house will be great, greater than that of the first" [Haggai 2:10], was fulfilled. For in fact in the diocese of Laon there emerged many monasteries that were not there before and from it there came forth across the world

---

191. This brief discussion glosses over the perpetually strained relations of Bartholomew with his cathedral clergy, whom he wanted to live more like the monks and canons he fostered elsewhere in his diocese. The failure of the canons to change their ways was the cause of the departure of Luke, who established what became the Premonstratensian house of Cuissy: see above, III, 16. Alain Saint-Denis suggests that the cathedral canons' continued resistance to reform may have played a part in Bartholomew's decision to resign as bishop in 1151: see *Apogée d'une cité*, 130–31.

192. Guy de Montaigu was elected bishop of the city now known as Châlons-en-Champagne in 1143. Herman's laudatory sketch is at odds with Guibert of Nogent's account of a much younger Guy: see above, note 56.

193. Haimo was Guy's nephew, himself elected as bishop of Châlons in 1153.

194. In 1144. On Thierry, see above, III, 18.

many with a new way of life, sprouting as it were in the resplendent brightness of new light.

Indeed, from the time of St. Genebald, the first bishop of Laon—there were forty-three bishops after him until the lord bishop Bartholomew, who was the forty-fourth to succeed them—we do not read of as many miracles the holy Mother of God performed in the church of Laon as in the times of Bartholomew. Yet in the time of Lord Helinand, who was the fifth bishop of the city before Lord Bartholomew, a miracle occurred in this church that we thought it worthy to memorialize in writing here.[195]

27. The woman from Chivy saved from fire by St. Mary

In a village near Laon called Chivy there lived a man by the name of William, the administrator of the village, with his wife Soiburge.[196] They married their only daughter, Guiberge, to a man named Albin. Loving them dearly, William and Soiburge had them live with them in the same house. Not long after, a foul rumor of disgrace began to fly here and there in the mouths of many and increased daily: the young man, forsaking his wife, violated his father-in-law's marriage bed in adulterous deceit and abused both mother and daughter in a forbidden fashion. When the rumor reached the mother's ears through the report of several people, she, inwardly stricken with the force of unimaginable pain and distressed by the false accusation of wrongdoing, began to ponder in great wrath how she might wash off the stain of this accusation. While in unbearable distress, nearly out of her mind, she roiled inside with extraordinary schemes and was finally corrupted by diabolical inspiration. Armed with that inspiration, already guilty, she turned over in her mind how to snuff out the innocent man, hoping, under diabolical seduction, that this alone would be the cure for her disgrace.

Already wintry cold was arriving and the time of autumn and the grape harvest had passed, during which, of course, many people from different regions were accustomed to flock to these places to pick

---

195. On Helinand, see above, I, 2 and II, 2. Herman's calculation is inclusive: as he notes at the end of the next section, Helinand (r. 1052–96) was succeeded by Enguerrand (r. 1096–1104), Gaudry (r. 1106–12), and Hugh (r. 1112–13) before the election of Bartholomew in the spring of 1113, meaning that Bartholomew was the fifth bishop from, not after, Helinand.

196. Chivy-lès-Étouvelles is a few miles southwest of Laon. The events described here took place in the 1080s, late in Helinand's time as bishop. Guibert of Nogent's earlier version is translated in Appendix 3.

grapes in exchange for wages.[197] Choosing from among them two poor
men and paying them for their services, she faithlessly demanded their
faith: they would cloak what they did in silence and ready their right
hands to commit the cruel and most wicked crime she had devised.
Therefore she named a place, fixed the day and the hour when, rising
stealthily from concealment, they would suddenly grab the innocent's
throat and strangle him. Now the fatal day arrived. In the morning, at
the first hour of the day, the woman's husband went out to do his business as was his daily custom, the servants were scattered here and there,
and the daughter left the house. There remained only Adam and Eve,
the innocent lamb and the savage lioness. At the woman's direction, the
two paupers secretly entered a hiding place in the cellar.

When she found that the hour appointed for the crime was upon
her, the woman first made pleasant conversation with her son-in-law
and at last told him to go down and bring some wine from the back
of the cellar. Suspecting no evil and innocently obeying as if she were
his own mother, he picked up a jar and hastened downstairs. As he de-
canted wine into the jar, the two men rose suddenly from their hiding
place, grabbed the innocent's throat, and strangled him. At their lady's
command, the pair picked him up and carried him to a bed where they
set him down, dressed in his clothes as if he were sleeping. Meanwhile,
her husband returned home, then her daughter and the servants came
back in time for the midday meal. When everything had been prepared,
the mother told her daughter to go wake her husband. Quickly reaching the bed where he lay and finding him dead, she screamed. Roused
by the noise, they all rushed in together. Postponing their meal, they
turned to funeral preparations.

Word spread rapidly through the whole region that Albin, in good
health a little while earlier, had been discovered dead in his bed. At that
time there was a vidame in Laon named Ilbert, a wise and very intel-
ligent man but more cruel than just.[198] When he heard the rumor, he
first marveled, then became suspicious. He held off that day, but the
next morning he went quickly to Chivy with his men before the dead
man was placed in his tomb. As if purposefully ignorant of what had
happened, he began to investigate carefully. When nobody's account of
the matter satisfied him and he was impatient to enquire further, he

---

197. In the Middle Ages migrant laborers made up a considerable portion of the grape
harvest workforce. This remains the case in the twenty-first century.

198. Ilbert, Helinand's vidame, died ca. 1089: see Saint-Denis, *Apogée d'une cité*, 81.

went to the bier, violently tore away the cloth in which the body had been wrapped, and instantly discovered sure signs of strangulation. At once, like a growling lion raging to avenge the crime, he dragged William with his wife and daughter, all three chained in dreadful fetters, to Laon for punishment.

While they were being dragged away in cruel discomfort, the woman said, "Don't oppress the innocent unjustly and harass those who know nothing about such a great crime with punishment and suffering. I am an accomplice in this crime, I am the man's killer, I alone am guilty. The weight of torture should be on me and blood vengeance exacted on me. As innocent people, these other two should be released." Hearing this, Ilbert sent them away and presented the guilty woman, who had confessed with her own mouth and was confined in strict custody, to the bishop. While different people offered various opinions in the presence of clergy and people, one of the clerics present was Master Quentin, highly educated but not well schooled in divine law nor inwardly moistened with the ointment of the Holy Spirit. He gave his opinion, judging that she should be burned. After hearing the judgment and at the insistence of the dead man's friends, the vidame hastened to carry out the sentence.

While the wretched woman was being led to her punishment, she asked that a moment be granted her to pray in the church of the holy Mother of God next to the bishop's house. Arriving in the sight of the clergy and people, humbly and in a pure confession she laid out the entire sequence of the crime she had perpetrated and turned many to compassion and the shedding of tears. Next, prostrate on the ground and weeping copiously, she commended her body and soul to St. Mary. Rising afterward and protecting her face and her entire body with the sign of the cross, she departed and was led to the site of punishment. There she removed all her clothing except a shift that alone covered her naked body and was taken into the house where she was due to be burned. Her ankles were tied with restraints, her hands bound behind her back, and she was strongly tethered with sturdy fetters to a post that had been placed in the middle and on which the entire frame of the house rested. Wood and straw were placed around the post, filling the entire inside of the house. After that, the door was shut and a flame pushed under it; without delay balls of fire rose toward the roof. However, as fire cruelly ravaged everything and the whole building was reduced to ash, still the woman seemed to stand healthy and still amid the embers.

In a rage, her enemies ran from all sides to the fences, carried away anything they could put their hands on, and heaped on the woman a much larger pile of wood and straw than before. Again a fire was lit, even greater than before. The wood and straw were consumed rapidly, yet she appeared healthy and unharmed. What increased the miracle even more was that the fire that had no power against her had consumed the fetters in which she had been bound. When for a third time the angry mob again tried to apply flames and violently pelted her with stones, she exclaimed in her misery, "Spare me, I beg you, spare me. Can't you see that the most saintly Mother of God, to whom I entrusted my body today, mercifully helps me?" On hearing this, they were moved to mercy and stopped their attack; the vidame ordered her to leave the fire at once. Once she had come forth, everyone surrounded her and marveled that her body, hair, and clothing were completely unharmed. Thus they returned joyfully to the church of St. Mary and took her to the high altar as she gave thanks to God and his gentle mother. Nobody could easily recount how many tears were shed there in great exultation nor how many praises were sung to the kind Mother of God.

Afterward, the vidame took the woman to his house, restored her fully with food and drink, begging that she pardon him for having raged cruelly against her. From there the woman was returned to her own house in Chivy, and after three days, summoned by divine mercy, as we believe, she relinquished her soul and crossed from labor to rest, perhaps "lest malice change her understanding or deceit further beguile her soul" [Wisdom 4:11]. Almighty God offered her such mercy through the intercession of his mother that all who heard about this would learn, after a true confession, to faithfully place their hope in the help of St. Mary and never despair of her mercy.

Not one, two, or three people saw this miracle worked at Laon in the time of the lord bishop Helinand: nearly the entire city of Laon witnessed it. Enguerrand succeeded Bishop Helinand, Gaudry, who was savagely murdered, succeeded Enguerrand, Hugh succeeded Gaudry, and Bartholomew succeeded Hugh. In Bartholomew's time, St. Mary worked the miracles in France and England that were described above.[199] But because the miracle that St. Mary worked for a woman who humbly invoked her in the time of Lord Helinand was recounted, now a miracle

---

199. Here again, Herman fudges the chronology to give Bartholomew responsibility for the two relic tours whose planning was accomplished by others and the first of which was completed six months before his election as bishop.

of vengeance that she took on a certain thief who presumed to put his hand into her treasury should also be related.

28. Anselm's theft

Not long after his consecration, the lord bishop Bartholomew saw himself in a dream standing in the pulpit in the cathedral of St. Mary along with some of his clerics one night. Facing the doors, he saw a most brilliant light emerge in the middle of the church as if from an opening in the ground, wondrously illuminating the entire church. After the light, there followed from the same opening in the ground something like the smell of the sweetest balsam that unbelievably refreshed not only him but also those who stood around him. When the bishop urged them to approach the opening with him and see what it was, but none of them wanted to obey him, it seemed to him that he alone came down from the pulpit and went toward it. But as he drew near, just as God had said to Moses while he hastened to look at the burning bush, "Do not approach, for the place where you stand is holy ground" [Exodus 3:5], similarly the bishop heard a voice speak to him from inside the earth. "Do not approach, because Almighty God is present here in his flesh and bones and nobody who seeks God bodily can live any longer. His holy mother Mary is also present here with God, and she commands you that her thief be seized and orders that you do not permit him to leave but do justice concerning him." Suddenly the bishop woke up and in silent wonder often pondered what this sort of vision meant for him.

At that time Anselm, surnamed Beessus, lived in the city of Laon. Much praised and honored by all thanks to phony piety, he was, as became clear at the end, far different in his heart than men saw in his face.[200] Because of that piety the treasury of the church was handed over to him along with other guardians for safekeeping since it was the ancient custom of that church that its treasury be entrusted to seven guardians: four clerics and three laymen. Thus Anselm, seeing that he was held in high regard by all, secretly stole no small part of the gold and gems from crosses that were placed on the altar during feast days and handed over his haul to a goldsmith to sell after obtaining a solemn promise from him that he would reveal to nobody that he was the doer of the deed. But when the goldsmith was selling the gold and gems in Soissons, by God's will canons from Laon arrived and recognized the

---

200. Guibert of Nogent tells a brief version of this story at the end of his account of events in Laon, translated in Appendix 4.

engraving on the gold. They made a complaint straightaway and had the goldsmith arrested by a judge. Seized and utterly terrified, he confessed that Anselm had given him his wares. Taken back to Laon, he met Anselm, who denied it all, in a duel. The goldsmith was quickly overcome and defeated—perhaps, as many thought, because he was guilty of violating the pledge made to Anselm that he would not expose him.[201]

Anselm, quite puffed up by this victory, was well aware that he had committed theft yet overcome his adversary, and he gained great praise from the people who proclaimed his innocence. He was enriched with numerous lands and vineyards and provoked more securely to greater accomplishments. However, Lord Guy, who was both archdeacon and treasurer of Laon's church, was disturbed by suspicion of Anselm, in fact certain of his thefts, and removed him from his office, that is, from the post of treasury guardian. Therefore Anselm, roused to great anger and nearly out of his mind, sought a time and place to avenge himself in the matter.

Meanwhile, it happened that Countess Sibylle, the wife of the most noble Enguerrand, castellan of La Fère, deposited numerous gold and silver vessels to be kept safely in St. Mary's treasury because of the security of the place.[202] Anselm, taking the opportunity thus offered, thought to steal these vessels so that when the countess asked Guy, who was in charge of guarding the treasury, to return them, she would accuse him of theft. So one night around the Lord's Epiphany, there was such hail, rain, and howling wind that hardly anyone could leave their houses.[203] Thinking that such a night would be opportune for carrying out long-plotted evil, and with everyone shut in at home, unable to hear

---

201. Guibert of Nogent says the more likely reason Anselm escaped punishment at this point is that church law does not sanction judicial duels (see Appendix 4). These were trials by combat, overseen by clerics, in which God's judgment determined the outcome. Twelfth-century churchmen were increasingly hostile to such trials. Ivo of Chartres, who as bishop welcomed the fund-raising party from Laon (see above, I, 13) was an especially vocal critic of the practice because it directly involved the clergy in bloodshed. Trial by combat was forbidden by Pope Innocent III in 1215 but lasted long enough to arrive in the Americas with Europeans.

202. Sybille (d. after 1117) was the daughter of Count Roger of Château-Porcien, about thirty miles east of Laon. She first married Count Geoffrey of Namur, a city about eighty-five miles northeast of Laon in present-day Belgium, then became the wife of Enguerrand de Boves, castellan of Nogent-sur-Coucy and La Fère, places not far from Laon to the west and northwest, as well as count of Amiens, about sixty-five miles northwest of Laon. Guibert of Nogent offers a damning portrait of Sybille, whom he cannot bring himself to name, as an adulteress, the inspiration for maiming and slaughter in her native region, and a very wicked stepmother: see *Monodies*, 110–12, 145, and 156–61.

203. The feast of the Epiphany on January 6 celebrates the adoration of the Magi after the birth of Jesus.

any sound other than that of the wind, Anselm hurriedly gathered ladders and gear now long at the ready, speedily scaled the tower in which the treasury was kept, entered a door he had bored through with expert skill, and stole all of the countess's gold and silver vessels. Noticing that the bag in which he had put them was not yet full and reluctant for it to be in the least empty, he put his hands on the church treasury. He tore up precious gospels covered in gold and gems and left the books, hiding the loot in his bag.[204] Next he broke apart gold crosses and phylacteries; while he was at it he also smashed a gold dove that was well known and honored for containing, it is said, the milk and hair of St. Mary, and hence was accustomed to be suspended above her altar on major feasts.[205] Therefore, grabbing the bag full of such great treasure, he descended and hid the bag not in his own house but in a place outside the city prepared and provided for in advance.

As the dark, rainy night passed and the wind died down, when the evidence of the broken door and the plundered treasury became clear, the entire city was suddenly disturbed at such sad news, the laity was no less upset than the clergy, and a more bitter night seemed to bear down on them. People ran to the bishop and announced the mournful report. The bishop was stricken with greater grief than everyone else because the treasury that a few years earlier God had spared from fire in the whole city and the church itself had now been secretly and wretchedly lost. A general assembly of the canons and citizens was called at once. They discussed what needed to be done and consulted above all others with Master Anselm, at that time the light of the entire city. As one most expert in divine law, he repeated the story of Joshua, that is, how God ordered him to investigate a theft in Jericho done without anyone's knowledge, working by lot: first by tribe, then by households and houses; finally men were questioned one by one.[206] On the model of this very subtle inquiry, Master Anselm advised that the perpetrator of this great crime should be sought through trial by water. One innocent child from each parish in the city would be placed in a pot full of holy water, then one child from each house in whichever parish happened to

---

204. In medieval Europe, the leather bindings of holy books were often adorned with precious stones: see the prologue to *The Miracles of the Church of Coutances* below.

205. That Herman makes this a report rather than a fact may suggest skepticism about the contents of the gold dove. When he mentions the dove later on, Herman again writes "was said."

206. Joshua worked by lot to uncover the identity of a thief, working through the tribe of Judah, the clan of Zerah, and the family of Zabdi, in the end accusing Zabdi's grandson Achan, who confesses and is stoned to death: Joshua 7.

be discovered culpable would be put in the water, then all the men and women of whichever house was caught would be forced to exculpate themselves through trial by water.[207]

When this advice of Master Anselm and his brother Ralph became known, terrified citizens, although aware of their innocence, flocked to the bishop and cried out that those who lived near the church, preferably its guardians, should be called to judgment first. The bishop agreed, and the six most suspect men were submitted to the trial. He compelled only Anselm by name, saying that he was motivated by suspicion of him. Anselm replied that he was very much amazed that the bishop could suspect him of such a crime, especially because he knew that Anselm was a servant of God and that he was aware that a few years before Bartholomew had become bishop, Anselm had bested in a duel the goldsmith who had disgraced him with the accusation of a similar crime. The entire populace applauded this response and, acclaiming him as a holy man and a worshipper of God, they also added in one voice that he should not be called to judgment.

Then the bishop seemed to change his former character. Never before or after was he found to be inflexible in any matter, always accustomed to change his opinion easily at the prayers or statements of others. But in this case alone he was so steadfast that when nobody accused Anselm, and indeed nearly all supported him against the bishop, by God's will nobody could convince Bartholomew to release Anselm.

Because the bishop had ordered him to be kept under guard until the appointed day of the ordeal, a knight named William who strongly favored Anselm asked the bishop that he entrust the accused to him for safeguarding, and thus, with the bishop's consent, he took the prisoner to his house. While confined there, one night Anselm had a great pot filled with water and himself, tied up, placed in it. That is, he wanted to test if he would be completely submerged in the water or float. When he had seen that the water had received him without any delay and he had sunk to the bottom of the pot, he said in delight that he had nothing further to fear but would freely go into the water.

---

207. Trial by water was a common practice in medieval Europe. In this case, the accused were tied up and submerged in holy water; if they sank, they were innocent, but if they floated, it was thought that the water rejected them and thus they were guilty. (Those who sank were fished out.) Like trial by combat that Anselm had survived unscathed, trial by water came under strong criticism in the twelfth century, and in 1215, while forbidding trial by combat outright, Pope Innocent III decreed that priests were not to participate in trial by water. The practice became less common in the later Middle Ages but did not die out entirely until the early modern period.

Why drag it out further? The appointed day arrived, and a countless multitude of clerics, knights, and peasants of different sex and age flocked to the church. Youths and virgins, older people alongside younger ones invoked the name of the Lord and his most glorious mother. The first man plunged into the water departed safely and joyfully, the second also sank, the third was saved, the fourth was found guilty, the fifth was freed, and the sixth, Anselm, was found guilty, thereby proving that he had done himself no good for having tested God before because this water was a great deal different from that in which he had had himself put before when he was in custody.[208]

Now chained up and ordered by the bishop to return the stolen treasure, Anselm immediately invoked God publicly to the effect that if he had any of it or had stolen it, he deserved to be hanged like Judas, who betrayed God. Seeing that exhortation was getting him nowhere, the bishop handed Anselm over to the castellan Nicolas, ordering that he be forced through torture to return the treasure.[209] While Anselm was naked, prostrate on the ground, and tied up, Nicolas had hot oil poured on him but could get nothing out of him. Then at the bishop's instruction, Nicolas had him hanged, not to kill him but only to torture him. He was tortured from morning to evening, hung up ten times and taken down ten times. When he saw that Anselm was dying, the judge ruled that if he allowed him to hang any longer, he would not thereafter be taken down alive.[210] At last Anselm asked what he would get if he returned the treasure. Hearing this instantly gave everyone hope for its recovery. He asked for one hundred pounds but was negotiated down to forty.[211] He said he would take it on the condition that he and the money be guaranteed safe conduct ten miles away from Laon in whatever direction he wanted. The judge ran to the bishop and reported the request. The bishop agreed and ordered that whatever Anselm had asked to be granted, on the condition that he return the treasure right

208. The difference was that the water that found Anselm guilty had been blessed. The guilty verdict on the fourth man is puzzling. Perhaps he was guilty of a different crime.

209. Nicolas was the son of Guinemare, the first man killed in the Laon uprising on April 25, 1112. In the vanguard of royal troops who violently quelled the revolt, he inherited his father's position as the chief royal officer in Laon. See Saint-Denis, *Apogée d'une cité*, 127 and 203.

210. Nicolas appears to have acted as the judge overseeing the proceedings.

211. Forty pounds was still a lot of money; what Anselm stole must have been extremely valuable. The thief is playing a masterful game: he knows that if his adversaries kill him, they will never recover the treasure and that he can extort a great sum of money in exchange for what he stole.

away: the bishop feared that if a delay, however brief, was allowed, Anselm would slip away at demonic instigation.[212]

By now daylight had passed and dark night came on. At the bishop's command torches, candles, and other sorts of light were lit around the city, so that in Laon at this hour the psalmist's word would be fulfilled: "And the night will be lit up like day" [Psalm 138:12]. Nobody stayed at home, all proceeding as if to a show. Anselm, like a bear brought out of its cage, was led forth, carefully surrounded by guards and people lest he flee. He went toward the church of Saint-Martin, located outside the city walls, and arrived at a place near the vineyards where a great pile of stakes with which vines were propped up had been heaped. He went down below on the slope of the mountain as if to hell. Putting his hand in the bag, he first produced a gold cover ripped from a gospel book and smirking at the bystanders said, "I made a good deal to turn over such a treasure for forty pounds because this cover by itself is worth a lot less." Thus the treasure was returned to the church of St. Mary at once to general cries of joy in the city. The streets echoed with the sound of exaltation and acknowledgment, and the bells of all the churches were rung in joy.

But I should not be silent concerning a great miracle. In the monastery of Saint-Vincent, a monk and goldsmith named Siger plied his craft one night. He opened the window of his cell through which the church of Saint-Martin was visible and saw what appeared to be a ray of the brightest light coming from the sky and reaching the place where the treasure had been hidden. Quite astonished, he pointed out the ray of light to some fellow monks, but although they heard that the treasure of St. Mary's relics was being searched for daily, none of them thought it was there. The monks saw the ray of light gleaming at night as long as the bag with the treasure stayed there.

Nor should I remain silent about another miracle that took place. Since Anselm smashed (along with the rest of the treasure) the gold dove mentioned above, which was said to contain some of St. Mary's milk and hair, in accordance with divine judgment, he could not sleep at all, as he confessed to the bishop later on. Whenever he closed his eyes, he saw the dove pecking at his eyes and opening them. Yet as the devil hardened his heart, he was moved to no compunction on this

---

212. Because Bartholomew was probably certain that Anselm had triumphed in the duel despite his guilt in the first theft, he had good reason to expect demonic interference.

account. After he returned the fragments of the dove along with other treasure, he regained the ability to sleep.

Therefore, coming to the bishop the next day, Anselm asked to be released from the excommunication imposed on him because of the stolen treasure, that a cross be given to him, and that he be permitted to go to the Holy Sepulcher in Jerusalem.[213] The bishop replied that he would do none of that because neither absolution nor pilgrimage to Jerusalem would do him any good as long as he kept the forty pounds that he had taken for returning the treasure. "You did not return it," he said, "as a penitent, and therefore you cannot be absolved, but remain under excommunication. However, if you return the money and make a true confession concerning the theft, indeed sacrilege, and then accept penance, then you can both be absolved and set out for Jerusalem." Yielding to the bishop's words, he publicly placed the money on the altar and agreed that the guarantors who had promised to escort him safely ten miles from Laon were freed of their obligation. And so, absolved by the bishop, he took up the cross and was permitted to go freely wherever he wanted. For some days he associated himself with the bishop on friendly terms. Yet terrified by scruples that tormented him deeply on the inside, he considered flight and at last wanted to run away from the city in secret. But when he had begun to descend, wonderful to say, he saw a sort of river, wide like the sea, flow toward him and force him back up the mountain. Stunned, he again tried to descend and flee through a different gate, but at once saw a river coming to rush over him, as before.[214]

While this was happening repeatedly to prevent Anselm from going down the mountain, he confessed to the bishop in private. Therefore the bishop, seizing the opportunity, urged him to return the entire treasure—some of which, as noted above, he had given to the goldsmith to sell in Soissons—to St. Mary so he might go more safely to Jerusalem. Repeating his usual denial, Anselm said, "Yes, I deserve to be hanged like Judas, who betrayed God, if I still have any of it. But if you don't believe me, I'm ready to undergo trial by water again, and if I'm

---

213. Anselm, shut out of the church and excluded from the sacraments, now asks to be taken back into the fold and to receive an official badge of pilgrimage, a cloth cross sewn onto the voyager's cloak.

214. Anselm's scheme is breaking down. His guilt causes such inward torment that he is willing to take the money he has extorted and leave Laon—and the portion of the treasure he has not yet returned. He is prevented by the miraculous appearance of rivers that threaten to drown him. Anselm is trapped.

found guilty or refuse to accept punishment, have me hanged." Then
the bishop asked him to return at least the gems that had been set in
gold crosses, with the promise that in exchange, he would do him no
harm. But Anselm wanted to surrender nothing to the bishop and denied to the hilt that he had anything else. Afterward, utterly terrified
that at the bishop's command the castellan Nicolas was threatening to
repeat his previous tortures, he took Nicolas to vineyards planted below
the mountain. Thrusting his hand into a hollow in the ground, he drew
out the gems from the now-rotted bag and gave them to the castellan.
This done, quaking once more in remorseful conscience, he again tried
to flee because he had concealed them from the bishop and given them
to the castellan.

When he had received the gems from the castellan and remembered the dream in which St. Mary had commanded him not to let her
thief escape unpunished but to do justice concerning him, the bishop
quickly called together his officers and commanded them to look for
Anselm, the sooner the better, and bring him back to him. They went
here and there and finally found Anselm in the valley below the monastery of Saint-Vincent. He tried to flee but was unable to because of
an overflowing river.[215] They ordered him to come with them to the
bishop. Pale and trembling, he asked them to let him speak to Lord
Adalberon, the abbot of Saint-Vincent. Not wanting to leave him, they
went along since the bishop had instructed them to guard him carefully. Anselm, prostrate at the abbot's feet, asked that he go with him
to the bishop. The abbot agreed and went with him. Anselm fell to the
bishop's feet, asking that his life and limbs be granted him. The bishop
asked, "So who is chasing you? Return the treasure to my lady St. Mary
and go free wherever you want." Anselm invoked his standard line: if he
had anything from the treasury, he should be hanged like Judas, who
betrayed God. The bishop replied, "It is obvious you are lying because
you gave the gems to the castellan and did not want to return them to
me. You promised me of your own accord that if I did not believe you
after that, you would submit to trial by water, and if you did not, you
agreed publicly to be hanged. So choose what you want. I tell you before
all that I do not believe that you do not have St. Mary's treasure. Either
return it or exculpate yourself through the trial by water, as you offered,
or you will be hanged, as you agreed. I give you the choice of these three

---

215. It appears that only Anselm can see these rivers.

options." Anselm replied that he did not have the treasure and hence would not undergo trial by water. Calling together a general assembly of clergy, knights, and citizens, the bishop brought the case before it. On their common advice, it was judged that the wretch should fulfill what he had proposed with his own mouth. He was led forthwith from the mountain to the valley below and hanged from the branches of a tree, offering manifest proof to all that God did not want one who harmed his mother to be released unpunished.

These are the things that happened in Laon in the time of the lord bishop Bartholomew.

Here ends Book III

Hugh Farsit, *A Little Book of Miracles of the Blessed Virgin Mary in the City of Soissons*

Introduction

The city of Soissons, about sixty miles northeast of Paris, is far less dramatic in site and twelfth-century history than Laon, its neighbor eighteen miles northeast.[1] Centered on the left bank of a windy stretch of the Aisne River, from ancient times it was a crossroads connected to several nearby cities—Laon, Reims, Compiègne, and Noyon—amid a rich agricultural region.[2] Soissons was the seat of a bishop perhaps as early as the late third century and an important late Roman city and early medieval royal center. Pepin the Short (r. 751–68), the founder of the Carolingian dynasty and father of Charlemagne, was consecrated king in Soissons. Although badly damaged in royal dynastic wars in the late tenth century, the city recovered into a period of relative peace and prosperity in the eleventh and twelfth centuries. In this era, Soissons was the center of a small county within the orbit of the kings of

---

1. The secular history of Soissons in the central Middle Ages is not well known: most surviving historical writing focuses on religious subjects. The last extensive treatment is more than one hundred years old: Bourgin, *La Commune de Soissons*, happily a rigorous piece of scholarship on which I rely in the next several paragraphs.

2. The main commodities were grains and wine. As with the region around Laon, Soissons viticulture has virtually disappeared since the Middle Ages.

the Franks, but not in their direct control.[3] Across the Middle Ages, some dozen families had short-, medium-, or long-term control of the county. At the time of the events Hugh Farsit describes, the count was Renaud III (r. 1118–41), whose ancestors came from Normandy, the powerful duchy north and west of Paris. Renaud retired to a monastery in 1141, and he was succeeded by his cousin Yves of Nesle (r. 1141–78), marking a peaceful transition of control of the county from the house of Normandy to the house of Nesle-Soissons, installed by the time Hugh wrote *A Little Book of Miracles of the Blessed Virgin Mary in the City of Soissons*.

Since the end of the tenth century, political and economic power in Soissons was disputed between the counts and the bishops, with the latter usually maintaining the upper hand.[4] Kings were sometimes drawn into these struggles, which seem to have turned violent relatively rarely, even though the bishops, like the counts, had a military entourage and vassals. Nor were there great tensions between the bishop and the cathedral clergy, its canons, as was the case in many other French cities. Soissons, like Laon, became a commune town. The build-up was gradual, stemming as in Laon from the resentment of citizens and the local peasantry of arbitrary exactions by secular and ecclesiastical powers. The commune appears to have come into effect, more or less peacefully, in the late 1110s.[5]

Soissons was a notable ecclesiastical center in the central Middle Ages, during which a great deal of hagiography was produced locally.[6] Josselin of Vierzy was its bishop from 1126 to 1152. Josselin's early career was as a Paris-trained theologian, student of canon law, and schoolmaster. As bishop, he was a noted preacher and became an important judge in disputes between churches during his long episcopate, sometimes delegated by popes to carry out such duties. He was a close colleague of Bishop Bartholomew of Laon, a neighboring diocese. The two collaborated, often joined by two successive archbishops of Reims, Renaud II (r. 1124–39) and Samson (r. 1140–61), on numerous ventures. Between 1126 and 1151, Josselin and Bartholomew appear together in dozens of surviving documents in the context of monastic

---

3. See the introduction to *The Miracles of St. Mary of Laon* on the limits of royal power in this era.

4. For what follows, see Bourgin, *La Commune de Soissons*, 16–34.

5. Bourgin, *La Commune de Soissons*, 57–89.

6. Bourgin, *La Commune de Soissons*, ix–xvi.

foundations, mediation of disputes, and the business of new and existing monasteries.[7] Josselin was also a friend of Abbot Suger of Saint-Denis from his years in Paris; Suger dedicated his biography of Louis VI to the bishop of Soissons.[8] Somewhat surprisingly, Hugh never mentions Josselin.

Twelfth-century Soissons was also home to four important religious houses. The first, just to the southeast of the medieval city walls, was Saint-Crépin, founded in the fifth or sixth century (its early history is obscure). It was dedicated to the martyred brothers Crispinus and Crispianus, the patron saints of Soissons. On the right bank of the Aisne was the abbey of Saint-Médard, which King Clotaire I founded in 557 to house the body of the recently deceased Médard, bishop of Noyon (d. 545). It retained its royal connections throughout its long history. Largely destroyed by Norman and Hungarian raiders in the ninth century and undergoing eclipse in the tenth, its recovery began after 1000, and by Hugh's times Saint-Médard was an extraordinarily wealthy monastery, maintaining close ties to Frankish and French kings throughout its history, and even minting its own coins. Its abbey church, the fourth on the site, was dedicated by Pope Innocent II in 1131.[9] Of much more recent date was the third significant community in Soissons, Saint-Jean-des-Vignes. Founded in 1076 as a house of regular canons, located just to the south of the medieval walls, it rapidly became wealthy and prestigious.[10]

The fourth house was the abbey of Notre-Dame, the only one within the medieval city and the only one for women. It was founded in the mid-seventh century and came into royal control under the Carolingians.[11] Charlemagne's daughter Rotrude was a nun at Notre-Dame and his sister Gisela its abbess. In its compound were four churches: Notre-Dame, for the nuns; Saint-Pierre, for the canons who served them spiritually and practically; Sainte-Geneviève, for pilgrims and the ill; and Sainte-Croix, for funerals. This house, closely linked to royal families throughout its history, is the setting for the miracles Hugh

---

7. On Josselin, see Ott, *Bishops, Authority and Community*, 47, 133, 272–76, 278–81, 302–6, and for the times Josselin and Bartholomew appear together in the documentary record, an appendix, 318–26.

8. Suger, *The Deeds of Louis the Fat*, 23–24.

9. On Saint-Médard, see Becquet, *Abbayes et prieurés de l'ancienne France*, 177–83.

10. See Bonde and Maines, eds., *Saint-Jean-des-Vignes*. Hugh of Farsit's name does not appear in this substantial volume, a telling indicator of his obscurity.

11. Becquet, *Abbayes et prieurés de l'ancienne France*, 169–73. The only detailed history of the abbey is Germain, *Histoire de l'abbaye de Notre-Dame de Soissons*.

narrates. It was a very large community by medieval standards: in the later twelfth century it was limited to eighty nuns, so as not to strain resources, suggesting there may have been more in Hugh Farsit's time.[12] A new abbey church for the nuns was under construction from circa 1130 to circa 1160.

Hugh, known as Hugh of Soissons or Hugh Farsit (Latin *Farsitus*, "stuffed"), was a canon of Saint-Jean-des-Vignes. Of Hugh's life almost nothing is known. He must have been born in the later eleventh century since between circa 1111 and circa 1115 he wrote four books entitled *Otium* ("Leisure") dedicated to his sister Helvide, whom Hugh calls a chaste virgin and who was almost certainly a canoness in Mons, about eighty miles north-northeast of Soissons in present-day Belgium.[13] As Hugh explains, he will write when it is suitable—when he has the leisure—or God inspires him, and he will divide the work by year. Four books survive, a total of 135 chapters written from 1111 to 1114 or 1115.[14] Most of *Otium* is comprised of theological and moral meditations that also serve in part as Hugh's spiritual autobiography. It is by turns cheerful and gloomy, the commentary of a man of great faith and in great fear for his soul, with a heavy emphasis on the figure of Christ and the sacraments of baptism and the Eucharist. In *Otium*, Hugh notes he had earlier written a verse account of one vision that he now repeats in prose, a longer *Progress of the Inner Man* that was at least six books long, a book on Jerusalem, and a long letter concerning heresy addressed to fellow canons in Jerusalem.[15] None of these four texts has survived, nor anything else Hugh wrote until almost thirty years after the completion of *Otium*. In 1143, two factions of the Premonstratensian Order whose origins Herman of Tournai describes met in Coblenz, along the Rhine, to settle differences in matters of religious practice.

12. Venarde, *Women's Monasticism and Medieval Society*, 156–57. In the ninth century, there were more than two hundred sisters: Bourgin, *La Commune de Soissons*, 45.

13. T, fols. 49r–106v, contains the full text of *Otium*, which has yet to be edited. See Vernet, "Les 'Loisirs' d'un chanoine de Soissons" (which relies on the Troyes manuscript) and Giraud, "Écrire l'histoire d'une âme au XIIᵉ siècle." Giraud casts doubt on the traditional assumption that the author of *Otium*, who calls himself "Brother Hugh of Soissons," is the same as Hugh Farsit, but he does not go so far as to claim they were different people. I follow the standard view that they are one and the same.

14. In *Otium*, I, 57, Hugh writes in 1112. But I, 43, is a prayer for Christmas Eve, so Hugh probably started writing in 1111. At III, 13, he gives a date of 1114. There were originally at least six books (Giraud, "Écrire l'histoire d'une âme au XIIᵉ siècle," 650).

15. The hexameter version of his vision: *Otium* I, 27; the books on the progress of the inner man: *Otium*, preface, I, 8, and I, 28; the treatise on Jerusalem: *Otium* I, 28; and the letter to his brothers in Jerusalem: *Otium* II, 16.

Hugh wrote a letter urging unity and fidelity to the intentions of Norbert of Xanten.[16]

Hugh probably wrote *A Little Book of Miracles of the Blessed Virgin Mary in the City of Soissons* shortly after his letter to the Premonstratensian abbots. The likeliest scenario is that the nuns of Notre-Dame commissioned Hugh to compose the collection on the occasion of Abbess Mathilda's death in December 1143, a way of preserving the memory of the miracles that took place in Mathilda's time, sometimes under her supervision, and that she may well have recorded in part.[17] In one case (section 7), Hugh himself saw a woman who had been cured; he may also have worked from the testimony of other eyewitnesses since he was writing less than twenty years after the events. The date of Hugh's death is unknown: the obituary of Saint-Jean-des-Vignes, the list of departed members of its community, notes that he had given books on religious and secular subjects to the house.[18]

The miracles Hugh describes center around an outbreak of what he calls *ignis sacer*, "holy fire," a medieval term for ergotism, a disease brought on by eating rye or other cereals infected with fungus. Ergotism takes two forms: convulsive (characterized by seizures, diarrhea, and mental disturbances) and gangrenous (characterized by festering and rotting tissue). What Hugh describes is usually the gangrenous type; he lays heavy emphasis on the bad smell associated with gangrene.[19] Many of the miracles he describes are related to cures of ergotism that was widespread across northern France in the late 1120s.[20] Hugh dates the miracles from 1128 to 1132, but those in 1131 and 1132 are not healings of ergotism.

---

16. Gerits, "La lettre de Hugues Farsit," which includes an edition of the letter. For commentary, see Constable, "The Letter of Hugh of Soissons."

17. Clark, "Guardians of the Sacred," 728: "With [Mathilda's] death, the community would likely have desired to create a more stable repository of their history." Giraud notes that despite the scholarly consensus that the abbess had died when Hugh wrote, internal textual evidence does not rule out Mathilda being alive and that the collection could date to any time after 1132, when the last recorded miracle took place ("Écrire l'histoire d'une âme au XIIe siècle," 654). I find Clark's argument that Hugh's text most likely dates to shortly after the abbess's death convincing.

18. Giraud, "Écrire l'histoire d'une âme au XIIe siècle," 656.

19. Contrary to a prevalent myth—a remnant of the characterization of medieval Europe by the nineteenth-century historian Jules Michelet as "a thousand years without a bath"—medieval people, especially lay elites, churchmen, churchwomen, and city dwellers, bathed regularly, even frequently: see Black, *The Middle Ages*, 49–68 (chap. 3, "Peasants Never Bathed, and They Ate Rotten Meat"). The foul smell of rotting flesh would have stood out, if not as much as it would today.

20. On this outbreak, see Foscati, *Saint Anthony's Fire*, 80.

The focus of the Marian cult in Notre-Dame-de-Soissons is a relic: Mary's slipper.[21] How and when the nuns obtained this relic is unknown. It appears in Hugh's account for the first time. The nuns, in particular Abbess Mathilda, are its caretakers, and there was some sort of healing ritual associated with it; Hugh is vague on its nature. The slipper was also brought around the church for those cured to bless and kiss it. One healed woman tried to chew off a piece of the relic, whether to swallow it or keep it for herself is unclear. Elsewhere, Hugh remarks that pilgrims to the nuns' church would often return home with soil, wood, or bread that had touched it, creating contact relics. The slipper goes in and out of the narrative, perhaps indicating Hugh's discomfort with a healing ministry, a quasi-sacrament, carried out by women: the nuns fade to the background in the latter portions of the collection.[22]

Hugh provides a vivid account of the disruptions that came with being a shrine church: it is clear that the noise, smell, and press of the faithful were a source of considerable annoyance to the male and female religious there. The slipper is withdrawn from circulation at one point; at another a pilgrim is shooed away because the crowd is simply too large; the harmonious chanting of the nuns had competition from the laity's din; several days of ravings of a woman possessed by the devil become a "nuisance"; a man with a putrid foot is expelled from the church because the stench is unbearable to those around him. Those living and working at a shrine made a trade-off: the stream of people was profitable—Hugh frequently mentions the donations of the faithful—but this account of miracles shows it was a trial to keep some order and carry out the round of daily prayers. Present day and night, loudly lamenting or rejoicing, banging drums, and blasting trumpets, the faithful must have been a real bother. Hugh was aware of the challenge of maintaining some semblance of order in a shrine church in a way most narrators of miracles were not.

Like the collections by Herman of Tournai and Abbot Haimo, Hugh's has as its context the construction or reconstruction of a church. Creating a sort of canon of miracles that could be read and, probably at least as important, recounted orally was a fund-raising tool. It may have been effective as such; a new abbey church, begun in the times of Abbess Mathilda, was completed under her successor, a second Abbess Mathilda (r. 1143–62), the niece of King Louis VII. Sadly, all that

---

21. Clark, "Guardians of the Sacred," on which I draw in this paragraph.
22. Clark, "Guardians of the Sacred," 737.

remains of what must have been an impressive building are two arched window frames.

Text: *PL* 179:1777–1800 is a defective reproduction of an imperfect seventeenth-century edition: Germain, *Histoire de l'abbaye de Notre-Dame de Soissons*, 481–504. Fortunately, the Bibliothèque nationale de France has made available online reproductions of five partial or complete versions of Hugh's text in twelfth- and thirteenth-century manuscripts: P, P2, P3, P4, and P5. Appendix 5 provides a list of manuscript readings I prefer to those in the *PL* edition.

A Little Book of Miracles of the Blessed Virgin Mary in the City of Soissons

Here begins the prologue of the little book written by Hugh Farsit of blessed memory concerning the miracles of Mary, the holy Mother of God, that took place in the city of Soissons[23]

For the praise and glory of the blessed, glorious, and ever-virgin Mary, Mother of God and our Lord Jesus Christ, God deemed it worthy in our times to show his people the power of their miracles, to give believers the inheritance of nations and to those who love him the good things he promised Israel [see Psalm 110/112:6–7; James 1:12 and 2:5]. Therefore, once illuminated they were made sharers in the Holy Spirit and already tasted the virtues of times to come, partaking no less of the good word of God [see Hebrews 6:4–5] and therefore scornful of and indifferent to present concerns. It was granted them by the gift of consolation to taste the power of the invisible kingdom in a hoped-for vision and drink in with their eyes the fear and love of divine severity and mercy. This is the great strength of God through which he restrains evils and lavishes invisible goods and the riches of his glory on those who love him. This is, I say, the great strength of God and the greatest might of his kingdom: invisible power, hidden power to curb evils that flourish like disease in his kingdom unless restrained, and the power of grace and mercy from his realm that reveal his works inexpressibly, through which assurance, once fear is driven away, he rejoices with his chosen people as he offers overflowing love. But I write of these things elsewhere.[24]

Here begin the miracles of St. Mary of Soissons

1. The first series of miracles

Therefore in the year 1128 of the Lord's incarnation—by what judgment of God and for what reasons let him understand who is able to—the capacity was granted to the hostile power to strike people of different age and sex in the region of Soissons with an invisible plague: once their bodies had been inflamed, they burned with intolerable torment to the point of death unless the medicine of God alone resisted it.[25]

---

23. Title from P.
24. Hugh is perhaps thinking of his *Otium*.
25. The "hostile power" is the devil.

This is a wasting disease, separating flesh from bones under stretched, bluish skin and eating it away. As time passes, the increase of pain and heat seizing them at every moment drives the wretched to die. Yet such a cure is denied to those who desire death until, once the limbs are consumed, the swift fire attacks the vital organs. Extraordinarily, this fire is effective at consuming without heat, spreading through the wretched with such cold, like ice, that no treatment can warm them. What is no less wondrous is that once the temporary cold is driven off, annihilated by divine grace, such great heat penetrates the ill in the same parts of the body that tumors very often accompany the burning unless counteracted by medicines.[26] It is a horror to look at both the sick and the recently cured and to cast eyes over the traces of death escaped in their ruined bodies and faces.

Yet the greater the misery, the worthier of thanksgiving the mercy. So it happened that in such urgent need—while the plague still raged and collective danger was at hand—in which human aid could not be considered, those in whom the fire was still rampaging resorted to the kind and gentle Mother of God, the ever-virgin Mary. In the end, their hope was not in vain. For six days in September, they were in the church of the Blessed Virgin located in Soissons. Their anguish persisting and the number of the enfeebled growing every day, they could not be quiet, and through the constant, horrible cries of the sort death is accustomed to produce, they allowed no peace to anyone who heard them. Renewed fear thrashed the city, and hearts however hard were stricken with fear: of imminent danger, of the fire attacking those so nearby, and of the plague wasting those who did not expect it. All the people gathered in that church, congregations proceeding not only from other churches but also from the cathedral. Barefoot, they were armed with humility on the model of the Ninevites, binding themselves with an abundance of penance in order to fight with the kind and merciful God—to fight, I say, and to be victorious.[27] For he is kind and cannot long endure assaults of heartfelt distress and great misery, but immediately falls in defeat, because he is kind. These are the heavenly weapons that protect, these the heavenly weapons that teach how to stand firm, engage boldly, and overcome.

---

26. Hugh likely means the divine medicine mentioned earlier in the section. Secular medicine at the time was of little help in cases of ergotism.

27. The ancient city of Ninevah was in what is now northern Iraq. God, angered at the wickedness of the Ninevites, sent Jonah there to preach. Its king and people repented by donning sackcloth and fasting, and the city was spared disaster (Jonah 3).

Therefore a battle station was set up in the church of the Blessed Virgin and Mother of God so they might enlist her aid, too, amid such great need. Once a priest had made a sign, he said, "Now is the time for them to come out and attack with prayers, the ravaging sword." Then they loosed the reins with their tears, and proffering the shield of faith, they took a stand in ardent desire, and their shouts ascended to heaven. And behold, the mighty queen and Lady of the angels was there as an auxiliary force, bringing with her mighty armies of heavenly spirits in whose presence hell should be afraid, the gates of death should tremble, and no adverse sickness nor any sort of plague-bearing power could remain.[28] It should not seem extraordinary to anybody that as a precursor of her arrival, such a great trembling filled the church that everyone, thinking there was an earthquake or the church was knocked off its foundations, took flight; it seemed to each one of them that they could not find doors and passages quickly enough. The substance and minds of men ought to have felt awe for such power and mortal hearts to have been cast down in the face of divine might.

But when they perceived there was no danger at hand and returned to their senses, they discovered that all the fire of the ill had been quenched and all pain put to rest with the deliverance of the swiftest sweetness.[29] Thus in this sudden liberation, the groans of sufferers that had a moment ago been unbearable now became boundless cries of happiness sent to heaven, and as popular exultation joined with them, it seemed that praises, tears, and thanksgiving could not be finished in what was left of the day. Bells and drums echoed and great, competing harmonies sounded the glory of God's victory as they increasingly encouraged a new spirit to take hold and for Christ to roar in the hearts of the faithful. Who then ceased to praise Christ? And your name, glorious Virgin, how many times was it repeated, how many times invoked? "Kind Lady!" was said a thousand times, "Kind and gracious Blessed Virgin!" shouted ten thousand times.

2. The splendors seen the day before

They say that on the day before these heavenly blessings were granted, a great brightness was seen by some of the ill, falling from heaven through the church's window-glass, a herald, as it were, of the largess to follow.

---

28. The language is thoroughly martial. The faithful use the weapons of penance like the ancient Ninevites against an angry God (who is quickly moved to mercy) and recruit Mary to help them. A priest signals the beginning of mounted warfare in the form of deafening prayer, and Mary enlists divine spirits in the ultimately successful battle that appears to be against both God and the devil.

29. Hugh uses "sweetness" (*suavitas*) and "good health" (*sanitas*) more or less interchangeably.

3. A girl healed by the slipper

A few days before the kindness of the same glorious Virgin had motivated the bold venture of asking for this collective gift, a girl was blessed and healed by the slipper of the Mother of the Lord kept in that same church. Abbess Mathilda, who then presided over the place, weary of the unseemliness and shrillness of the girl's incessant cries, took up the slipper of the Blessed Virgin and went forth with her escort. And as soon as she was blessed, the girl became well at once, her pain driven away and sweetness recovered.[30] Henceforth in her lavish kindness the Most Blessed Virgin, the Mother of Compassion, quenched the fire and healed however many arrived each day and they went home, all their pain driven away. Nor was there now any difficulty in maintaining health.[31] Night and day, again and again, drums echoed, and very often praises to almighty God resounded in harmonious sweetness from those staying in the church. The ones who had already departed for their homes and hearths could not contain their tears and proclamations of praise. What more to say? Within two weeks, 103 people noted by name had the fire in them quenched, and three girls with crippled limbs who had arrived were restored to the blessing of health.[32]

4. Stars that dispersed fog

Concerning a dark all-night fog at this time, many affirmed that they had seen stars of wondrous size pursuing and chasing that same fog away from the church.

5. The woman who bit the slipper

It was the custom that the sick, once restored to health, would stay there for nine days. On those days they were blessed by the slipper one by one as it was carried around and they kissed it. When one of the women who had recovered her health kissed the slipper, inflamed with excessive religious zeal she bit it. Moved by righteous anger, the

---

30. Hugh does not specify the nature of the ritual with the slipper, although it was clearly organized by Abbess Mathilda in concert with others, perhaps nuns and clerics working together. Although it would seem likely that such a fragile relic was preserved in some sort of reliquary, it was unprotected at least some of the time, as section 5 shows.

31. That is, those healed through Mary's intercession did not relapse, which regularly happened: see section 9.

32. The names of those miraculously cured were often written down at cult sites by those who guarded relics; perhaps Abbess Mathilda had a record like this. The 106 healings mentioned here must have come at least in part after those in section 1 because they took place across the course of two weeks, and the healings were bolstered, as is clear in section 5, by the mysterious slipper ritual.

slipper's bearer and guardian, in a rage, began to inveigh against the woman guilty of such a crime, bitterly reproach her for what she had dared, and state that because of excess of this kind she would no longer bring it out to them.[33] But the woman, aware of charity yet fearing her accuser and indeed praiseworthy for such ardent love, fell silent. We confess that we are entirely overcome by the material relating to those whose fire had been extinguished because I believe no man can convey anything but this: the renown of such copious grace roused all as far as the shores of the ocean and the banks of the Rhine, and however many came were healed.[34]

6. The people's great devotion

But who would dare even to begin a narrative of popular devotion, the immense throng, and reverence of men and women, rich and poor, the old, the young, and children? Who could tell of the tender, frail people, not only men but even young girls, their soles hardened, overcoming winter's harshness and the difficulty of travel? They offered soft flesh preserved in this world, designed to cut through the cold and bleeding, as a very sacrifice vowed to God.[35] What was in their hearts, Lord, how much desire, how much charity, how much frenzy in love for you? Who knows the tears, prayers, the sighs heaved from the depths of their hearts, and the roar of penance except you alone, Lord, who moved them through your Holy Spirit and received them mercifully? Let those who want to marvel at bodily miracles, as is truly just. We, Lord, marvel more at your grace working in sinners worn away in fear of you and turned to devout penitence. As if raised from the tomb and because of the remembrance of grace, they boil over with grateful tears and humility in love for you. These are our miracles, which are especially in our hearts. For these we glorify, praise, and worship you, Lord Jesus,

---

33. The "bearer and guardian" was mostly likely Abbess Mathilda. The final "them" is feminine (*eas*), suggesting that many of those cured were women, although the syntax of the first sentence of the section shows that the newly healed were both male and female.

34. The "ocean" here is probably the English Channel. The point is that people came from far and wide (contrary to Herman's peculiar insistence in Book II of *The Miracles of St. Mary of Laon* that people could only be cured in their own diocese).

35. The events with which Hugh began in 1128 extended into 1129 (in section 7, a penitent bewails that the spring equinox has not yet arrived). These two sentences, divided for readability from one in the Latin text, are Hugh at his most maddeningly dense and telegraphic. The point is that men and young women travel to the nuns' church in terrible weather. Their frail bodies endure the trek, despite the cold and feet bloodied during a winter pilgrimage, evidence of exceptional faith and devotion.

Table 4.   Places mentioned in Hugh Farsit's miracle collection

PLACE	APPROXIMATE WALKING DISTANCE AND DIRECTION FROM SOISSONS
Arras	74 miles north-northwest
Audignicourt	14 miles northwest
Autrêches	12 miles northwest
Avesnes-sur-Helpe	66 miles north-northeast
Blérancourt	15 miles northwest
Chelles	15 miles west and slightly south
Clermont	44 miles west
Coucy-le-Château-Auffrique	12 miles north
Crouy	3 miles northeast
Douai	78 miles north and slightly west
Jouy	13 miles northeast
Lagnicourt-Marcel	64 miles north and slightly west
Laon	22 miles northeast
Le Mans	190 miles southwest
Mortiers	30 miles northeast
Nesle	38 miles northwest
Rumigny	64 miles northwest
Saint-Quentin	36 miles north
Saint-Riquier	88 miles northwest
Vaux	4 miles west and slightly south

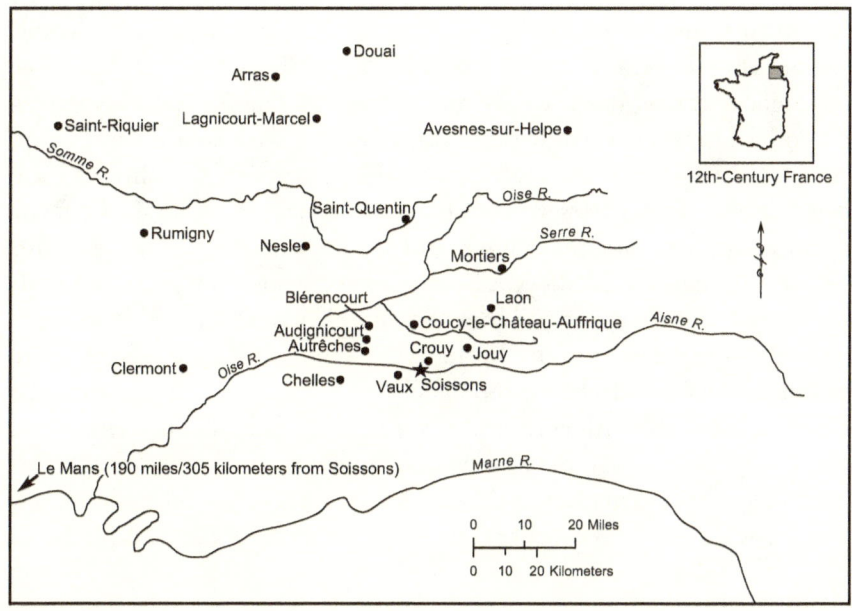

MAP 5.   Places mentioned in Hugh Farsit's miracle collection

because this is the full reward that remains in eternal life: the piety and humility that grow hot in you.

7. The woman who recovered her nose

I recount one miracle the likes of which I do not know if I have read was ever seen or heard of in ages past. A woman named Gundrada and her husband Theodoric lived in the region beyond the Aisne River that flows by Soissons in a village called Audignicourt. Among others whose limbs the pernicious fire was consuming, she had come to the church of the blessed, glorious, ever-virgin Mary, Mother of God and our Lord Jesus Christ, entreating the aid of medicinal grace through that same Mother of Mercy. For the fire had attacked the woman's face and mouth and now, to the horror of onlookers, some fleshy cartilage stuck out from her nose, and the wasting, ravaging fire had deformed the upper lip below the nose down to her teeth and gums. Why say more? She asked for and received mercy, and the wasting fire on her face was extinguished.

But because the miracle was common and ordinary, it was counted as if lesser, for greater ones followed and unusual power was made famous in the same person. Meanwhile, although she was spared such great distress through the favor of grace, she nevertheless did not escape the horror of being seen as she carried your mercy and judgment, Lord. She was now made troublesome and hateful to all who met her, forced to return to her family so that the blessing of kindred would temper the unbearable alteration in her appearance.[36] But this did her little good: it was hard for anyone to look at her. Therefore she was compelled to veil her whole face except her eyes with a damp cloth. She succeeded very little through this artifice by which she should have been able to shelter herself from hatred and nausea through the favor of humanity and kinship. What could she do, where could she go, from whose company could she not be cast away as one now spattered with the hatred and curses of even her servants? Thus, so cut off from every necessity, despairing of any human assistance, she took advice more advantageously and encountered help more fully. Calling back faith that was now growing cold and disappearing, she blamed herself for being, as it were, forgetful of previous blessings, and that through forgetfulness she had neglected the Mother of Mercy abounding in mercy, that is, Mary, Christ's mother. Therefore, renewed in faith and hope as

---

36. Gundrada's illness had been cured, but her disfigurement remained.

if girded with weapons, she prepared to go again the next day to the church of the blessed and glorious Virgin in Soissons. So, having made the candle that she in her poverty planned to offer, she went to sleep.

That night, waking up rather early and concerned that it would get light quite soon, mindful of her promise and plan, she bewailed nights that were too long (as it was before the spring equinox). Then she felt the cloth that had hidden her face slacken and hang loose. When she tried to tighten and cinch it back up, she had little success. She was driven to implore the help of those lying around her. While they delayed, slowed by cold or sleepiness, she nonetheless asked a lamp be lit and brought to her as an aid. Meanwhile, when she felt flesh that pressed under her fingers and the cloth was growing, she did not know that it was the flesh of her restored nose and lip. But while she repeatedly cinched the cloth and repeatedly touched the formed matter through it, she said, "God and St. Mary, help, God, St. Mary, help!" Disturbed and roused at this sound, those around her quickly brought a light. Then they were astonished at the new matter, the proof of renewed resurrection in the form of her restored nose and lips was celebrated, and there was joy as if she had been returned to life from the dead.

When daylight arrived, to offer a candle as thanksgiving, she departed for the city as she had intended in her vows.[37] What wonder if she was now a fresh miracle for those who recognized her, she who, carrying around such mercy of God for her whole life, openly provided evidence of divine grace? We, too, saw her, and she in no way suffered further harm in the restoration of favor, but the new flesh was like what had remained, except that it seemed brighter to those who looked at it carefully. Therefore, people's fervent ardor and fervent faith did not blush to kiss her nose and face, as if this miracle had been worked just now by the hands of God himself.

8. The faithless but punished artisan

A blacksmith from the region of Laon had an annual contract: remaining there in Soissons he would repair the masons' tools and fulfill his duty and do as ordered for a whole year.[38] But afterward he was regretful and thought himself cheated in the agreed-upon wage. The opportunity presented itself for him to see and put in order his little family's

---

37. That is, Gundrada, although healed at home, honored her pledge to return to Soissons.

38. As becomes clear below, these were masons working on the reconstruction of the nuns' church.

house. It being no secret that the quarrel over his wage bothered him, he returned home, as if to come back right away and continue what he had agreed to more or less seriously. He is said to have obtained leave in this way: because he did not have bail money to post for himself, he gave the holy lady Mary as bail for his prompt return and the fulfillment of his contract.[39] Thus, such bail accepted, he was released. But then, little mindful of the kind of collateral he had left for himself, he stayed away longer than expected and returned when it pleased him—since he announced that he did not want to serve all year for the contracted salary, that is, sixty solidi. Then the chief of works, with whom he had made the agreement, accused him of lying and warned him of the punishment that would justly come to him because he lied not to men but to God and St. Mary. The blacksmith promised to work there two weeks for nothing as if by this show of servitude he would deservedly be freed of the year's service he did not want to complete. When two weeks were up, he departed under the protest of the chief of the works, who was incensed that the vows of good faith and agreement with him were violated and reminded him of the pledge he had given. The blacksmith, however, persevering no less in his plan, went away.

When he had passed by the village called Crouy that is beyond the abbey of Saint-Médard and now climbing a mountain, while laboring to reach its height, his hands and feet began to become useless and his limbs seize up to the point that any possibility of continuing his return journey home was denied.[40] He was forced to return in tears to Soissons and the church of the Blessed Virgin Mary—whom he in his mendacity had left as bail—and to solicit her help. For the obstinate and faithless man had more than once tried to shake off the sluggishness as if it were fortuitous and accidental. The more he strained, the more he was hampered until his distress alone gave meaning to what he heard: that he was able to return to the monastery easily, but any capacity to go home was denied him. Returning at last and bound in the chains of his faithlessness, or rather by the power avenging his faithlessness, he was taken back to the church of the blessed Mary, Mother of God, and while he embraced the altar in tears he was recognized by the chief of works. "Is that you, our runaway, lying blacksmith?" he asked. "The

---

39. The blacksmith was expected to provide some kind of bail to ensure his return. Having no cash, he made Mary his bail, a pledge in her name.

40. Crouy is just outside Soissons toward Laon. The route rises quite steeply from the valley of the Aisne River. On the abbey of Saint-Médard, see the introduction and section 22, below.

very one," he replied, "a miserable wretch, prisoner of the Blessed Virgin, who now demands my just deserts, as you see at present. So yes, so God has treated me. But now I make a promise to God and the Blessed Virgin and I am prepared to serve her the whole year or my entire life if only the gentle and merciful Lady deems it worthy to be mindful of me and have mercy on such a sinner." While embracing the altar and making these supplications with tears and groans, he was freed from muscle contractions and remained firm in service, not now daring to lie again.

9. A boy taken in a vision

Among the first of these blessings poured forth from heaven, a herder boy of eleven with burning feet was brought by his mother. After passing a few days there and obtaining a cure for his pain, he was taken home. He was from Vaux, a village beyond the lower Aisne near the bank of the river. But when by divine will the same boy, mindful of such great favor, burned with desire to see the church of the Blessed Virgin, he pestered his mother every day on the subject, insisting that they should return to Soissons for thanksgiving, as it were. She was having none of it because, she said, the opportunity is not given to the healthy unless the necessity of renewed illness compelled what was being denied to the boy who truly desired to return. "Let the one who sees the hearts and desires of sinners hear me." At these words, the boy began at once to be troubled by his former torments, the wasting fire already consuming his flesh. His mother was quite afraid. Putting all responsibilities aside, they returned together to the city and church of the Blessed Virgin. Now the boy's limbs were rendered useless from the former suffering and its present renewal, yet he received the grace of liberation from illness for the second time and had sweet dreams.

At the entry of a procession into the mother church, accompanied by a great crowd, the boy was shaken from sleep because of the thanksgiving and burst open the sky with his cries and bore witness again, in himself, to famed blessings. And he told everyone that he had been taken before God and seen Our Lady, Mother of God, supplicating on behalf of the people that God deem it worthy to destroy this sickness and take away the spark that had befallen them. At this request she had received a kind reply from her son: "Mother, you are the star of the sea, may your whole will be done."[41] While this same Blessed Virgin likewise

---

41. In the twelfth century, "the star of the sea" (*stella maris*, the latter word close to the Latin *Maria*, "Mary") was already an old epithet for Mary.

lamented about her church, which was more lowly and abject than others, she likewise heard from her son that he would have money brought from across the sea and across the Rhine with which her church would be rebuilt and he would light it up with great brightness and glory in the eyes of all who looked on it.[42] He proclaimed on God's behalf that bad fortune had come to the people of Soissons because they were not repairing his mother's church.[43] And indeed the fire attacked many from that city, and we do not know which and what sort of other things are still to come.

There are as many witnesses of this vision—as much for the splendor with which it is honored by every age, sex, and condition as for the abundance of gifts and offerings—as there are people remaining today who want to see. The boy swore that he was going to die soon after, and so it happened. He did not survive a month. This, too, was a great marvel about this boy: weaving together the entire Old Testament from the beginning of the world, he quickly arranged the entire narrative rhythmically. From the New Testament, he set out gospel texts and the deeds of the Lord in such order that it was as if he were reading it all from a book and pronounced what was declared by others. Concerning the holiness and virginity of Joseph, the guardian and husband of the holy Virgin, he said, among other things, "He who holds the scepter of the blooming branch was the guardian of the glorious girl." It is a marvel when we read that Joseph had maintained the flower of virginity through which he accepted the declaration of the virginity of the blessed Mary.[44] Here is the renewal of the ancient gifts of the Holy Spirit, which filled up a shepherd-boy and made him a harpist and prophet.[45] While this boy was narrating these things so fully, like a rushing river the Lord's spirit

---

42. By "the sea," Hugh probably again means the English Channel. As the canons of Laon knew, England was quite wealthy by twelfth-century standards.

43. Hugh, while claiming at the beginning of section 1 that he does not know the cause of the epidemic, has now offered three: general sinfulness, demonic interference, and Mary's distress at the neglect of the material state of her church.

44. A genre known as "infancy gospels" dates to the second century. These texts offer more detail on the family—especially Mary—and early childhood of Jesus than is found in the canonical gospels of Matthew and Luke (and about which Mark and John say nothing). The so-called Gospel of Pseudo-Matthew, which originated in the seventh century, contains the germ of the widely known story Hugh refers to here. A priest sought a husband for Mary and assembled the male descendants of King David, instructing each to bring a branch. The one whose branch flowered was said to be ordained to become Mary's husband. Joseph's branch bloomed at the instruction of the Holy Spirit. The boy's words are very close to those of an antiphon, a brief prayer said or sung, on the feast of St. Joseph.

45. That is, the biblical King David.

drove forth, his eyes closed as if he detested ephemeral light. He who heard great and profound words inside himself did not see the light of this world, scarcely deigning to speak to the laity and the illiterate, as if disgusted by their ignorance. And he who "made the tongues of infants eloquent" [Wisdom 10:21] and "chose the weak things of the world to confound the strong" [1 Corinthians 1:27] also deemed it worthy to make the boy a witness to his glorification. Therefore, the time of his appointed witness finished, he died soon afterward, as we said. Such grace had spread over his face that it conferred I know not what angelic or divine appearance in its splendor and brightness.

10. A mute man healed through a vision

Three mute men had come to the same church of the Blessed Virgin Mary. While they lay slumbering in the church at night, one of them, disturbed by a vision, was roused from sleep. Rushing to the altar, he began to speak profusely (with a tongue unused to speaking) to thank the Blessed Virgin and explain the process of his liberation. Namely, while he was fast asleep, two doves, as it seemed to him, began to pluck at and scratch his ears. Wakened by this incitement to fear and rejoicing in the gifts he had received while asleep and unknowing, on waking he bore witness. This sign blunts the foolish heresy that tries to claim that the grace of the Holy Spirit works nothing for children because they cannot at the time understand the baptism that they accept. Here the Spirit worked in one sleeping and unknowing. The other two mutes departed without gaining the use of their tongues. He who said that only the Syrian Naaman was cured when there were many lepers in Israel in the time of the prophet Elisha knows best why this happened.[46]

11. Another deaf and mute man healed through a vision

We also saw another man from the region of Laon above the little Serre River who was deaf and mute from infancy. He was named Christian and he was about eighteen. He among others also came for intercession from the blessed and glorious Mary, Mother of God. He saw himself in the church mingled with very packed crowds, calling out to God only with his mind and gestures since he could not do so with his tongue. Therefore he was always present, awaiting the time and the hour when

---

46. See Luke 4:27, where Jesus summarizes a story told in 2 Kings 5:1–14 of the general Naaman, cured of leprosy by bathing in the Jordan River at the advice of the prophet Elisha. Hugh's point is that the failure to heal some seekers is a mystery known only to God.

divine grace would turn its attention to him. While staying put and looking around, he was shooed away from the shrine by a sacristan who could not tolerate the unseemliness of so many people. He was leaving, unwillingly, when behold! God turned his attention to the man's unfailing faith, revealed after a period of testing. It seemed to the man that two people crowned in the manner of bride and groom descended from above and a gleaming light filled the whole church. Moreover, there was an appearance of the glorious Virgin, with wondrous brightness of both garments and face: it is fitting that such heavenly beings and dwellers in eternal light appear in this way. Then she, caressing the throat and mouth of the afflicted man with a gentle touch, unfastened the fetters from his tongue and ears. The stream of blood that spurted from his nose, ears, and mouth attested to the power of the mighty Lady. Then, having received such favor, he rejoiced but said nothing, withdrew in silence, and on returning home bore witness that he had received the gift of speaking—with a stammer, because he was only now learning to talk. Word quickly got out among his contemporaries and fellow countrymen that God and St. Mary had taken pity on Christian.

A priest of this village, called Mortiers, scoffed at the rumor going around and denied that Christian could either speak or hear until the man was led into his presence. Afterward, the priest, drawn to repentance and reproaching his lack of faith, was stricken with fear and went to the church of the Blessed Virgin. Prostrate before the altar, flat on the ground, in the process of making himself whole again he poured out great grief, tears, and groans, adding that in his sins, he had dared to doubt the power of the Lord and his mother. It got to the point that onlookers suspected that he was being burned by the fire or tormented by some kind of suffering until he told everything, in order, to those inquiring and promised that on a given day, he would bring Christian. This, too, was done. Christian spoke for himself and about himself, along with neighbors who testified to everything they knew had been done. Because he was deaf and mute from infancy, they bore witness to God's grace in the outcome of the matter, for evidently he was hearing and speaking. Then praises were sung to God on high, then there was the beating of drums and air mimicking the blaring of trumpets, then there were prayers, tears, and thanksgiving from people of every age, sex, and condition as the glory of God was announced generally.

12. A peasant's foolhardiness is avenged

The serf of a knight of Soissons, assigned peasant labor yet idle a number of times on feast days, had been accustomed to go to the church of the blessed Mary, Mother of God, in the company of fellow villagers. But while the others made whatever offering they could afford and paid honor to the Blessed Virgin Mary's slipper, he offered nothing. When they were returning to a certain quarter, speaking of the slipper among God's other wonders, Boso—this was the serf's name—remarked, "You're really stupid if you thought that's St. Mary's slipper, because, duh, it would have rotted away a long time ago." He had scarcely finished his statement when behold! his blaspheming mouth was twisted up toward his ear with such violence and pain that owing to the tightness, his eyes seemed nearly to have popped out of his head. As that tightness pressed on him, his whole face caved in and became a tumor, its human use destroyed. Striking fear into onlookers, his breathing became labored to the point that he had been handed over to his tormentor.[47] He just barely managed to burst out that he should be taken back to the church of the holy Mother of God. And so it was done. Cast before the altar, for some time he offered the spectacle of his madness and the avenging power to which he had been handed over. He was twisted, his body contracted into a tumor. Air from his belly fouled nearby ears with steaming vapors.[48] His voice was like a roar, and he lost the use of his tongue and mouth. Then, moved by piety, Abbess Mathilda and others who were present directed him toward an altar. Embracing it, he was blessed with relics and the slipper and began to recover, released from the oppressive tumor. What more to say? Both his face and body were restored to complete health. This Boso, mindful of the blessing—in that he had been snatched from the jaws of death—asked for and got his lord to release him from servitude. From then on he did not want to serve a man, but to give himself to her through whom he had kept his health and put himself in the service of the church.[49]

13. The blind woman who recovered her sight

A woman had a painful eye and applied celandine and other herbs to stem the pain. Not only did this do no good, but the destructive force of the herbs squeezed the eye, now turned into a tumor, out of its socket and her entire head.[50] Tucked into a little sac of membrane like a sort

---

47. That is, he seemed nearly to have died and been sent to hell.

48. It would be expected that the nose, rather than the ears, would be offended, but both printed texts and manuscripts read *aures* ("ears"). This may be an error for *nares* ("noses").

49. Boso, released from his obligation to the knight, became a serf of Mary as the nuns' property.

50. Medieval physicians prescribed celandine for eye ailments. Hugh appears to be taking a swipe at the limitations of secular medicine.

of blister, it hung down onto her face and mouth and so she had lost all hope of seeing. Thus, altogether deprived of any human help, she gathered together the strengths of faith and hope and gave herself over to divine aid; together with her relatives she approached the church of Mary, the Mother of God, and remained there with the others asking for Mary's help. On the night when the woman recovered her sight, a boy of seventeen with crippled feet was being attended to there by his mother. There was also a crowd of people keeping vigil, some out of devotion, others serving their sick companions. The boy's mother, finished with her vigil and lamentation, had gone to sleep when suddenly the boy arose, upright and healed, and began to walk to the altar. Then the people standing around him raised a great shout, then the name of the Blessed Virgin was repeated a thousand times, to the point that the already fragile walls of the church seemed to be shaken off their foundations by the clamor of people and the sound of drums. Good Jesus, were you not present at this miracle of the kind you yourself so love, when burning faith and the passion of the faithful take you zealously and the sacrifice of a contrite spirit is seasoned with the offering of sweet tears?

The mother, awakened by these sounds, bewailed that she was cut off from her son and the people pressing around him with happy and excited shouting.[51] The woman who grieved that she had lost her eye was unhappy to hear these shouts of joy sent up to heaven, and hence she burst out these words: "O glorious and gentle Lady, now others rejoice and your praise-filled church resounds, but it is denied to poor me to share in such joy." When she was saying these and other things, dejection quickly followed. Thinking that she had entirely lost the eye that had slipped out and hung on her face, she cried out to those around her, "For God's sake, bring some light here at once, because my eye has just fallen into the dirt." For it had seemed to her that someone had been standing next to her and as he poked with his finger, the little sac that was like a blister popped. Bringing a light, they discovered the burst membrane and a stream of bloody and evidently putrid matter had flowed down her whole face all the way to the ground, moistening the dirt with its extensive sprinkle, but her eye, clear and bright, was sitting in its socket, completely whole. They cried out to her, repeated when she still did not believe, and kept insisting that she had recovered her health and her eye through God and the Blessed Virgin. When she

---

51. Reading *congemuit* ("bewailed") for *congeminat* found in the printed edition and manuscripts.

had found out and tested her eye, she was flooded with joy, and the church was filled with repeated praises.

14. A deaf and mute man cured

A deaf and mute man from the region of Arras learned that some people from those parts were going to Soissons to pray for the intercession of the blessed and glorious Mary, Mother of God. He, already known to them all from daily association, joined their company. On arrival, he entered the church with the others, and after staying there a short while, he indicated to some of his companions that he had recovered his hearing but the capacity to speak was still denied him. They rejoiced with him and after making the accustomed offering agreed that they would start on their way back, the mute man with them. Among the company was a group of clerics from Arras, who had also come together, but while they were in Soissons, intent on seeing and hearing other things, they did not yet know anything about the miracle that began with the mute man hearing. Now on their return journey, as their companions told about and the man himself gestured about the ability to hear he had received, the clerics marveled, rejoiced, then took themselves to task because, the miracle being silent, they had not given any praises of thanksgiving to God. Therefore, they returned quickly—they were on horseback—taking with them the man in whom the miracle of hearing had been celebrated. They reported what had happened, showed the man hearing acutely but not yet speaking, and gave thanks to God and the Blessed Virgin, through whose merits these blessings were bestowed. Then the good, sweet Lord and the blessed Mother of Mercy no longer tolerated that the faith and devotion of those whom it did not trouble to delay a journey already begun would be empty and sterile as they gratefully fulfilled the duty of piety. While the party paused and delayed, and while, with the man standing amid them, they mentally gazed at God and the Mother of Pity, suddenly the fetter on his tongue was loosened and he spoke correctly. At this sight, these clerics, now delighting in the fruit of faith, gained the strength to raise praises to heaven with zeal, and as bells rang and a chorus of God's handmaidens raised the *Te Deum laudamus* to the heights, the noise of a devout crowd and blended voices joined in, but all sounding together the praises of God.

15. A mute boy from Cologne cured

A certain boy born in Cologne was raised in the region of Beauvais in the castle of Clermont. His mother, a poor little woman, had taken him as a young child with her from the Rhineland, but the gift of speech was not granted him by God, and he passed from birth to age twelve a mute. It seemed to the protectors of the boy, named Vasselin, on whose charity he had already been supported for five years or more, that they should take him with them to the church of Mary, the blessed Mother of God, in Soissons. So on the night of the Purification of the Blessed Virgin, although he was sunk in deep sleep in the way of children, nonetheless they forced him to keep a vigil with them, for the entire church was filled with those doing the same. Now in the course of the office of Matins, when the response "See the miracle of the Lord's mother" was begun, the boy was disturbed by sudden fear from a dream.[52] It had seemed to him that a dove flew around his head and then plucked at his lips and tongue, seeming to rage and threaten. Roused by this vision of the dove's anger, the boy, in a most delicate and keen voice that seemed to be more of the Spirit than of man in that it overcame both the women's harmony and the whole crowd's din, cried out, "St. Mary! St. Mary!" Who did not fear and marvel at this voice, angelic and newly formed, distinguishing itself completely among all people of different age and different sex, and overcoming the keen and more than keen melodies of the virgins? At once those who were nearest and the protectors who were looking after him for God's sake first cried out, then the whole crowd cried out, and the multitude of the ill entreating similar help for themselves joined in. The noise of the whole church and the sound of trumpets now echoed, and the passion of those who love you, God, broke through heaven itself.

The boy was taken to the altar of the exultant church with joy. Lord Jesus, who then refrained from weeping? Whose hearts, even the stony, did not break when they saw you again walking among men? These are the solemn feasts of the sort you commanded your people to make for you, these the festive days on which true worshippers worship the Father in spirit and truth. The whole church rejoices and equally makes vows for those who are to be healed. The boy's protectors, whose faith and work shone forth, marched in triumphal procession and led him, and others to whom he had been known the day before, to the abbess.[53]

---

52. The feast of the Purification of the Virgin Mary, also known as Candlemas, is on February 2. A "response" is a special prayer said or sung by monks and nuns during a given feast day, this one during the first in the cycle of eight daily prayer services. His benefactors apparently did not succeed in keeping the boy awake until dawn.

53. Here is a hint that Hugh worked from notes jotted down by Abbess Mathilda or someone in her circle shortly after the miracles. The boy, now hearing and speaking, would have

16. A woman freed from a demon

Before the praises for that miracle were even finished, a certain woman possessed by a demon when she had barely recovered from childbirth had already lain in the same church of the Blessed Virgin for some days, raging most savagely. It had reached the point where she had become a nuisance known to all because of her constant agitation and endless shouting. Therefore, she was freed from the demon through the great operation of God's grace and the cooperation of the blessed Mother of Mercy. She proceeded to the altar in no need of anyone's help, reproaching herself and confessing her guilt because out of ignorance she had both said and done many things against God and his glorious mother with a raging mouth. Her friends rejoiced and piously wept along with her. Then, with the power of faith and love not yet growing cool, the blessing of divine grace poured forth anew and gave perseverance in joy, and a sort of commonwealth of people and angels joined together was created in vigils during the entire holy night.

17. A rich madman from Douai

Meanwhile, a certain madman named Gaurin was led from the castle of Douai, facing the region of Arras, his hands tied behind his back and his neck bound with iron and a great shackle. Five men could scarcely drag him along, even though they drove him forward with both whips and rods.[54] He was a rich man, strong both in body and hardy age, and hence the fame of his miracle does not permit concealment. For some reason the devil had taken power over him, whether out of anger or smarting from being cheated, as some say, I have not been able to discover for certain. In any case, his insanity and the healing that followed through God's grace is very well known. God allowed him to lie ranting in the church for several days to offer a spectacle to all: either he would be overcome with shame after recovering his sanity or, as one handed over to the devil for his sins, he would suffer punishment, so that as long as the enemy was bending him to his will, once satisfied he would send him away more easily—or, while the sorrow of a repulsive sight would be prolonged in the eyes of all, the grace of liberation would be sweeter and better known for having been postponed and God be glorified more frequently. Fastened to substantial pews with a fetter and, it

---

had no need to see or ask anything from the abbess, so it seems that he went to her to make a report and brought witnesses of his former affliction along with him.

54. This was a long way to escort a strong man resisting his captors: it is almost an eighty-mile walk from Douai to Soissons.

was said, tied with ropes, he nevertheless repeatedly dragged the pews over and nearly overcame his guardians.

But what need is there to recount the madness of his words and the savagery of his deeds? After it seemed like enough to you, Lord Jesus, and to your holy mother, the enemy power in him was subdued. Returned to his senses, he lifted his eyes to heaven and glorified the one who lives forever, who can humble the proud, knock the arrogant down from their disdain, and set them before his face. The man proceeded to the altar, as was customary, honoring in great humility and devotion the image of his liberation with what vows and prayers as he could.[55] There is no need to say whether he brought joy to his friends, both those who were present and those he had left at home. Then, conducting himself like a man of a calm and sane mind and behaving wisely, he mounted a horse and returned to his homeland with those who had taken him away. Once and for all completely made master of his spirit, he was returned to his wife and his household and friends who all were grieving and mourning for him. Not only in Soissons, where the light of joy was first born in him, but also in those parts praises were rendered to God and his health was celebrated with such happiness that it was as if life had been brought back from the dead because of God's love and glory and the reverence and honor paid to the blessed and glorious Mother of God and our Lord, the ever-virgin Mary.

18. Some wanderers led back to the path by the blessed Mary
Because word was spreading of these and other very well-known miracles of the god Christ and the virgin mother, people of different ages, both sexes, and different conditions assembled and gathered in Soissons from far and wide for the love and kindness of the holy Virgin. Then also up to about twenty-five men and women called forth from the hills of Hainaut took to the road that leads to Saint-Quentin. While they hurried along the road as night was already approaching, fear of bandits drove them to speed up: that region was exposed to robbers. They reached a forest where, because of a very dark night and ignorance of the roads, they lost their way. As they wandered, not only did they hope to secure lodging as quickly as possible, but also they were uncertain about location or progress. They were all perplexed, doubtless because they (mostly the women) were tired from a long day's travel

---

55. By "image of his liberation" Hugh probably means an artistic depiction of Jesus in two or three dimensions.

extended into the night, and their spirits were worn down within themselves from fatigue and weariness. So in their exhaustion, they had sat down in a thicket, some of them fearing all the things that could happen, some others, stronger and more vigorous, looking here and there for the lost path, when behold! not far off, they saw a gleam of great brightness, all the more visible for the darkness of the night, that portended more delight than fear. And in the middle of this splendor they saw, as it were, a female likeness of virginal beauty, whose whiteness of snowy garment and flash of divine and differentiated and shaded heavenly beauty seemed to have as its purpose a brightness that surrounded it in dutiful service.

So sure and so manifest was this vision that those seeing these things retained them most powerfully in their minds; they narrated from memory the bearing, clothing, and linen sleeves fanned by breeze. All saw and all cried out in wonder. Their common decision was to go where God was calling them. They got up, much improved by a good hope, without any expectation that better could follow. For the love of the vision that they would soon recount, they made their way quickly, although through rough places bristling with thorns, as if in the same moment they grasped the location of the light placed there. Nevertheless, they secured the public road with the greatest certainty. Once gathered together, they rejoiced that they had returned to the way they had lost. Walking along the path and arriving at a house of hermits along the roadside, they got the answer that this was the surest public road that led to Saint-Quentin. We add this miracle because it had as many witnesses as there were people present, no fewer than twenty-five, as we said, who all arrived at the church of the blessed and glorious Virgin with gladness and returned home with joy after fulfilling their vows. No less amazing is what followed.

19. The woman who gave birth to stones

In the village of Chelles in the territory of Soissons, which was a property of the cathedral of Sts. Gervaise and Protaise, a woman was in labor and because of the difficulty of the birth began to be in danger.[56] Weakened by three weeks of constant pain, she was very close to death. Persuaded by neighbor women, she vowed that if she were freed from the danger of imminent death she would go barefoot to the church of

---

56. The cathedral of Soissons was dedicated to the Christian martyrs Gervaise and Protaise.

the blessed and glorious Mary, Mother of God, of pious memory. She was saved but in an amazing fashion.

First, three stones emerged from her womb. The first was the size of a goose egg, the second about the size of a hen's egg, the third not less than the size of a nut. Once these stones had poured out, there followed at once the birth of a baby, who received the grace of baptism and survived a few days. Therefore, as soon as she could, after recovering from her illness, she went as promised, barefoot and clad in wool, carrying the stones with her as witnesses of the critical moment and proofs of divine work. Accompanied by the neighbor women who had all been present when everything happened, she reached the church of Our Lady (indeed of the whole human race) and the home of the queen of angels. She offered at the altar a candle with wick and proportion to the measure of her body that she had made while still endangered in labor and that she had kept until then.[57] She herself was the most truthful narrator of her peril and the release accomplished through the Blessed Virgin. "These stones," she said, proffering them, "bear witness even as I am silent." Thus, once praise had been given to God on high, as is the custom, and the wonders were quite evident, the stones were bored through and hung up. For a certain time they served as a manifest memorial of this deed.

20. A paralytic healed

A paralytic lay for a very long while in the narthex of that same church, the strength of his whole body so destroyed that he had even lost the ability to speak.[58] Every hour was evil to him, but he was tormented more in the harshness of winter, the cold doubling his affliction and dire circumstances while as his limbs stiffened from the force of disease, prickling pain as if from spears seemed to pierce his bones and marrow. At these times he began to hurl wretched sounds and sigh out dreadful groans to the sky since he was unable to speak. Many people, moved by pity, stopped in the face of his anguish, but soon terrified by the horror of this inhuman sight they passed by, nonetheless offering vows, prayers, and sympathy on his behalf in the hopes that God and the Blessed Virgin would come to his aid. When their devotion and the distress of the wretched man found favor, in the end divine grace turned its attention and healed the sick man completely: all his pain

---

57. The offering of a candle the same height as those healed was very common in medieval Europe.

58. The narthex is the area between the main part of the church and its entrance, a sort of porch.

was gone, and he recovered his bodily strength and the full ability to speak. Those who had taken pity on the sick man wished him joy once he healed, and because so manifest a miracle that could not be hidden was celebrated, praises and thanksgivings were rendered to God and the Mother of the Lord on his behalf.

21. A blind woman who regained her sight

A woman, the mistress of a household in Blérancourt, a village near Coucy-le-Château-Auffrique, was stricken with blindness. She was persuaded to ask for the intercession of the Blessed Virgin and sat there for several days, awaiting and asking for divine aid to the same degree. She had sat before the presence of Truth for a while to no purpose, for as long as she wanted to conceal the truth. One day it happened that a priest from Autrêches, accompanied by crosses and a crowd of parishioners, entered the house of the Lord's virgin mother, offering praises. Once prayers and vows were finished, the mayor of the village, that is, Autrêches, recognized the woman embracing the altar there as a blood relative. Asking the reason for her presence, he learned of the misfortune that had befallen her. In the presence of Abbess Mathilda, he said, "You, my kinswoman, have deservedly been stricken with blindness of this sort because although you are a serf of Our Lady, St. Mary, you have deprived her of lordship and denied that you are hers and of her household. So if you want any help from the Mother of Truth, confess the truth." At the word of one who loved her, she was alerted to divine punishment and believed this advice. Once the truth concerning the power that she was denying was recognized and professed, immediately her eyes and face were bathed in brightness. Her faithfulness restored and needing no guide, she returned home rejoicing.

22. A woman who had not been able to go to church

In the year 1131 from the incarnation of the Lord, on the feast of Luke the evangelist, God once again did not refuse to glorify his name even with an unaccustomed miracle.[59] Pope Innocent, chased out of Rome by his rival, was welcomed honorably by the cisalpine churches and the kings and princes of the land.[60] He had recently dedicated the monas-

---

59. The feast of St. Luke is on October 18.

60. Cardinal Gregorio Papareschi was elected pope in early 1130 amid dispute, taking the name of Innocent II. A majority of cardinals preferred a rival, historically the antipope Anacletus II, so Innocent was forced to flee north ("cisalpine" means "beyond the Alps"), where he secured the support of numerous rulers and Bernard of Clairvaux.

tery of Saint-Médard of Soissons, right across the river, in a ceremony thronged with such a great crowd that it cannot easily be said either what great thanksgiving there was for that dedication or how many vows and prayers were rendered to the blessed Virgin Mary, the Mother of God, in her church. Among others present was a woman from the region of Laon, specifically the castle of Rumigny. Mindful of her sins, she was processing with others into the monastery of the Blessed Virgin when lo! she was prevented from entering by an invisible power. Trying a second and third time, she was thrust back more strongly. Mixing in with the crowd and shamelessly rushing forward, she got the same result. But then, at the urging of divine judgment, the present trouble gave meaning to a rumor while (too late) her conscience finally accused her. Moved by the enormity of her guilt to tremble all over her body and in her limbs, she began to be troubled with great fear. Prostrate and feeling the hand of divine justice on her, with loud cries she urgently beseeched those around her for aid and that they earnestly pray to God on her behalf.

The guardian priest was there, having just prepared to celebrate Mass.[61] Relying on his office and the priestly vestments in which he was clothed, he lifted the miserable woman from where she lay; holding her hand as the crowds pushed around them, he tried to enter the church. But as she recounted afterward, her feet were made so very heavy that she thought lumps of lead were attached to them. Nothing worked, either her own efforts or priestly assistance, but she was ravaged by the violent pushing. She was drawn this way and that and made unimpeded progress like the others, but a hidden force violently blocked her as she prepared to enter the church. Then the people raised a great cry, the grief and tears of the crowd bewailing their sins and the judgment against this woman. What, then? What else was there to do except to soothe the divine countenance through confession and thus beg for its mercy more freely? Therefore, she wanted to confess to that same priest, yet—by what judgment this was done we are uncertain—as she said herself, she absolutely could not do it. Grief and fear goaded her; she wanted to confess her sins in public but was prevented. Yet she confessed with sighs and grief to another guardian priest, as truthfully and sincerely as she could, for certainly she needed to be reconciled to the Truth through the truth. She asked the priest to speak in public so

---

61. The guardian priests in this section seem to be men charged with supervising the altar on which the faithful left offerings—also, perhaps, with guarding the slipper.

God would spare her to the same extent as she was filled with confusion and shame in fear of him. Looking at her for a while, he put a stop to it and told her what she was ordered to do there. On receiving absolution, reborn and restored, she tearfully offered supplicant hands to the crowds around so that she who despaired of her own merits might be helped by theirs. She pleaded that the abbess come, and she did. Offering her hand, the abbess began to lead her from where she was. But now a great clamor, now the tears and sighs of the packed crowd, now the frenzy of ardent love and mad piety followed her as she went. It burst the air and reached heaven itself and imposed the sort of force it wanted to bring to bear on God himself, prying from him the mercy that he willingly showed. Therefore, once the woman was taken into the church, how many praises and thanksgivings were rendered to God and glorious Mary, Mother of God, cannot be made known because it is unsayable.

23. A woman's swollen womb healed at Eastertime

At the castle called Nesle in the Vermandois region, a woman suffered anxiously with a great distended swelling of her womb and limbs. When her husband hastened to bring her the help of physicians, she said it was not possible to wait long. Spurred by the violence of the illness, she asked that a horse be readied for her as soon as possible, already faithfully confident in the deliverance of the Mother of God if she deserved to reach Mary's dwelling-place. Therefore, she set off for Soissons with her husband. Taken to the altar of the Blessed Virgin, she placed hands heavy with fear upon it. Delighting in faith, she solemnly requested that a ring no force had been able to twist from her finger be squeezed off, saying, "Sweet Lady, take this ring off my finger and it will be yours." So it was done at once. From the fifth day before Easter she endured a womb swollen to the point of bursting until, sleeping in the church over the holiday and the following night, she was completely healed. Awakened and feeling no heaviness whatsoever, she rushed to the altar. Her husband, roused from sleep and disturbed, asked, "Where are you running off to, a miserable woman on the brink of death?" "I'm not," she replied, "because I'm already completely freed through the grace of God and the mercy of the Blessed Virgin, and I suffer none of the former pain and sickness." Thus she whose former illness was very well known had her cure made famous in a short time, and what the Lord had worked in the present was widely reported among all. On this account praises were given to God and the blessed Mary, Mother of God, and the joy of Eastertime was increased.

24. A sick man healed with bread that touched the slipper

"Say," it says, "to the just man because he is well, because he eats the fruit of his labors" [Isaiah 3:10]. For he is just in faith and "the just man lives through faith" [Romans 1:17] and the fruit of his faith is justice. There is no fruit of justice except from the root of faith and therefore a rich faith must be sought so it can bear fruit.[62] It did not suffice for the faithful to come and ask for cures in the place dedicated to the Blessed Virgin, where she is accustomed to offer blessings, but there are also those from remote regions who despaired of ready access to that church and made a habit of bringing back with them some memento from the same church—wood, earth, or bread that had touched the Blessed Virgin's slipper—after they were healed. Made safer by this protection, they do not fear ill-health.

There is a place near the castle of Baupaumes called Lagnicourt-Marcel where a youth verging on adulthood was so vexed by epilepsy that about once every ten days his wretched limbs were afflicted, striking the ground to the horror of onlookers. What of his unhappy mother, who was driven to consider death in her family every day? What spirits was she in, forced to caress her son's frothing mouth and joints stiff with lethal cold in her lap and, reviving him with her natural heat, giving birth again, so to speak? One day it occurred to her that one of her neighbors had returned a few days earlier from the church of the Blessed Virgin Mary, Mother of God, and brought back with him some bread that had touched her slipper, which he often distributed to sick people when they asked and it cured them. Hastening to the man's house, burning with faith of a sort that inner womb pain stimulated and acting as a mother intent on calling back the life of her dying son in his anxious suffering, she asked insistently, in her maternal affection, that she be worthy to take a little of that bread sanctified by God, to aid her son, to remedy his pain. But he tried to brush off her lack of manners: he set aside barely a little piece to keep for himself, having distributed most of this health-giving bread to those who were likewise ill. At last, defeated by the distress and the perseverance of a raving woman, he took a little bit of it and bestowed it on the wretched mother.

---

62. At the beginning and end of this section, Hugh offers religious musings of the sort that characterize his *Otium*.

Judging herself blessed by so great a gift, she figured she had received her son's life in this crumb. Already improved in the joy of faith and hope, she flew to her son, carrying the food of life and health with her. When he had chewed on what he was given, the youth suddenly recovered, becoming perfectly cured of so great an illness. Just as it is God's way to give without reserve, so he seemed to have sensed no trace or remnant of his former suffering thereafter. These are the fruits of rich faith. He who cultivates his fig tree eats its fruit. Through these short-lived fruits, we are invited to those that give eternal life, if only we have faith according to those fruits. Each person is rewarded according to the measure of faith. Whence there is a faith that merits these temporal things and a very different one that merits eternal things.

25. Of the two shield-bearers freed from captivity

Two boy shield-bearers from the region of Laon were captured and taken beyond the forest of Thiérache to the castle called Avesnes-sur-Helpe. Each was put in fetters.[63] While they were under guard there, the elder of them remembered that for the construction of the church of the Blessed Virgin Mary in Soissons, among other things needed was that someone bring and offer iron nails. So he vowed that he would bring one hundred nails there if the blessed and glorious Mother of God would help him and free him from captivity. Immediately he saw with his own eyes the wooden clasps coming apart, and he wriggled his foot out. Some of the day remained so he stayed put, waiting for night, better suited for escape. Then he said to his companion, "By the grace of God and the help of St. Mary, Mother of God, I'm free and I could leave if it weren't still daylight. Look, I vowed to the Blessed Virgin that I'd bring a hundred iron nails to build her church and as you see, I'm free. If you do the same according to the faith you have in her, she will set you free." "Sure," said the younger one, "I'd bring not just a hundred but another thousand nails there if she takes pity on me so I'm set free." On the night the first one had been freed, he passed by the gates and the guards and escaped to safety with no resistance from anyone.

The one who remained, having learned from experience how great the goodness of faith is, deprived of his companion and called to better things by a manifest blessing, with a solicitous heart appealed to Our

---

63. Shield-bearers, also called squires, served knights by attending to their horses and carrying their armor and weapons. They were usually aspiring knights in their teenage years, as the ones here probably were.

Lady, St. Mary, that she bring aid to his sinful self. Shortly thereafter, the man who held him captive, moved by fear and worrying that the boy would be taken from him, decided to transfer him to a safer guard. While he was doing so, the captive escaped safe and sound through the grace of God. He was the nephew of Milo of *Asceaco*.[64] Traveling barefoot as much as he was able, he arrived at the church of his liberator, not ungrateful for such a blessing, and he quickly and gladly recounted in order everything that had happened.

There are many matters we cannot set out in order since they are numerous and defeat our limited talent. And yet so that we might at least speak succinctly, we must pass over certain things in silence.

26. A mother who regained her son

At Saint-Riquier in Ponthieu, which is in the region of Amiens, a noble woman with little money had handed over her son as a pledge to a moneylender and fierce tax collector in exchange for many marks of silver. As time went on, the total of the interest grew until it was the case that unless his parents sold their land, they would not be able to redeem their son. Then his mother, the more heartbroken of the couple, abandoning all hope of human help and in despair, turned to divine aid and the gracious Mother of Mercy, accustomed as she is to listen to the contrite in spirit. Therefore, one day, with the incitement of maternal grief nobody could lessen, she was forced to go where her son was held under guard and in fetters so that at least she could refresh her wretched eyes with the sight of her son as he paid the penalty for parental need. Coming to Saint-Riquier, a city crowded with people, she quickly found her son in the middle of a street, bound with iron straps suited to his small size to keep him there. In the view of the people, she picked him up, and without anyone's interference and with no difficulty, she lifted him onto her horse and took him back. It is not easy to say what joy, what happiness she poured forth, how many thanks she gave to her benefactress, the glorious Virgin, as she went to Mary's house in anxious spirit and humble body.[65]

---

64. The manuscripts spell this word *Asceaco* (P), *Archeiaco* (P3), and *Asceto* (P4). It could refer to Assis-sur-Serre, about twenty-five miles north-northwest of Soissons or to a place that has vanished since the twelfth century.

65. The mother, then, subsequently went to Soissons to give thanks.

27. A blind woman who received her sight

A blind woman from the region of Le Mans heard rumors of the miracles that the Lord was doing in Soissons through the grace of his mother, the Blessed Virgin. She vowed that she would go barefoot for Mary's intercession, vowed it with a contrite and faithful heart, and at once she received sight.[66]

28. Ralph Cantellus

Thomas, lord of Coucy-le-Château-Auffrique in the region of Laon, was on his way to the king of the English. He decided he wanted to take along with him one of his vassals, Ralph, surnamed Cantellus, because he thought Ralph very faithful to him.[67] The lord ordered his vassal to prepare. When everything was readied for the journey, this Ralph was suddenly stricken with ill-health. All his sinews began to contract, his limbs rendered nearly useless. He had sharp pains that bored holes, so to speak, in his bones and marrow. Given his distress, Ralph received a dispensation from his duty to travel. The illness that wandered around his limbs was very similar to the plague of fire, feeding under swollen skin and tearing flesh from bones. Hence for the moment, Ralph suffered the most severe pains, but he escaped any external signs of deformity, thanks to a remedy of swift assistance. For as soon as possible he sought the house of the blessed Mary, Mother of God, seeking help for his miserable self.

It was the day before the vigils of Christmas. Ralph sat facing the altar, decked out in elegant clothes and shoes, and troubled by a very fierce attack of pain, sweat dripping from every pore. Now brought to self-knowledge, in place of the atonement of an offering, he was driven to confess his sins, saying, "You suffer deservedly, wretched man, and you eat the fruit of your impiety. You sowed pain, you reap it, and you receive it as is fitting. What crime have you ever failed to commit, what evil have you not perpetrated? With what sexual sin are you not polluted and which woman have you ever not dishonored? With how many

---

66. The woman's commitment was notable: Le Mans is a journey of nearly two hundred miles from Soissons.

67. Thomas of Marle (ca. 1073–1130) was the most infamous castellan of his day. Guibert of Nogent describes his sadistic cruelty, faithlessness, and depravity (*Monodies*, 143–45 and 156–62); Abbot Suger calls him "the vilest of men and a plague to God and men alike" (*The Deeds of Louis the Fat*, 37). On Thomas, see Bisson, *The Crisis of the Twelfth Century*, 231–43 passim and 280–84 passim. According to his confession quoted below, Ralph Cantellus does not appear to have been much different from his lord.

killings are your hands stained with blood, by your direct action or your advice? How many arsons and violations of churches did you preside over? How many thefts and highway robberies have you incited, how many wars and feuds have you incited by your counsel, with your tongue? How much gluttony and drunkenness have you gorged yourself with? Which deceits have you not practiced? Now they are rightfully turned back onto your head, wretched man, now you pay deserved penalties. You are just, Lord, and you will be just justice against me. I have always been a standard-bearer of every evil and leaving you behind, my creator and redeemer, I have always done the will of the enemy.[68]

"And you, Blessed Virgin, kind Lady, Mother of my Lord, although I am the greatest sinner, now you demand just punishment from my body, filthy body, stinking body, body worthy of sulfur and hellfire. Now you demand just punishment from my deceitful soul, faithless soul, soul that in its pride bears the likeness of an unbridled devil, soul foul like that of horse and mule, filthy with lust. Come, Lord and come, Lady, double and triple my pain and torment, because no man's body ever deserved more justly to suffer the punishments of hell. The earth should not have been able to support or carry so great a sinner, and it would be right if it swallowed up such a sinner right this minute. Pitiable tears, why do you cease? Why do you not chase a deadly body, already dead, to the grave? Devote yourselves as is fitting to the funeral rites for one sinful and hateful to all and for which, with good reason, no human would pay. Come, miserable soul! Look, there you see your wretched body—the body that always obeyed your desires, the body that always indulged your wickedness—prepared for a death that is much to be feared. Swollen with infernal heat, it is now burning up, but soon enough you will endure horrible fires and globes of flame. Alas, miserable me, both for the hardship I suffer and the eternal death I expect! Woe, woe, woe to a wretched sinner, most justly damned!"

While he was saying all this and things like it before everyone in a voice all could hear, sweating from every pore, he drove those who saw and listened to him to grief and tears when behold! suddenly the good Lady and the good Lord, who does not want the death of a sinner but rather that he convert and live [see Ezekiel 18:23], brought sweetness with the cessation of pain. He began to improve and to put forth

---

68. That is, the devil.

different words, words of joy and exultation: thanksgiving and a voice of praise were heard from his mouth. It was the hour of Vespers. Jumping up on his healed and whole feet, he ran to embrace the altar. Not unmindful of so great a blessing, he set out on pilgrimage to Jerusalem not long afterward.

29. Two women attacked by the fire that is extinguished

There were two women from the monastery of Nider.[69] One had a cheek consumed by the fire, making her a spectacle of horror, and the other carried in front of her a hand and arm eaten away by the wasting fire, putrid and sallow flesh that made everyone nauseated. They went to Soissons, fulfilled their vows in the house of the Blessed Virgin, and were completely healed. Only a little redness remained on the surface of their skin, as if tokens of the praise they had once given, a memorial of the miracles of that powerful Virgin. She, most worthy of all praise, did not want these tokens destroyed or forgotten. They remained as if marks of life and death.

30. Fresh light

It was the beginning of the year of our Lord—counted from his incarnation—1131, in the twenty-third year of Louis and the second of his son Phillip on the feast of St. Vincent the martyr.[70] While Mass was being celebrated and the cleric was sitting after the introit, one of the two candles that usually sat on the altar until the end of each day had totally burned out while the other held steady.[71] The sister who was serving at the altar, hastening in her fear, zealously busied herself looking for a substitute candle. After retrieving one lying in a box and trying to light it, unsuccessfully, in careless wickedness she knocked over and put out the candle that was still lit. Disturbed and thinking herself dead, she was driven to the kitchen for a light. But the deacon, fearing that light would be absent from the office of the Mass, leaped up and grabbed the candle that was lying unlit.[72] When he gave it to the subdeacon so he

---

69. I can find no trace of a women's monastery of this name or variations on it in the five manuscripts consulted.

70. That is, January 2, 1131, the feast day of St. Vincent of Zaragoza. Louis is King Louis VI, who made his eldest son Philip coregent in 1129. Philip died accidentally late in 1131.

71. The introit is part of the opening of the liturgy of the Mass.

72. By tradition, there are at least two lit candles on the altar at Mass; the priest was afraid that there might be none at all.

could quickly seek a light, as the candle was passed from one hand to the other, suddenly it was relit. The deacon, having seen this miracle in his hands, stricken with faintness and drained of strength, was forced to lean on a nearby chest. This event became so noted and renowned because there was no hour of the day without a crowd of people at that spot. Therefore, they praised God on high and as drums echoed far and wide in melodious air, the harmonious sweetness reached the sky, and the whole city resounded with praises of Christ. Indeed, all the lamps in the church were illuminated with this fresh light and many of the faithful hastened to take it home.[73]

31. A man miraculously freed from a foot ailment

But in the year of the Lord's incarnation 1132, while lying among others in the church of the Blessed Virgin, a man named Robert from the village called Jouy, a church property, pursued healing for his foot in this sequence. There was an incurable disease in his whole foot, which had turned into a tumor marked by numerous pustules. It got to the point that constantly leaking bloody matter fouled the adjacent air with such a stench that it became intolerable for everyone. Hence the guardians were forced to tell him to leave because they were not able to bear him any longer. Completely despaired of by physicians, he had already stayed there quite a while as his whole foot melted into rottenness. Therefore he unwillingly left the church on his way to his family, whom he hoped, because of kinship, would offer him indulgence and compassion. Yet as he departed he appealed to the Blessed Virgin in this way: "O glorious Lady, although for many days here I've waited for your help that I've yet to attain, even as my limbs withered and putrefied my soul's faith neither withered nor failed. Thus I leave against my will, but I'm forced to go. But you, kind, gentle, powerful Lady, can obtain health for me through your son wherever I am. I am yours, your humble dependent according to my ancestry, so I seek not only favor but demand the debt you are used to repaying those who belong to you.[74] My blazing flame, Lord Jesus, look on your mother's servant. See how I am departing and dying because I am torn away from you,

---

73. This seems to mean that people lit their own candles or lamps from the one miraculously relit before leaving the church.

74. The man, then, was a laborer, probably a serf, on the nun's estate in Jouy who thought that the lord of his village, in this case Mary, should take better care of him as such.

highest God. Be mindful of your servant and your mother's. My heart is downcast with renewed grief because I am leaving you. At the sight of her, my body's pain is lessened and almost forgotten." After saying these things he departed.

Once returned home, at first he was patiently carried about by his family as accustomed, but as time passed he became disgusting and nauseating. There was such a stench that at night when he put his foot out in the air to cool it, neither his wife nor his children could stand it. Yet he did not cease to pray, calling out to the Blessed Virgin with restless words. When it seemed to be enough, the kind Lady was enticed not by the patient's pain but the enduring faith of one who believed in her and loved her. One night as he slept she appeared to him in such splendor that human eyes could not have borne it. Heavenly light struck his glance as he looked on, unable to bear the brightness of her face. Then it seemed to him that she cradled his neck in one hand, ordering him to sit up on his bed, and with the other hand she took his foot and stretched it out. The man, awaked by the strangeness of the dream, tried to walk and learned through experience that he was completely healed. It is not easy to say how happy he was, what joy he gave to his little family, and what thanks he gave to God and the glorious Virgin.

Not remaining at home, he prepared for a return to the church of his Lady and healer. Because of his great exultation, nothing was done quickly enough and every delay seemed long to him. After entering the church he approached the altar, which he addressed in a loud voice, and what a quantity of tears he poured out there with joy and thanksgiving. Because with a constant and unwavering heart's faith he had attained bodily health, he knows better the God who shapes his words of devotion and holds them in himself with lively understanding. Torn away from the altar, like a reveler he began to run about the holy of holies and stamp his healed foot on the ground.[75] To those asking about the cause of such joy, he replied nothing other than, "This is the foot of my lady, St. Mary! This is the foot of my lady, St. Mary!" Repeatedly stamping his foot on the ground, he explained the order of events and the cause of joy to those following him around. "Aren't I the man of my Lady St. Mary, from Jouy, the one you threw out of

75. The holy of holies (*sancta sanctorum*) likely refers to reliquaries in the sanctuary, one of them perhaps containing the slipper not mentioned since section 24.

the church because of the unbearable stench of my foot? Didn't my kind virgin Lady, the Lord's mother, heal me in such-and-such order?" Following up on these words, he easily proved them true: he was a known person because he was a dependent of the church and served as evidence of a miracle. They had seen his putrid foot and stinking body and now saw that he was completely healthy and strong. A known person and an evident miracle! Soon the drums gave out their sound, and praise of the Lord and the glorious Virgin in her strength and mercy was celebrated by all.

Times of affliction and misery will come when pious minds remember these days, as we do in peace and abundance of worldly things, both because the church is venerated and cherished by all people and because devotion is greater than in former times. Therefore, reflecting on these events, when they compare their persecutions to these prosperous days, they will suffer more. For this reason in particular we believe that so many and such great miracles in the churches of the holy Mother of God should be celebrated especially in these days, while in signs, wonders, and various miracles God bears witness to the incarnation of his son and, because we hope that the dangerous time of the Antichrist is imminent, that the faithful may steadfastly die for that Truth to the same extent that it is celebrated by the certain testimony and praise of all nations.[76]

Here ends the book of miracles of St. Mary of Soissons[77]

---

76. As Christians had done for centuries, Hugh hopes for the Second Coming, the return of Christ to earth, during which the Last Judgment will consign all people to glory or punishment. The Second Coming was to be presaged by the appearance of the Antichrist, a person or people who will try to substitute themselves for Christ. In the first letter of the evangelist John, he specifically notes that the Antichrist will deny the identity of God the Father and God the Son (1 John 2:22). Hugh, then, in his final sentence encourages his audience to remember Mary's miracles and hold fast to the truth of the incarnation of God in Christ. In speaking of the death of the faithful, Hugh refers to the expectation of their resurrection at the Last Judgment.

77. Text in P.

Haimo of Saint-Pierre-sur-Dives, "Letter to the Brothers of Tutbury"

Introduction

Abbot Haimo of Saint-Pierre-sur-Dives narrates miracles in the form of a letter. Saint-Pierre-sur-Dives is in central Normandy, approximately 110 miles west and slightly north of Paris. The duchy of Normandy was "the most dynamic and powerful French principality of the eleventh and early twelfth centuries . . . a strong and for its time a well-controlled polity with a clear territorial definition in comparison with its neighbours" that included the lands controlled, if shakily in the first half of the twelfth century, by the kings of the Franks.[1] For most of the period from 1066 to 1204, the dukes of Normandy were simultaneously the kings of England, although the leadership of Normandy was disputed after civil war broke out among two factions after the death of King Henry I of England in 1135. Henry had designated his daughter Mathilda (ca. 1102–67) as heir, but her cousin Stephen of Blois (r. 1135–44) seized the throne and Normandy. In 1144, the year before Haimo wrote, the French king Louis VII, following on the victories of Mathilda's husband, Count Geoffrey of Anjou (r. 1129–51) against Stephen's forces, recognized Geoffrey as its duke. This was not a peaceful

---

1. Hallam and West, *Capetian France*, 51.

time in Abbot Haimo's Normandy, then, but the duchy was nonetheless a much more centralized principality than the lands under the kings of the Franks.

The abbey of Saint-Pierre-sur-Dives was founded shortly before 1050 by Lesceline, the wife of Count William of Eu and great-aunt by marriage of William the Conqueror.[2] By coincidence, Lesceline and William's son, also William, became count of Soissons thanks to his marriage to Countess Adelaide of Soissons. William and Adelaide were in turn the parents and grandparents of three subsequent counts of Soissons.[3] Another of Countess Lesceline's sons, Bishop Hugh of Lisieux, assisted in the foundation of Saint-Pierre-sur-Dives. Lesceline endowed the new house with numerous properties and rights in the vicinity; she also gathered its first community, comprised of monks transferred from Fontanelle, an abbey near Rouen about sixty miles northeast of Saint-Pierre-sur-Dives. She was buried in the monastery she founded on her death in 1058.

After nearly two decades of construction, the first church at Saint-Pierre-sur-Dives was consecrated in 1067 in the presence of Duke William, who the year before had become king of England via the Norman Conquest. The abbey prospered in the following decades but was burned down in 1106 during the successful campaign of King Henry I of England (r. 1100–1135) to take the duchy of Normandy from his older brother, Duke Robert (r. 1087–1106). Some of the monks died in the fire. Henry, at whose behest the fire was started, subsequently became a patron of Saint-Pierre-sur-Dives, reaffirming and extending its properties and rights. Rebuilding was a long process well underway by the times of Abbot Haimo, who mentions a complete or near-complete "great tower" in section 13.

Of Haimo we know nothing except that he was a monk of Saint-Pierre-sur-Dives and then its eighth abbot from sometime between 1140 and 1143 until his death in 1148. In 1145, he wrote a letter describing numerous recent miracles to the monks of Tutbury Priory, in the central English county of Staffordshire. Tutbury was founded in the late eleventh century and by Haimo's time was a dependent priory, that is, its properties were under the ownership of the abbey and its head, a prior, answered to the abbot of Saint-Pierre-sur-Dives.

---

2. On the origins and early history of the abbey, I mostly rely on Bouillie, *L'Abbaye de Saint-Pierre-sur-Dives*, 7–16.

3. The last of these was Count Renaud III: see the introduction to Hugh Farsit's *A Little Book of Miracles*.

Haimo offers a contemporary account—he describes events of recent months—of a penitential practice that Arthur Kingsley Porter first called "the cult of carts" over a century ago.[4] This was the practice of faithful lay people who carried materials for building or rebuilding churches. It first appeared at the central Italian monastery of Montecassino, where in 1066 a crowd of laypeople carried a marble column recently purchased for rebuilding. This one-time event is echoed in an account from the abbey of Sint-Truiden in present-day Belgium that recalls events from the second half of the eleventh century when its abbey was undergoing restoration. People brought building materials and piled them in carts to take to the construction site. A few years before Haimo wrote, Abbot Suger of Saint-Denis reported, perhaps drawing on the Montecassino account, that a crowd of people of all classes dragged some Roman columns newly excavated in Pontoise to carts on which they could be loaded for the journey of almost twenty miles southeast to Saint-Denis.[5]

The classic form of the cult of carts, however, first appears in Haimo's account, which is centered around pious laypeople who dragged laden carts to Saint-Pierre-sur-Dives in the year 1145. This was an extension of a practice developed a year earlier when the cathedral of Chartres, some eighty miles southeast, was undergoing extensive renovations. There is a brief letter, also from 1145, from Archbishop Hugh of Rouen to Bishop Thierry of Amiens describing the phenomenon, like Haimo (see the end of his sections 1 and 3) stating that it began in Chartres and spread throughout Normandy. Hugh says that some of his flock went to Chartres to participate.[6] The practice was short-lived: when Robert of Torigni reported it in his chronicle completed in the 1180s, it is clear that the cult of carts was a thing of the past.[7]

The first several sections of Haimo's letter describe the cult of carts and some healing miracles in a fairly general way before moving on to more specific miracles. Some of these are directly related to cart-dragging: people who fall from or in front of a cart but are spared serious injury or death. Others have little to do with the cult of carts,

---

4. Porter, *Medieval Architecture*, 2:151–60. Here I draw on Porter and on Barnes, "The Cult of Carts."

5. For a translation of Suger's account of this incident, see *Gothic Art*, ed. Frisch, 13.

6. Archbishop Hugh's letter is edited and translated in Porter, *Medieval Architecture*, 2:156–57; the translation is reprinted in *Gothic Art*, ed. Frisch, 25.

7. Writing in the 1180s, Robert remarked of the phenomenon, "He who has not seen this will not see the like" (*The Chronography of Robert of Torigni*, ed. and trans. Bisson, 1:143).

miracles that heal complaints familiar from the collections of Herman and Hugh: paralysis, motor impairment, deafness, muteness, and blindness. There are also numerous instances of nonhealing miracles—here most of them protection from danger—of the sort that account for more than 40 percent of nearly five thousand miracles recorded in eleventh- and twelfth-century France.[8] Furthermore, the cult of Mary at Saint-Pierre-sur-Dives did not have relics like the cathedral of Laon and the nunnery in Soissons. In these ways, Haimo's letter is different from the cults and miracles Herman and Hugh describe, which center around relics and overwhelmingly concern healing.

Especially in the early sections of his letter, Haimo often writes in the present tense, suggesting that the miracles related directly or indirectly to the cult of carts were ongoing. How long this penitential practice flourished is unclear since the end of the abbot's letter has not survived. It is unlikely the cult of carts itself greatly benefited the building project at Saint-Pierre-sur-Dives: people do not make very good draft animals in comparison to oxen or horses. However, the novelty of such a spectacle and the miracles associated with it may have increased donations; certainly it gained the monastery patrons like their once skeptical neighbor Robert of Courcy (see sections 9 and 12).

Saint-Pierre-sur-Dives was rebuilt in the thirteenth and following centuries; all that remains of the twelfth-century construction is a single west tower—perhaps the one where a boy who had miraculously gained hearing and speech saw Mary in section 13.

Text: Delisle, ed., "Lettre de l'abbé Haimon," 120–39. Delisle, a master medievalist, edited what he considered a reliable seventeenth-century copy of a medieval manuscript since vanished. There are partial English translations of early sections of the letter in Porter, *Medieval Architecture*, 2:151–53 and 155, and *Gothic Art*, ed. Frisch, 25–26. A full if very loose French translation is Glanville, *Histoire des miracles qui se sont faits par l'entremise de la Sainte Vierge*.

---

8. See the tables in Bartlett, *Why Can the Dead Do Such Great Things?*, 343–44, summarizing the massive survey in Sigal, *L'homme et le miracle*.

Letter to the Brothers of Tutbury

1.

Brother Haimo, humble servant of the servants of the blessed Mother of God in the monastery of Saint-Pierre-sur-Dives, to his sweetest brothers and fellow servants in Christ at Tutbury: may they merit the salvation promised to those who love God.

Rejoice, brothers, rejoice and exult in the Lord, because the one rising from on high visited us, visited us clearly not according to our merits, but he poured the heart of his mercy into us out of an abundance of grace and accustomed compassion and did not, in his anger, limit the gifts of his kindness. O what a great sweetness was shown in our times to a world weakened by sins, wounded by crimes, despaired of in the vastness of its wickedness, a world that plainly was nearly godless recently because through its guilt it was estranged from God. Human ill-will had advanced to the point that had that kind one rising from on high not hastened to visit us, had he not mercifully come to the aid of that collapsing world, coming to earth he would have found very little faith.[9]

But where guilt was abundant, grace was superabundant [see Romans 5:20]. The kind Lord looked down from heaven on the sons of men—because there was nobody who understood and sought God and, since nearly all had turned aside from him and become abominable in their sins, there was not one among them who reflected in his heart and said, "What have I done?"—and drew back those rejecting him, called back those going astray, and made a new posterity from what he sought, a posterity, I say, both new and unheard of throughout the ages.

For in all preceding generations who ever saw, who ever heard tell that mighty lords, princes, people powerful in worldly honors and puffed up with riches, men and women of noble birth, submitted their proud and haughty necks, now bridled to carts loaded with wine, wheat, oil, limestone, rocks, wood, and other things necessary for sustenance and the building of churches and dragged them to Christ's refuge like brute animals? In the towing, moreover, this is wondrous to see: while for some time a thousand or more men and women were bound to a cart—so heavy the load, so great the apparatus, and so great the burden imposed!—still

---

9. Haimo refers to the Incarnation, that is, the appearance of God on earth in the form of the human Jesus and probably also to the Last Judgment or Second Coming (see the end of Hugh Farsit's *A Little Book of Miracles*). He may also be making an oblique reference to the recent end of military conflict in Normandy (see the introduction to this collection).

they advance in such silence that nobody's voice or even murmuring is heard. Unless you saw it with your own eyes, you would think no such crowd was present. While they stopped along the road, nothing resounded except the confession of wrongs and supplicant, pure prayer to God to obtain pardon for sins. As priests preach peace, hatred is lulled to sleep, quarrels averted, debts forgiven, and the unity of souls restored. If anyone went forth in such bad spirit that he does not want to renounce the sinner in himself nor obey the priests when gently admonished, then his offering is thrown out of the cart as impure and he is severed from the company of holy people in great shame and disgrace.

There alongside the prayers of the faithful you might see the ill and those weakened by various ailments rise healed from the carts in which they had been placed, the mute open their mouths to praise the Lord, and those harassed by demons recover a sounder mind. You might see Christ's priests in command of each cart exhorting all to penitence, confession, lamentation, and resolve for a better life; you might see them lying prostrate, completely flat, kissing the ground for a long while, old people with younger ones and children of a tender age crying out to the Mother of the Lord and directing to her in particular sobs and sighs from the depths of their hearts in a voice of acknowledgment and praise. It is evident that these prayers to her, after those to her kind son, were the most needed. She especially gave herself to this labor after her son. She first lit up the church of Chartres and then ours, dedicated to her, with so many and such great virtues and miracles that if I wanted to describe the things that I was deemed worthy to see in one night alone, memory and tongue would utterly fail. These things would seem to have exceeded enumeration or belief, but from those powers God has given, what follows is as truthful as I have been able to make it.

2.

To go back to the beginning, when the faithful people returned to the road to the sound of trumpets and the raising of banners that preceded them, wondrous to say, the matter was accomplished with such ease that nothing slowed them on their journey, neither the steepness of mountains nor deep water between them but—just as it is read of the ancient Hebrews entering the Jordan River in throngs [Joshua 3:15–17]—in the same way each of them on arriving at a river that needed to be crossed suddenly went forward from dry land, without delay and with God's guidance, to the point that even the tide at a place called Sainte-Marie-du-Port is faithfully asserted to have stood still while they were crossing it on the way to us.

Table 5. Places mentioned in Haimo of Saint-Pierre-sur-Dives's miracle collection

PLACE	APPROXIMATE WALKING DISTANCE AND DIRECTION FROM SAINT-PIERRE-SUR-DIVES
Argentan	21 miles south
Bayeux	38 miles northwest
Bellengreville	12 miles northwest
Bures-sur-Dives	17 miles north-northwest
Caen	21 miles northwest
Chartres	89 miles southeast
Courcy	5 miles south
Écajeul	4 miles north
Garnetot	8 miles south-southeast
Le Mesnil-Mauger	6 miles north-northeast
Mézidon-Canon	4 miles north-northwest
Montpinçon	8 miles southeast
Pierrepont	18 miles southwest
Poussy-la-Campagne	11 miles northwest
Saint-Clément	58 miles northwest
Saint-Léonard-des-Parcs	36 miles south-southeast
Sainte-Marie-du-Port	25 miles north-northwest (the village has since disappeared)
Tournai-sur-Dive	16 miles slightly east of south
Trun	14 miles slightly east of south

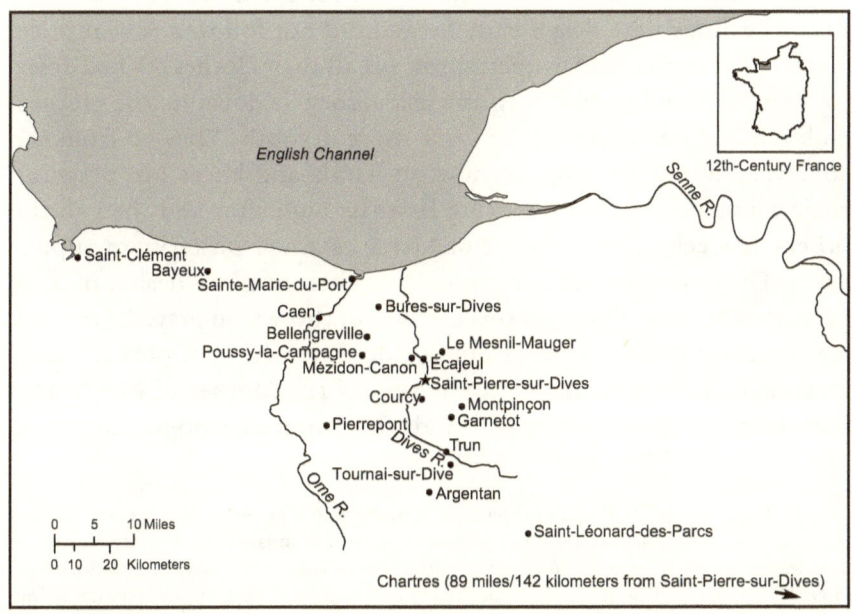

MAP 6. Places mentioned in Haimo of Saint-Pierre-sur-Dives's miracle collection

It is clearly no wonder that older people, those of mature age, take up this labor and burden because of the multitude of their sins. But younger ones and children: What compelled them to do so? Who led them except that good teacher who brought about his praise in the mouths and works of young children and those still at the breast? He brought it about, I say, so that things begun by adults would surely be known to have been completed in all ways by children. You could see them, attached to their laden carts alongside their kings and dukes, not dragging them along bent over like adults, but going along upright as if bearing no burden and, what is more wondrous still, outdoing the adults in eagerness and speed. This is the character of the journey, one indeed much more glorious, holy, and devout than we could express in words.

3.

But when they had arrived at the church, they arranged the carts into a circle, like a spiritual fortress, and during the entire night that followed the Lord's army celebrated a vigil in psalms and hymns. Now candles and lamps are lit in each cart, now the sick and weak are gathered one by one, now the relics of saints are brought to aid them, now rites are carried by priests and clerics in procession, the people following like-wise in the greatest devotion and as one, most intently entreating the mercy of the Lord and his blessed mother for the healing of the weak. But if healings were delayed briefly and did not follow a vow at once, you would see men and women throw off all their clothes. Naked down to their loins and all blushing cast aside, they lie down on the ground, children and babies doing the same more devoutly. They go from the courtyard of the church, not now on hands and knees but dragging their whole bodies along, seeking first the high altar and then all the others, beseeching the Mother of Mercy as a new posterity of suppli-cants. There they forcefully obtained from her the pious desires of their pleadings at once. What did this method of those who prayed, groaned, sighed, and begged not force out—I would not say "not obtain"—as it ascended all the way to the kindly ears of the Mother of Mercy who harbors the greatest feelings of kindness?[10] Indeed, who would not be

---

10. Haimo is more explicit than Herman or Hugh, who also report instances of what ap-proximates nagging, that extraordinary human works and actions can extort Mary's favor. On the measures medieval people took to get the attention of saints, see Geary, *Living with the Dead in the Middle Ages*, 95–124 (chap. 5, "Humiliation of Saints" and chap. 6, "Coercion of Saints in Medieval Religious Practice").

moved, indeed the stony heart of which onlooker would not be softened by the pious humility of those dragging their bared sides though
the dust? Whom would the piteous voices of those crying to the heights
not inspire with devotion? Whom, I ask, would the hands and tender
arms stretched out for whipping with rods not overcome? It does not
suffice, this great weeping cry, something surely to be marveled at in
those of very tender age; it does not suffice, I say, this outpouring of
tears, unless voluntary bodily affliction, quickly effected to heal the
frail, is brought to bear.

Therefore, tearful priests stand above those submitting their very
tender limbs exposed to whips, beseeched by those being thrashed not
to be spared—lest the priests wanted to be gentle in the beating. All
spoke in one voice: "Thrash, strike, beat, and do not spare us." There
you could see a thousand and more hands held out for a whipping.
They even bare their ears, eyes, and tongues, saying, "Let hands that
have sinned be thrashed and let the ears that have heard vain things, the
eyes that have seen them, and tongue and lips that have uttered lying,
idle things be struck." Here indeed, I ask, who is so hard-hearted that
he would not be moved to tears? Who is so savage and callous that he
would not immediately be moved to mercy at such a pious spectacle?
The Mother of Mercy is assuredly moved at once and has gentle compassion for those afflicted in her presence. The efficacy of the healings
that follow at once bear witness that she was moved and had heard
those crying out. Soon the ill and weak jump out of each cart, healed.
They toss aside the staffs with which they had supported their formerly
weakened limbs and run unencumbered to the altars to give thanks.
The blind who had received sight find the way without distress. Those
with dropsy put aside harmful thirst, their bowels now emptied.[11]

What to say? Which individual healings should I enumerate when it
is impossible to enumerate them because they are innumerable? Amid
separate processions to the high altar, Masses are performed, bells
rung, praises and thanks conveyed to the Mother of Mercy. This is the
due measure of vigils, these the divine night watches, here the provi-
sion of the Lord's fortress, this the appearance of new faith, here the
rite of holy nighttime prayers established from above. Nothing carnal,
nothing in any way earthly is seen here, but everything done is divine,

---

11. Dropsy, what is now called edema, is the build-up of excessive water in body tissues
and cavities. The people referred to here suffered from gastrointestinal edema, which has
various causes.

everything heavenly. The heavenly vigils are truly of this kind: nothing is heard in them but hymns, praises, and thanksgiving. This ritual of holy custom began at the church of Chartres, then it was strengthened in ours through innumerable miracles. Finally, it grew strong far and wide throughout almost all of Normandy, taking hold especially in nearly every place dedicated to the Mother of Mercy. In fact, that gentle and most kind Lady has lit up our church, or rather hers—the church in which we, however unworthy, serve her after her sweetest son—with such glory in the form of miracles (as we said above) and has lifted it with such brightness of signs to her eternal memory and that of her kind son that a great crowd of the faithful from various and far-flung parts of the earth gather to this church. There the crowd obtains quick fulfillment of their prayers concerning whatever need they had cried out. So the beginning of this blessing was made among us.

4.

Since the fame of the miracles in which the blessed Mother of God and ever-virgin Mary offered her kind presence and her son's was spreading far and wide and, ever more celebrated by the witness of the faithful, word had reached us, her servants, although unworthy, great devotion to her began to grow and daily increased her cult and veneration among us much more than was customary. But we also learned that newly out-fitted carts made in Gaul, laden with things necessary for the improvement of the cathedral of the kindly Mother of the Lord, were being pulled by Gauls to Chartres.[12] Our people, too, having learned about the new kind of carts the Gauls made that they dragged to Chartres laden with materials for the improvement of the church of God's merciful mother, built a cart in honor of that same Mother of God with great care. They have most devotedly dedicated themselves to the completion of this new work, begun in the times of King Henry but interrupted for many years.

On the day the cart was built and blessed, how gratefully and how kindly the Mother of Mercy accepted it and immediately made evident through the application of the blessings of her gentleness. Meanwhile, they readied another cart, laden with stones to begin construction, which, already mostly filled, the people drew along.[13] A very

---

12. Where this new type of cart came from and what the modifications were are mysterious.

13. Haimo implies that without the carts dragged by the faithful, there would have been no reconstruction. In reality, it had already begun, and a small crowd of people is no substitute for sturdy animals.

large stone, suddenly falling out of it, seemed to have destroyed the foot of a certain Andrew, but with Jesus protecting him through the intervention of his mother, he was only slightly injured. On the same day when people dragged a loaded cart to the church door with mighty force, it happened that a man pushed out of the crowd fell in front of it. The Mother of Mercy freed him from the danger of imminent death as all those in attendance tearfully cried out, "Help, Lady, be kind, save him!" In a flash, the cart broke into pieces and the man thought already dead was saved.

5.

But now greater things follow lesser ones. The next week, on the Friday when the martyrdom of the holy apostles Peter and Paul was being celebrated, our people were again leading a cart from the forest, so laden with large branches that even the hardest rocks on the road were shattered under it.[14] When it had approached the village, the women got down from the cart and began to drag it most devoutly. A certain Odo fell under one of the wheels and what? Thought dead for having been pressed under such weight and force, there could have been absolutely no hope for his life unless he was saved by divine intervention. Therefore, while all cried out as usual, and loudly repeated amid tears the name of the most kindly intercessor, the Mother of Jesus, immediately the one thought dead rose unharmed. Running before the cart like a fawn and taken to the altar of his most merciful emancipator by the monks who met him, he devotedly delivered himself to her service.[15] Thus the blessed Mother of God, through her good son Jesus, entrusts her perfection to us little by little, by increments as it were, and thus the good son called the souls of the faithful to the worship and veneration of his mother.

6.

But look, while we linger in small matters, we are called to greater and more glorious ones. For just after what had already happened, on the next day, when Saturday had passed, the faithful gathered in church at Vespers and on that night they first celebrated devout vigils in praise of the Lord and his holy mother there. They had brought with them—or

---

14. The only year in the period Haimo was abbot and the feast of Sts. Peter and Paul fell on a Friday was 1145. This incident, then, took place on June 29, 1145.

15. In thanksgiving, Odo made himself a servant of the monastery.

to put it more truthfully, they had carried in—a virgin girl, the daughter of a priest named Herbert. She was known and brought up among us to that point.[16] From birth her feet were so crippled that she could never stand, never walk at all; she carried herself along the ground only on hands and knees. As Sunday dawned, as if enraptured three times, she appeared dead from such great pain. Why say more? The Mother of Mercy gazed on her and lifted her up, for at once her soles and heels were made strong, and she who had never put a foot on the ground then began to stand and began to walk. The crowd of the faithful that was present burst into tears in their great joy. What thanksgivings they proclaimed and what words of confession and praise they sent forth cannot be described. The girl, rejoicing, returned to her people on foot. From that time forward a Saturday gathering of the province's faithful began the Sunday vigils. Word of what was being done circulated not only in neighboring areas but those further afield, and as it grew and grew the news reached everywhere.

7.

On Monday of the following week, Ralph of Saint-Clément, a village in the region of Bayeux located above the Vire River, was brought to us.[17] For five years and more he had lost the ability to walk. The miracle worker, the kind Mother of the Lord Jesus, healed him the moment he entered the church door so that, lifted on his feet before all the people, he proceeded to the altar, and thus rejoicing and giving thanks he returned home unimpaired.

On that same day, Rohaisa from Caen brought her ten-year-old daughter Hadvise, who had not walked the earth for three full years and whose whole body was bent almost to the ground. Promptly led in, the girl was carried to the altar in the arms of the faithful and healed. Turning to those standing nearby, she declared in repeated words of exultation that she was completely cured. All marveled, weeping with joy and praising the Lord. The outcome of the matter proved itself, for that night she kept vigil in hymns and praises in the church of the Lady who had saved her. Early the next day, safely on her feet, she took to the road toward Chartres, to which her mother

---

16. In theory, priests were not to marry or have children. Haimo's casual mention of a priest's daughter shows that the prohibition was frequently violated.

17. Monday, July 2, 1145. The events recounted in sections 7 through 16 can all be dated to July 1145.

had first vowed her in exchange for recovering her health, accompanied by her mother.[18]

On that same day, too, a deaf woman from Caen came to the church, seeking along with others the protection of the kind Mother of the Lord, and there she immediately received the hearing she had desired.

Still on the same day, a man from a village called Pierrepont in the region of Bayeux was present. He was so lame and had so lost the ability to walk that he could scarcely be supported even with a staff. The moment he entered our village, he recognized the power of the gentle protector, and soon tossing his staff aside, the healed man began to drag a cart with the others. Indeed, with these four miracles, the kind Mother of the Lord showed her favorable presence on the day the triumph of Sts. Processus and Martinianus was honored among us.[19]

8.

The next day, that is, on Tuesday of that week, a large stone from a cart fell with great force on the shoulder of our servant Berenger, but with the aid of his Lady, the Mother of God, he escaped unharmed.

9.

When miracles and signs were daily events, when people came eagerly from everywhere to see them, nevertheless many local people did not believe them, but as is commonly said, they wholly doubted even what they held in their hands and understood by its benefit. Among them was Robert of Courcy, our neighbor, still so obstinate that he could not easily be led to the church, nor could the malice of his disbelief in all these things be softened. Rather he reproached believers, opposed those who narrated miracles, and stated that he would absolutely not believe unless he saw a great thing with his own eyes, something quite difficult at that. Therefore, the blessed Mother of God, the gentle mother of believers, very quickly turned her kindly eyes on him, looked down, and discovered a glorious proof near at hand with which she put an end to his disbelief. In Robert's house there was a girl named Mathilda, more than twelve years old, who was among the poor who obtained a daily

---

18. Having traveled less than a quarter of the way from Caen to Chartres, where her mother had pledged to take her, Hadvise was healed at Saint-Pierre-sur-Dives. Haimo's account smacks of a competitive spirit: he wanted his monastery to become an object of pilgrimage for those seeking Mary's favor to rival Chartres.

19. Processus and Martinianus were martyrs of the first-century church whose feast day is July 2.

offering from his table. She was so deprived in her limbs that she could not even lift herself from the ground or creep along on her hands and knees. She carried herself along the ground with side and shoulder in the dirt, a wretched spectacle for all. As she hauled her whole body, stuck to the dirt through muddy streets and even swamps, so pitiful, so pitiable was she that those who saw her very often dissolved in tears.

Consequently, Robert's wife insisted that transport be prepared in which they could send her to Chartres. "By no means," he said derisively, "but have her sent to Saint-Pierre, where new miracles are taking place—or that's the story." What more to say? At once Mathilda was taken and lifted into a cart that at the moment happened to be dragged by women. Lest she fall, since she had no to way hold herself in, our servant Roger held her in his hands. Without delay, the kindly eye of Jesus's mother looked down on her, did not despise her but looked down, I say, and lifted her up.[20] Quickly her now dead limbs began to warm up as if kindled by some invisible flame; muscles loosened from bones soon joined together and were restored as if in an instant her whole body flourished in wholeness. She raised herself up in the hands of the one who held her and announced in a loud outcry that she was healed.

Roger, stunned, ordered those who were dragging the cart to halt. As was customary, all stood still at the voice of the one crying out, knelt, and in a sort of stupor began to marvel at what had happened. They were suspicious about seeing the girl they had formerly seen lying flat and, wonderful to say, now saw upright and did not believe she was standing up. Instead, they thought that their eyes were being deceived. They marveled at her, or rather were insufficiently able to marvel at this sign from heaven. But she said, "Put me down, quickly, because I am healed, because I am completely saved. Put me down and I will haul along with you." Put down at once, she stood on her feet. Moving toward the cart, to give proof of what she had said, she, too, began to drag the cart along with the others without any trouble whatsoever.

Then, to be sure, with a shout raised to the sky, all wept for joy, all gave thanks, all glorified the Lord and praised the kindly Mother of Jesus for the blessings procured. You would surely have seen a wellspring of tears run down the faces of every single one of them. People flocked together, surrounded the girl, and fixed their gaze on her most intently as if they had never seen her before, for her face, too, seemed

---

20. Haimo's rhyming Latin in this sentence (*non despexit, respexit eam, inquam, et erexit*) is impossible to duplicate in English.

much more beautiful than usual, and something heavenly glowed red in her altered appearance. Why delay any longer? Soon better dressed in clothes women eagerly offered and welcomed by the monks and people coming out to meet her, Mathilda was taken to the church amid hymns and praises and thus presented most devotedly before the altar of her most gentle healer along with the people's offerings. Meanwhile, bells were rung and thanks given to God quite readily. The whole church resounded with praises, filled with the glory of the Lord.

Word of this miracle came to Robert's ears, yet he had still not been able to put aside his hardness of heart. He sent a messenger to inquire very scrupulously about whether it was true or not. On returning, he announced what his lord had heard was true. But Robert did not yet believe it and sent another messenger, who affirmed like the first one that it was true. Even so, still he could not be persuaded to believe. But finally, inspired from above, he got up, went to the monastery, saw the girl coming back healed from the altar, and, marveling, was very afraid. Greeted by her, he greeted her most humbly in return and wept for joy as he praised the Lord for his work, fell on his face, and gave thanks not only for the restoration of the crippled girl but also because his hardness of heart had now been softened. Therefore, from that day forward Robert became a devoted defender of the miracles of which he had formerly been a most bitter assailant. Wherever he went, wherever he turned, he invited all alike, indeed urgently advised them that they should make haste, they should hurry. They came one by one, they came devotedly, they came and saw the mighty works of God.

But the girl, mindful of her healing, or rather her healer, did not leave the church at once, staying there forty days, most devotedly ministering to the ill and weak who came or had already come from various provinces to seek health in that church. She knew better how to have compassion for a condition she herself had suffered, she knew from miseries experienced what would be useful to the miserable, and she knew from her own needs how to serve the needs of sufferers. The day she obtained healing was the feast of the translation of St. Martin, but her glorious restoration was much more celebrated among us.[21]

---

21. Wednesday, July 4, 1145. It was on this date that the relics of St. Martin were transferred ("translated") to a new church in Tours, where he had served as bishop. Again, there is an implied competition here: a miracle effected through Mary was more important to the monks than the translation of one of the most important Christian saints.

10.

The next day, there arrived a woman from the village called Bures-sur-Dives named Murielde, so bent over from the age of twelve that she could scarcely support herself on two staffs. Along with her came a man whose hand was so withered that he could not lift it to his mouth. So when both had gotten onto a cart that was being dragged with the utmost devotion, at once the Mother of Mercy, in the sight of all, both lifted up the crippled woman and restored the man's hand. The monks went out to meet the pair most joyfully, welcomed them as they proceeded with the people, and took them to the church amid hymns and praises and great jumping for joy, giving thanks to God.

On the following night, a certain Robert from England, whose hand had likewise withered, was healed before the altar of the blessed Mother of the Lord. Then on Saturday night, Christ deemed it worthy to show so many and such great marvels for the praise and glory of his mother that their number would almost seem to have been beyond belief—except for those who do not doubt that for God all things are possible [see Matthew 19:26].

11.

But whoever you are who love the Mother of Mercy, direct yourself in faithful spirit to what she deemed it worthy to work on that same Saturday for one of her servants, and on this account incline a spirit more readily inclined to the worship of her.[22] A woman called Emma had been enfeebled in half her body, rather completely robbed of it. Taken from Bayeux to Chartres, when she could not be healed there in two weeks and having used up everything she had brought as provisions for the journey, she was carried back to us.[23] Placed in a little bed in the church of the gentle Mother of the Lord before the cross of her kind son, she had already spent three days there. So on that Saturday, around Prime, she was taken in rapture and seemed to have drifted off a little when the Mother of Mercy appeared to her and with her holy hands stroked every part of the sufferer's body in which she was weak or rather deprived,

---

22. Haimo echoes the prologue of the Rule of St. Benedict (ca. 540): "Listen carefully, my son, to the teachings of a master and incline the ear of your heart. . . . To you, therefore, my word is now directed—to whoever, renouncing his own will in order to fight for the Lord Christ, the true king, takes up the brilliant and mighty weapons of obedience" (*The Rule of Saint Benedict*, ed. and trans. Venarde, 3).

23. That is, having traveled about 125 miles southeast from Bayeux to Chartres, Emma had returned well over halfway back toward Bayeux to Saint-Pierre-sur-Dives.

simultaneously performing the duties of both fellow sufferer and physician. "Here," she said, "and here and here, daughter, you are weak, as it seems, and deprived in all ways." As she spoke, as was said, she caressed each weakened limb, and Emma replied, "Even now, lady, even now pain has filled everything and has completely taken over for itself this part and that, as you see." "Do not, daughter, do not despair of your health. The Lord can help you presently, and I, leaving here now, will return shortly. When I do, I promise good health both now and in the future." Having said this, taking hold of Emma's withered arm and pulling it toward her, for a little while the Mother of Mercy lifted it off the body to which it had stuck and still holding the arm vanished from sight, away from the high altar.

Immediately woken up by the strangeness of the vision and great joy at the promises, she returned to her senses and began to look everywhere, peering very intently at the place by the altar from which, as it seemed to her, the vision had departed. She asked the people surrounding her, "The lady who was here just now and spoke with me—where did she go?" She explained to them what she had seen. When they had heard, immediately some of the monks present who had been accustomed to come to her quite frequently with a kindly feeling of mercy heard from her what she had seen, then asked about Mary's face and clothing and the manner in which she had appeared. "Her face was most serene and sweet, her attire was beyond all whiteness, she caressed each part of my body where I suffer with a most gentle hand, and she promised she would come back soon to offer good health." The brother responsible for the church answered, "Be certain now and have no doubt whatsoever. It is the Mother of Truth. She will not be able to fail in what she promised but do what she pledged. So now be in no way doubtful about the expected outcome because soon you will feel the effects of her mercy, just as she promised."[24] Without delay, after drawing away from the altar, she again closed her eyes in sleep and behold! suddenly, mindful of her promises, the Mother of Mercy stood nearby and lifted up and stretched the withered arm now reattached to Emma's body. But, awakened by the intensity of the pain, Emma gave voice to such great lamentation and complaint that she made everyone in the church and cloister run toward the crying voice. Among them was the brother who had left her just a little while earlier. He took her arm in his outstretched hands, clutched her as she threw herself about in torment

---

24. This monk seems to have held the office of cellarer, the guardian of church property.

from great pain, and applied whatever words he could, as is customary in such cases. Suddenly, still in the hands of the monk who held her, wonderful to say, a thumb began little by little to lift itself from the middle of the palm to which it had been stuck for a long time, and then each finger in order began to rise up after the thumb. Then the moisture formerly drained out bathed the withered arm and renewed heat quickened dead joints. Why linger? At once there was a rush of people to the church. The cries of all were lifted to heaven and praises to God on high and the Mother of Mercy were repeated for a long while. In the sight of all around her rejoicing and glorifying the Lord in her, Emma rose from her bed, went up to the altar in the company of the people, and having finished the praises of her Lady savior stayed there through the night that followed, then returned home healed the next day.

On the night of the same Saturday she was healed, eight people were set upright and three who had been quite blind received sight. The other great miracles effected were so many that it would be impossible to count them.

12.

On Monday, a blind man who had come with his wife wanted to buy a candle to offer at the altar, but the one who sold candles was absent.[25] So he hastened to the market of St. Peter, prince of the apostles, near the monastery and sent his wife to buy a candle. But while she waited a little while in the marketplace, her husband suddenly fell before the cross of the Savior and after a brief while regained the sight he had lost long ago. On seeing this, an astonished priest ran at once with those who accompanied him and set the man who had been brought to us before the altar of the blessed Mother of God. At the report of this miracle, the entire crowd that had come to the marketplace that day immediately flocked together. Robert of Courcy, along with Earl Roger of Hereford, came quickly, and there was a wondrous joy in all and great exultation.[26] Each one rejoiced and magnified the Lord in his work, and in the sight of all the Lord magnified his mercy and revealed the accustomed grace of his kindness. For as all who were present looked on, he healed a nephew of Richard Bigod, who was deprived of the use of half his body, and also restored a boy's thumb that had swollen

---

25. It appears there was usually a merchant at the church to provide candles for pilgrims.

26. On the former skeptic Robert of Courcy, see section 9. Roger Fitzmiles was the second earl of Hereford from 1143 until he died in 1155.

enormously.[27] Furthermore, he freed Adelmus, the brother of one of our monks, from the pain he had long suffered after being struck by a horse.

13.

But see how greater things follow lesser ones. A noblewoman from Caen, Rohaisa, the wife of Ralph, brought her twelve-year-old son with her.[28] Since he was deaf from birth, he was so mute that he had almost no tongue. To tell it briefly: his mother had announced that he was deaf and without a tongue. Many knew him, many had very often put their fingers in his mouth, for they scarcely believed their own eyes and therefore tried to see if they could grasp something of a tongue with their fingers. Thus, as often as he opened his mouth a great chasm was exposed, he could scarcely swallow, and he consumed only soaked crumbs, just barely and in distress. This was his food and drink. People interacted with him only through nods, which he both readily returned and easily understood. The blessed Mother of the Lord repaired him little by little and over time so the miracle would be greater. She renewed him in this way: she gave partial hearing immediately while he was among us, then the rest in Chartres, where his mother had vowed him. He indicated with new nods that he could hear and in sudden wonderment trembled in fear as much at the words of those who spoke as the sound of things. After returning to Caen, whence he had come, he was received with popular exultation and rejoicing for the gift of God he had already received. They rejoiced because they saw he could hear, but they entirely despaired of his ever being able to speak since, of course, he lacked the tool of a tongue. Who would have even dared to consider that he would have a tongue when they knew that nature had entirely denied it to him?

In the meantime, a cart to be brought to us was prepared by the noble people of Caen, and the day arrived when they would take to the road. The woman who had brought the boy up went to her husband and said, "My lord, I am taking him with me to see if perhaps my Lady, who deemed it worthy to show him mercy in the one way, would still deem it worthy to look upon him." He replied, "Are you crazy, woman,

---

27. *Richardus Bigot* is unknown. Haimo may have meant Roger Bigod (d. 1107), a Norman knight who joined Duke William of Normandy in the conquest of England in 1066, earning him substantial estates in East Anglia.

28. If this is the same Rohaisa named in section 7, she was the unlucky mother of two children with significant impairments.

or joking? Perhaps you will make him a tongue? How will one who has no tongue be able to speak?" She said, "I am absolutely not crazy, nor am I joking, nor will I make him a tongue, but my Lady who gave him hearing will also give him a tongue. I am certain, I am sure, that 'with God all things are possible'" [Matthew 19:26]. Therefore, animated with this firmness of faith she went with the people and dragged the cart with others doing the same, accompanied by the boy. I am about to speak of wonders. As they approached the village called Bellengreville, just about halfway to us, a new tongue began to be formed in the boy's throat and to enlarge little by little as if in secret: it did not arise in its entirety at one time, yet grew gradually larger—in order, that is, that the miracle would be increased and in it the magnificence of God understood as greater. But what thanksgiving all those present poured forth in that place, what wellsprings of joyful tears they shed, is not for us to tell. They paused in a church of the holy Mother of God, where they passed the night in vigils of praise.

Meanwhile, his tongue was fully formed, yet the boy did not speak for a while. Then as dawn broke the next day, Saturday, they continued their planned journey to us. Nothing along the way was difficult, nothing perilous, as they took refuge in the fire of their faith and the greatness of their joy. The crowd went forth in great acclaim, great glory, meeting people who had already happened to have heard what had transpired. All hastened together, coming from the fields and villages at the rumor of such a miracle to see that it had happened. They received the party coming along with great joy and exultation and joined those dragging the cart, vying to take their places in turn. What more? Night fell and the cart was parked at the church door, as was the custom, and the ill and weak were placed in it. The mute boy with a tongue now whole was lifted into the cart. Lamps were readied in the circle, candles lit, vigils kept by everyone, and the mercy of the Lord prevailed upon quite profitably. The church was filled with countless people, and the churchyard was full, too: the place could not contain the multitude, so great was the crowd of those arriving from everywhere.

Amid all this, the mute boy, getting up and standing in the cart, lifted his eyes upward to the top of the great tower and poked a sick girl lying next to him with his feet while she frequently cried out in anguish. But since it seemed he could not do much to heal her, in the end the priest in charge of the cart approached the screaming girl and scolded the boy quite severely. When he paid no attention to what he heard and stood still, keeping his eyes fixed on the tower as before, the indignant priest asked, "What is going on that makes you look up this way, as if mad or insane, and pay no attention to us when we speak to you?" His tongue let loose at once through divine influence, he said, "Don't you see my Lady, St. Mary, standing there?" The cleric, stunned at the boy's first utterance, asked, "And where?" The [former] mute said, "You really don't see her standing there in the opening of the tower, holding a little boy under her clothing?" At the same time, he pointed her out with his finger, so to speak, but only he who recognizes power sees it. Clearly he saw her standing there because she was his helper, clearly saw her with a boy, but the boy that was the Word, the Word made flesh [John 1:14], because he, too, was a boy recognized by the mouth of one who had never spoken yet formed words. At once the entire multitude of those who had come from everywhere flocked together, all lifted a cry to heaven, the entire church echoed with the praise of God, and celebration of thanks and praise were offered to God.

The boy was carried off to the altar, no longer mute but speaking and giving thanks. So great a crowd surrounded him as he spoke that they nearly suffocated each other in their passionate desire to see the tongue and hear the new speech. It is hard to say what they marveled at more, the speech or the tongue. Meanwhile, the boy greeted everyone in the name of his saving Lady, quickly and lucidly pouring forth words that he had not learned from men nor through men. But she who had brought him, she who had brought him up and loved him more than the rest, profiting from good judgment and fearful lest something happen to him, suddenly removed him from the hands of those who were holding him and asked that first he be protected with the Lord's sacrament. This was done, and soon he was returned to the crowd to be gazed at, returned to be heard. They could not be satisfied by seeing or satisfied by hearing. Each of them fixed their gaze on him and could not keep themselves from staring at him. Each beheld him as if he were dispatched from above, each marveled at him as if he were sent from heaven, and he was asked repeatedly to open his mouth and display his tongue, indeed he was incessantly beseeched by all that he not leave their sight. Each one busied himself most attentively not only to see the tongue but also to kiss it and rejoiced to see and venerate in it something special from God. But now it was not enough to see, not enough to hear: they all picked him up and lifted him onto their shoulders. One by one, they carried him around the whole church and monastery with the utmost devotion. And to put it briefly, whoever was able to touch him believed they sensed that something truly great and divine had been done in him.[29] But also during that same night, in the other carts that were around the church and in particular those inside, Christ deemed it worthy to show so many miracles for the honor and praise of his most glorious mother that it would be entirely impossible for us to recount them. We have rather lengthily pursued the miracle of the mute boy, very special among the others, indeed more special than the others, not only because it is marvelous enough that the ability to speak was given to one who did not speak, but because it is much more miraculous that a tongue was made for someone utterly without one.

14.

Although he was given a tongue first while among us, as was said, let me return to matters omitted. The Lord raised a crippled woman before the altar as people stood by. Furthermore, on the following Friday a woman's hand was restored and a bent man made straight at the church entrance. Also that day, our women carried to the altar in wondrous fire of faith a woman weakened in all her limbs who had been lying in the church a while. Soon they merited to obtain the joys of the healing hoped for her from her kind Lady, the Mother of the Lord.[30]

15.

One day, our men brought back from the forest for the first time the new cart they had made—we mentioned it earlier—and destined for this new work. It was filled with wood and other building materials.[31] When they had come into the territory called Saint-Léonard-des-Parcs, the Lord, at the prayers of his mother, so restored a man bent over for many years who had been placed in the cart that without delay he not only dragged the cart along with the others but even surpassed some of our people with his quick step. Seeing this, the local lord Robert and his wife, a good woman among the many who were there dragging the cart, were afire with such veneration for the Lord's mother about what had happened that they made a pious vow that they would immediately make a cart to bring to us. Not long afterward they devoted

---

29. Amusingly, this claim to brevity comes in the longest section of the letter. Two sentences later Haimo admits he has gone on for quite a while about this miracle.

30. It is unclear who "our women" were. They may have been members of the local community or dependents of the abbey.

31. This is the cart mentioned in section 4. "Our men," like "our women" just above, could be locals or serfs.

themselves to this purpose. But our people, now moving more briskly, came along as they greatly praised the magnificence of the Savior as well as his mother, whose kindly presence they sensed was among them with such great miraculous power. On that Friday night, they rested in a village called Trun. The priest as well as the entire populace welcomed them with great joy. The next day, on departing they took with them a woman from Tournai-sur-Dive, long bent over and known to all. As they looked on, the gentle Mother of the Lord powerfully lifted her up and soon had her join, now unimpaired, those dragging the cart. Then, in renewed joy, all of them repeated praises and thanks to God. By this time, they recognized with certainty that God was present in his works and rejoiced. Accordingly, everyone in the villages and fields, on hearing of their approach, came out to meet the party. Coming along, because God was with them, they departed in good and eager spirits, and by now there was an innumerable crowd that followed in faith with wonderful devotion. All along the way, the crowd was wondrously increased in every single place until they reached the monastery.

When they had almost arrived, so great was the multitude of sick people in the cart that it was necessary to unload some of the construction material. Those already present and those who joined devoutly picked it up and carried it on their shoulders. A small child missing a hand approached along with others and—I am about to speak of marvels—bending to the ground at once took up some of that material in his hand. As all looked on, he carried what he had picked up in a hand now restored. Then you would have seen all weep for joy, then rejoice in a way that cannot be described, give thanks, and at the same time express their delight in a great, exultant dance. The monks and all the people received them with great veneration, welcomed first because of their reverence for the holy work performed for God, then because of the mighty deeds that the Lord had seen fit to show on their behalf, for in addition to those three healings we have already mentioned, two other people were freed at home and presented unimpaired at the altar of the blessed Mother of God.

16.

On the following Saturday night, the gentle Mother of God raised up a crippled child in the presence of the people, but also restored hearing to Mathilde of Mézidon-Canon. She likewise cured Albereda, a cripple from the village called Poussy-la-Campagne and also in the sight of all restored Emma of Garnetot, who had been deprived of movement in half her body. Another small child, who had been blind for five years, received sight here. And also Gisea of Montpinçon, likewise blind, merited to have her sight restored here. In addition, Roland of Caen, who was deaf, heard as he stood here. In addition, the gentle Mother of the Lord kindly raised up two crippled women from known places, and she restored the missing eye that one of them had lost and had all those healed return home whole. Thus, thus the blessed Mother of God lit up her church with divine works; thus she offered her son's name, glory, and magnificence to those coming to her; thus it is plain that the gentle and very powerful Lady called forth people from everywhere to come, rather to flock, to her churchyard; thus the kindest mediator offered those taking refuge in her medicine for both bodies and souls.[32] For hearts' secrets were revealed here through confession, and matters hidden in souls that shuddered to hear were laid bare. Thus each one of them was in fear for both himself and others and busied himself lest on account of the stains of his sins God's blessings be denied to others.[33]

When the healings of the ill seemed to be taking a while or were only partial, the priests immediately sought the remedy of confession, and after throwing off their clothes in the sight of all exposed their bare sides to very severe discipline.[34] Nothing among them was shameful, nothing indecent, no foul thing was done through sin.[35] Coming along with the people in their care, they carried switches, even whips, with which they chastised not only those subject to them but also, as was said, inflicted the voluntary discipline of flogging on themselves. The whole crowd carried very rough cuttings of thorns and brambles in their hands in public, and anyone they spared in the floggings thought them unmerciful.

You surely would have seen blood flowing from the sides of not only the men but of those of the weaker sex. You would have seen both sexes, here and there throughout the church and the churchyard, exposed to whips and humbly beseeching in sobbing, prayer, and tears that they not be spared a beating. Seeing the signs and miracles being worked, they gave and received punishment in the fear and love of God. Thus,

---

32. "Mediator" is the feminine form (*mediatrix*). The healing she offers is *medicinale*, medicine for body and soul.

33. Another early reference to lay confession: see note 84 to Herman of Tournai's *The Miracles of St. Mary of Laon*.

34. The narrative takes a sharp turn here, from accounts of miracles to penitential acts even more extreme than the dragging of carts. Haimo explains his reasons for digressing a bit further on.

35. Haimo is at pains to insist that there was nothing untoward in all this baring of flesh.

in treading on the dirt, they made the dirt of their bodies the spirit of salvation. Nobody should be amazed if I pause a little while in this digression, rather that I pause only a little because these things must be explained in relation to the miracles revealed: these matters are much greater, much more glorious, because they are spiritual. In one case bodily afflictions are removed but in another mental ones; in one case mortal bodies accompany the healing of the weak, but in the other healing that saves is delivered to a soul that will be eternally victorious.[36]

In fact, up to now we have kept to the order of events as far as possible, without reporting everything.[37] But henceforth there was such a countless multitude of miracles that in no way could we touch on them through memory—to say nothing of describing them in words. Still, we will proceed concerning outstanding ones performed for the benefit of those who had lived among us or those from nearby whom we know unmistakably because there cannot and should not be any doubt that we may proceed most truthfully about these matters, with the one who worked them also bestowing this capacity.

17.

One Saturday, when as usual a rather large crowd of the faithful had assembled for vigils, there happened to be sitting in a cart laden with branches two little boy brothers whom their mother had declared were mute from the womb. Leaving her sons behind, she had hastened into the church to see the many miracles that were being performed there, when through divine aid their tongues were immediately loosened for use in speaking. One of the boys asked, "Brother, where's our mother?" The other, at once surpassing the first through God's gift, burst into speech. "I don't know where she went, brother, I don't know where she left for." "I'd really like to see her," said the first brother, "but where will we look?" Hearing this exchange, everyone around them immediately lifted a cry skyward. Flocking together from all sides, they snatched the boys off the cart and carried them in great joy and exultation to the

---

36. Haimo thinks that miraculous healing, something divine power can easily bring about in a mortal body, is one thing, but spontaneous, dramatic acts of penance on the part of humans that lead to salvation and eternal life are another. The dragging of carts would seem to belong to the second category.

37. In sections 7 through 16, Haimo has reported events in chronological order from July 2 to July 22, 1145. Those recounted in the remainder of the letter took place later, but their exact timing cannot be determined. It is likely they followed shortly after those from the first three weeks of July 1145. Like Herman of Tournai and Hugh Farsit, Haimo specifies that he does not provide an exhaustive account.

altar of the blessed Mother of the Lord, whose work this was through her sweetest son, as both boys glorified him in her. She who had borne the boys ran to meet them, and when she heard those she had just a little while earlier left mute were now speaking, it is not easy to say what wellsprings of tears she poured forth on the spot in the immensity of her happiness or with what thanksgiving and celebration she offered praises to the most gentle Mother of the Lord Jesus. The whole crowd gathered to see and hear the boys speaking, and they most readily exalted the greatness of both the Savior and his blessed mother in them. The younger they seemed, all the more outstanding the miracle was judged. They proclaimed that a mother unfortunate in birth was fortunate in the advancement of so great a miracle.

Meanwhile, she first fell on her face, then rose from the ground, weeping and kissing her children's necks, and once again fell prostrate. She was from nearby, namely the village of Le Mesnil-Mauger. The place and the situation were known so there was no need for testimony, although there were just as many witnesses of the miracle from all over as there were from the village, from which numerous inhabitants were present. Count William of Ponthieu had also come that night and along with him all the nobility of the region. He arrived with a cart led by the people of Argentan, along with whom both he and his companions, barefoot and humbly attired, had most devotedly hauled.[38] Indeed, there were some significant healings in that cart after it entered the town even before it reached the monastery itself. You would have seen everyone lying on the ground, none of them shrinking even from stretching themselves out in the mud, kissing the dirt and planting their faces in it, having no doubt that the ground the Lord—to the glory of his name and his mother's—had deemed worthy to light up with such miracles was holy ground.

18.

On that same night boys from the village of Écajeul were likewise present with their cart. A number of them brought five sick people in the cart with offerings and gifts. The kind Mother of the Lord received their offering, made as it was in the purity of innocence and odor of sweetness. Immediately she revealed herself through the mercy granted

---

38. William III, count of Ponthieu, ca. 1093–1172. What is now called Crécy-Ponthieu is about 120 miles northeast of Saint-Pierre-sur-Dives, but apparently William also held lands much closer to the monastery.

to the sick people to whom the boys were tending. She restored four of them to health on the spot, and while she put off the fifth, immediately the boys all threw down their clothes at the church doors and surrendered their bared bodies to the ground. Crawling on the floor as a pitiable spectacle for all, they reached the altar, and as they wept there, they brought the great crowd present to tears.

After great cries, after long supplications, they turned at last to an image of the gentle Mother of the Lord sitting on the altar, and they began to dispute with it as if alive and—like someone rebuking a male or female servant—to argue quite vigorously that she had put them off.[39] They asked, "Why, Lady, do you refuse to heed the prayers of your servants? How is it that you in no way take pity on the afflicted in your presence, people stricken in body and soul, as is your custom? Behold, we are naked in your sight, we sigh, we wail, we are beaten, we are flogged, and you disdain us? Why, Lady, do you not devote attention to those of such a tender age? Why have you no regard for the devoted service of your innocent ones? Where is your mercy, your affection, your gentleness, your kindness? You have already granted us the healing of four sick people. Why do you delay in the case of the fifth, Lady, since you could do it most easily? If it is because of our sins, behold, we promise repentance for past deeds, we pledge before you in a vow that henceforth we will never steal fruit, vegetables, or grain from the fields."[40] Meanwhile she did not spare them, and although wounded, they prayed that she not spare them in any way whatsoever.[41]

Then they crept to the altar of the Holy Innocents in the fashion already mentioned and repeated the same things there as if in the presence of the innocents themselves, adding that these saints should not avert their eyes nor disdain those of their own age.[42] And thus they returned to the high altar, prostrate on the ground, and repeated everything as above with most ardent crying and groaning. Why should

---

39. See note 10, above.

40. As children, the boys' only sin to date was petty theft.

41. That is, as Mary allowed penitential acts to continue, the boys begged her to continue punishing them if that was necessary in order to effect the fifth cure.

42. The Holy Innocents were little boys massacred by King Herod of Judea as recounted in Matthew 2. At the time Jesus was born, the Magi had promised Herod they would tell him when they found the infant king of the Jews in Bethlehem. Warned in a dream not to make their report, they slipped away from Judea. God appeared to Joseph, telling him that the king intended to kill Jesus. Herod, enraged that the Magi had tricked him, ordered all male children two years old or younger to be murdered: surely one of them would be Jesus. But Joseph and Mary had escaped to Egypt with their infant son. The altar dedicated to the Holy Innocents is a fitting place for children to seek divine favor.

I delay further? The Mother of Mercy could no longer contain her gentle heart with regard to the afflicted, indeed could not refrain from fulfilling such pious desires of her innocents. What did she deny, or rather what did she not do for those praying this way, contrite in this way? What, I ask, would she not have offered to those weeping this way, crying out this way, afflicted in this way? To act thus was indeed to use violence, if I may put it like that, to extort through force. What would people praying thus, wailing thus not extort by force? . . .[43]

---

43. Here the text breaks off. It is impossible to know how much longer it was originally. It seems safe to assume that the fifth patient in this story was promptly healed.

John, son of Peter, *The Miracles of the Church of Coutances*

Introduction

The city of Coutances lies on the Cotentin Peninsula in northwestern Normandy. It is approximately sixty-five miles west of Saint-Pierre-sur-Dives, 170 miles west of Paris, and about seven miles inland from the English Channel. Its first bishop is said to have been St. Ereptiolus (mid-fifth century); the medieval diocese included much of the peninsula. After several centuries of dominance by Frankish kings, Coutances was largely destroyed by Vikings in 866 along with its cathedral. It came under the control of what was then the kingdom of Brittany to its west. The city was a bone of contention among various kings, dukes, and counts for nearly two hundred years, only coming firmly into the Norman orbit during the time of Bishop Geoffrey de Montbray (r. 1048/49–93).

Geoffrey, whose interest in having an account of miracles concerning his cathedral lies at the origin of the collection translated below, was a colorful figure.[1] His brother Mauger bought the bishopric of Coutances for him, probably from Duke William I of Normandy. Geoffrey found himself accused of simony, the purchase of ecclesiastical

---

1. Concerning Geoffrey, see Allen, "The Norman Episcopate," 1:176–203.

office, at a church council in Reims led by the reforming pope Leo IX (r. 1048–54). Geoffrey confessed to the arrangement but said he had not initiated it and in fact the office had been violently forced on him. He was allowed to remain bishop.

Geoffrey did not return at first to Coutances. The city was in poor shape, and its bishops had resided elsewhere for 150 years. However, Geoffrey's predecessor, Bishop Robert I (r. ca. 1023–48), had begun to rebuild the cathedral with the support of the Norman countess Gunnor (d. 1031), and Geoffrey wanted to ensure the work continued. He proceeded to Italy, where he was welcomed by his kinsman Robert Guiscard, a Norman adventurer in Sicily, of which Robert became duke in 1059. Geoffrey managed to get Robert to supply him with money and precious items that he subsequently used in a vigorous campaign to continue restoring the cathedral and city of Coutances with additional help from Duke William. He saw to the creation of a considerable cathedral library and established a school. The new cathedral was dedicated in 1056 in the presence of the duke, the archbishop of Rouen, other Norman bishops, and many lay noblemen from Normandy and Brittany. In the next decade, Geoffrey continued to assemble a considerable patrimony for his church, again with the help of Duke William, to whom he became a trusted advisor in the years leading up to the duke's invasion of England in 1066. Geoffrey was present, in probably both spiritual and military capacities, at the Battle of Hastings in October 1066, after which Duke William became the king of England; he played an important role in the coronation of William at Westminster Abbey in London two months later.

From this point onward, Geoffrey was far more visible in England than in Normandy, from which he was absent for long periods. During this time, he served King William as a warrior and judge as well as advisor. After William died in 1087, Geoffrey's position was difficult: the king had chosen to leave the kingdom of England to one son, William Rufus (r. 1087–99), and the duchy of Normandy to another, Robert Curthose (r. 1087–1106). Geoffrey's personal property in England was much more substantial than that in Normandy, so he had to remain on good terms with both king and duke. Archdeacon Ralph, who eventually succeeded Geoffrey as bishop, managed the diocese in his absence. Geoffrey's definitive return to Coutances did not take place until 1091, only to have an earthquake damage his cathedral. It was perhaps after this catastrophe that Bishop Geoffrey first commissioned a collection of miracles that, as will be explained below, was not completed until decades after he died in 1093.

Much of the information about the rebuilding efforts in Coutances early in Geoffrey's tenure comes from a short account called *On the State of this Church from 836 to 1093* (*De statu huius ecclesiae ab anno 836 ad 1093*), written by a cathedral canon known as John, son of Peter, probably not long after Geoffrey's death. John was also the author of *The Miracles of the Church of Coutances*. It was likely originally appended to *On the State of this Church* because in the prologue to the miracle collection, the first reference to John's father Peter, also a cathedral canon, calls him "the aforementioned treasurer Peter." *The Miracles of the Church of Coutances* must date to 1106–35, the dates Henry was both king of England and duke of Normandy. It was almost certainly late in that period: in section 27 John refers to the widespread outbreak of ergotism across France in the late 1120s that Hugh Farsit describes. John calls himself an old man and rues that many miracles have been forgotten because the people who witnessed or knew about them are dead, which also suggests a late date. The miracles recounted, then, mostly took place in the late eleventh century, although John is clear that some occurred after Bishop Geoffrey's death.

The thirty-two accounts John gathers are a heterogeneous collection. Mary and objects related to her slip in and out of the narration. An image of Mary (a presumably painted wooden statue, as section 14 shows) appears eight times. Oddly, in section 22 Bishop Geoffrey discovers what he believes to be some of Mary's hair, which a subsequent test of its power shows to be genuine—and then the relic is never mentioned again! Ten sections are about things other than the healings that are standard elements of Mary's repertory: John describes a white dove that frequents the church, a canon's theological doubts, bright light in the cathedral at night, and bookends his collection with appearances of mysterious tapers descending into the cathedral from the sky. In sum, John's collection is less focused on Mary than the first three in this book. Like Haimo's, John's stories do not center around a relic, but unlike the collections of Herman, Hugh, and Haimo, it does not have the reconstruction of a church as a context.

The titles and subtitles may well be editorial, though it is impossible to know because no medieval copies of the text have survived. However, it is interesting that the entire work is called *The Miracles of the Church of Coutances* (*Miracula ecclesiae Constantiensis*) and that the prologue title provides the same description. At the beginning of the miracle accounts, the subtitle reads "Here begin the miracles of St. Mary" (*Incipiunt miracula sanctae Mariae*), but that could be shorthand for "Here begin the miracles of the church of St. Mary." The prologue says Bishop Geoffrey first commissioned a collection "for the praise of God, the honor of his Lady, the Mother of God, and the edification of his successors," broadening the focus from Mary alone. Mary's intercession is frequently secondary in the reporting of miracles that, after all, only God can perform.

Text: Allen, "The Norman Episcopate," 1:483–502, is the best edition of the *Miracula ecclesiae Constantiensis*. It is a marked improvement on the only printed edition: Pigeon, *Histoire de la cathédrale de Coutances*, 367–83. Allen's edition is largely dependent on a nineteenth-century transcription by Léopold Delisle, based on an early nineteenth-century copy of a now lost thirteenth-century manuscript and a seventeenth-century copy of (probably) that same manuscript. In a few instances, I have preferred readings from Pigeon or Delisle as noted by Allen or emended the text myself if sense calls for it. Pigeon provided an abbreviated French translation: *Histoire de la cathédrale de Coutances*, 97–115.

The Miracles of the Church of Coutances

Prologue to the miracles of the church of Coutances

When in the delightful times of Bishop Geoffrey of Coutances the church was thriving in worship and progress and flourishing far and wide in numerous manifestations of wonders and miracles, that bishop, a wise and foresighted man, decided that the mighty miracles seen in that church should be written with a truthful and worthy pen for the praise of God, the honor of his Lady, the Mother of God, and the edification of his successors, arranging and announcing that he would cover the book of those same miracles with imported gold and gems in honor of the Blessed Virgin Mary. On hearing this, a certain conceited youth, a relative of cathedral personnel—hoping more (so I believe) to procure for himself the worldly favor of the bishop and popular praise than to have obtained hereafter a worthy repayment from the Truth itself, which is God, and from the glorious Virgin—set himself to writing. Indeed, he wrote some true things, but because he surpassed the limits of excess with the adornment of words, habitual digressions, numerous asides, long comparisons, addresses to individuals, and lengthy conclusions, it displeased the judgment and dignity of his lords, so he abandoned it altogether.[2] All feared that an open attempt to accomplish the task would either rouse hostility toward themselves or displease the reverence of their friends. Hence it happens that only a faint glimmer of the miracles of that time is just barely known to us, and no wonder, since our memory would not suffice to pass along half of the ones we heard about or witnessed.

However, we, who are commanded to praise his wonders and recount his miracles that we know in full faith and that our fathers faithfully passed down to us, shall relate with a crude but truthful pen the Lord's praises, his wonders, and the miracles he performed for the benefit of the sons who are being born and growing up, who will tell their sons. Because those lords and masters, wiser and stronger than us, left the miracles completely untouched, and alas have passed from human concerns, and a whole generation of that era swiftly departed, like shadows, and also because old age now threatens us, who are like their dross or rust, and forces us toward death, therefore, I, John—canon, although

---

2. The author was likely a much younger John, who in his old age, as he says at the end of the prologue, will write truthfully and without adornment to earn God's reward.

unworthy, of the same church and son of the aforementioned treasurer Peter—by dint of necessity am driven to write this both because there is no one to instruct anyone to record these things, nor is there anyone among the wise or foolish who would take the care to do so, although they are all masters.[3] I prefer to adorn my lowliness with tokens of truth rather than the fancy language of artifice and rhetorical flourishes and write a few things in full truthfulness rather than, in going beyond the miracles' plain truth, I in any way offend God, who is the pure Truth, and from whom I believe I will earn a just reward for my work.

Here begin the miracles of [the church of] St. Mary

1.

In that time, by divine will heavenly tapers were accustomed to descend into the church in Coutances, especially on the night between Saturday and Sunday, and quite often stand and burn visibly before an image of the blessed Mother of God. When during the first part of the night a priest had seen a gleaming taper of this sort descend from above and go through the roof of the church, he hastened to run to it. When he had summoned Peter, then the church sacristan, both hastened to the Virgin's altar and saw a heavenly taper standing and burning with no visible support.

When the priest touched the taper with his hand, it immediately went out. But because he was soon penitent and beat his breast for the sin of such presumptuousness, the taper was relit from heaven and burned until after the early morning Mass, as many people saw. The church guardians rang the bells, and both clergy and citizens flocked to the church as usual, and people from the suburbs flocked to the church as usual when new miracles were worked. Bits of the substance of this angelic taper, whether wax or something else—God knows—fell to the ground little by little, as if in drops, which the fire from the taper, visibly slipping down, soon consumed. For that entire Sunday, the sweetest smell wafted from the same place.

2.

It happened that a woman humbly entered the church of the Blessed Virgin, carrying in her hand a candle as an offering. At the very moment

---

3. The last phrases of this long sentence are somewhat obscure. John seems to mean that although there are plenty of learned men who could write up the miracles, none of them wants to do so unless commissioned. *The Miracles of the Church of Coutances* is an old man's undertaking, an homage to those who have gone before him and their experiences.

of her entrance, when she asked if she would find a light in the church, the candle she was carrying was lit by divine fire. The woman and many others who were present at this wonder marveled, giving thanks to God.

3.

One Saturday, when Vespers was finished and still this solar light was burning, some people who had already left the church saw three tapers in the air, descending toward the central tower and getting inside through the tower's roof. On seeing this and alerting many others, they immediately went back into the church and discovered that the three tapers were burning and standing without human aid: one was before the high altar, the second facing the image, and the third above the church's well. Therefore, while they prayed and gave thanks to God, along with many others they observed the burning tapers and that the one that stood before the image on one side of the altar was quickly moved to the other, to the glory of God. And thus they burned that whole night but were so consumed by fire that they did not even leave for onlookers anything like ashes.

4.

During another service, it happened that a woman with crippled feet, unable to walk, was taken to the basilica of the Blessed Virgin and prayed while holding a lit candle. Suddenly returned to full health and the use of her feet restored, she rose and, passing quickly by the crowd of canons on her fortunate legs as clergy and people together marveled, she ascended to the high altar and placed on it the taper she was carrying, giving thanks to God and the holy Virgin.

5.

In a village called Saint-Pair-sur-Mer in the diocese of Coutances, a boy named Gisbert was so paralyzed that his left hand was curved into his chest and he carried his face backward and the back of his head forward.[4] When, I say, he had endured such misery for two years, he was told in a nocturnal vision that he would recover from all his infirmity through the merits of St. Mary, the Mother of God, if he prayed for her aid in her church in Coutances. Some way or another he came to Coutances, entered the church, and prostrated himself in prayer. He wept

---

4. The Latin text at the end of this sentence is scrambled, but the meaning is clear: the poor boy's head is on backward.

Table 6.   Places mentioned in John, son of Peter's miracle collection

PLACE	APPROXIMATE WALKING DISTANCE AND DIRECTION FROM COUTANCES
Agon	7 miles west
Amiens	196 miles east-northeast
Avranches	28 miles south
Bayeux	40 miles northeast
Froide Vallée	14 miles south-southeast
Isigny-sur-Mer	28 miles north-northeast
Mont-Saint-Michel	42 miles south and slightly west
Orval	4 miles south-southwest
Saint-Pair-sur-Mer	18 miles south and slightly west

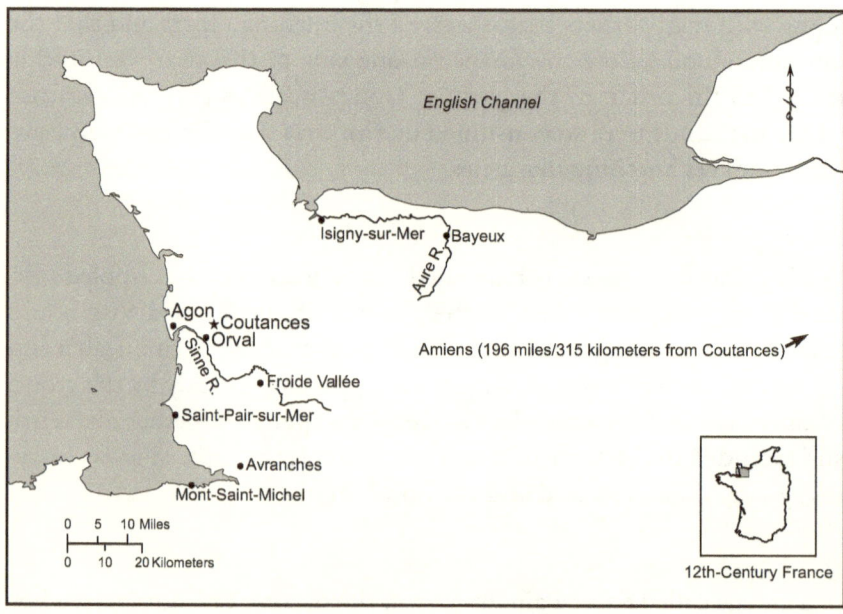

MAP 7.   Places mentioned in John, son of Peter's miracle collection

before the altar, and there by the mercy of God through the merits of St. Mary he was immediately restored to full health. As he lay down, weeping for a long while and bent down on the ground, the guardians of the church told him many times to get up. A priest of the village of Saint-Pair, who had come for a synod—it was the day of the synod— very carefully examined the boy and learned that he was free from all affliction.[5] On the spot, along with the priests and others present, the boy recounted the illness and misery he had suffered. Given the testimony of many people and the self-evident nature of the matter, Gisbert himself remained in the service of the church for many days as a mason. Later on, he had a wife and sons, as we saw, and was a shepherd for Bishop Geoffrey.

6.

A priest of a village called Isigny-sur-Mer, in the region of Bayeux, was returning to Bayeux with his parishioners on the Wednesday after Pentecost so they could make a suitable procession and offering as was due and customary to render to cathedral churches in those days. In exhortations and prayers, he reminded his flock that just as they had done for the church of St. Mary in Bayeux, rendering what was owed, they should also make a prayerful procession and offering to the glorious Virgin in the church of Coutances, showing through their common and spontaneous vow the holiness of that church for its great and famed report of miracles and as the dwelling place of the Holy Spirit: they all also should agree voluntarily and obligingly to give thanks to the blessed Mother of God and pay due tribute, just as they had then done [in Bayeux].[6] All agreed and willingly pledged to do as the priest advised. On the third day, a Friday, as said before, the priest and his people took to the road at the crack of dawn, and once at Coutances fulfilled their vows with prayer and offerings.

A parishioner named Vitalis, who had made the vow at the priest's instruction along with the others, was seized by a foolish thought. Turning over in his mind that St. Mary of Bayeux and St. Mary of Coutances were one and the same Mother of God and no gentler or more powerful in Coutances than in Bayeux, he put off fulfilling the vow he had made. Resting in bed, he stayed home on the day and hour of the procession. When he had fallen asleep, he heard a voice saying to him, "Vitalis, Vitalis, why did you break your resolve to join the procession? You have behaved badly, and the outcome of the first work you do will

---

5. A synod is a gathering of ecclesiastical officials; this one appears to have been a meeting of all the clergy in the diocese of Coutances.

6. The Latin here is suspect. It is clear enough that the people of Isigny recognized the special holiness of Coutances and happily agreed to make a second pilgrimage and offering, perhaps because Isigny was located on the border between the medieval dioceses of Bayeux and Coutances.

certainly prove it to you." Frightened by the voice, he considered and pondered whether what he had heard in the dream was true, but since he recognized that he had not behaved well, he decided that he would resolve to abstain from servile work and labor on his own behalf and first of all devote his effort and toil as a mercy to someone. He rose and proceeded, according to his resolution, to fence in the grain field of a poor little woman, his sister, which animals were trampling and devouring. Vitalis supposed that this was a good deed and that no harm could come to him from a good deed. He climbed a rotten tree trunk so he could sink stronger stakes made from wood further up but immediately he slipped and fell in such an unfortunate fashion that one of his thigh joints was completely sheared away from the rest of his body. There was now no hope that human medicine could put him back together. Upon hearing pitiably awful, loud, and disturbed shouting, some travelers ran to him, gathered him up, and took him home.

It was reported to the priest on his return from the pilgrimage how the wretched man had fallen and with what pain he was racked, almost dying. He hastened to the suffering man. The priest rightly began to reproach the wailing wretch's disobedience and transgression, gently called him to confession and penance, and promised pardon and bodily health if, while repenting, he hastened to fulfill the vow that he had arrogantly broken while praying for pardon and mercy in prayer. Vitalis, confessing and lamenting his guilty transgression, was taken to Coutances on a litter in the company of the priest.[7] All twisted, he was brought before the altar, and although under the influence of distress and loud cries, nonetheless as God's mercy led the way, his whole body was put back together that night as Sunday dawned.

The next day, Monday, Vitalis asked Lord Peter, the church's treasurer, dean, and distributor of alms, that he order a hatchet to be given to him so that along with other carpenters, he could exert himself mightily in work on the church.[8] When he had gotten it, along with others he spent that whole week and the next wisely and gracefully working on outlines for stained glass called frames, which were being made in those days.[9] This accomplished, when the treasurer offered

---

7. Here is another early instance of lay confession.

8. This Peter is the author's father. Since Peter had a family, the canons in his day were seculars rather than regulars, although John reports gatherings for communal prayer.

9. The process of making stained-glass windows started with heating a mix of sand and potash until it liquefied, then adding powdered metals to create colored pieces. The pieces were placed into a wooden outline and cut to size. Vitalis, it appears, made the wooden

him a worthy and rather generous wage for his labor as thanks, Vitalis utterly refused it, saying that he would be a pledged serf of St. Mary and her church and would, as long as he lived, pay a head-tax to the church every year.[10] He did this devoutly for a long time on the major feasts of the glorious Mary, Mother of God.

7.

While still in the bloom of youth, the wife of a man from the diocese of Coutances fell into the shadows of uninterrupted blindness in such a fashion that although she had clear, bright eyes and the ability to open and close them as before, she could not see at all. She remained blind in this way for some years and had used up a great deal of money and goods on medicine and physicians to absolutely no avail. But she had now also completely lost the beauty of her eyes and the power to move them. After much time had passed and she had thrown away all the medicines, she went to the church of St. Mary with her husband and many others on the eve of the feast of the Assumption of the glorious Mother of God.[11] She spent the night in prayer before the image of the Virgin, and when, the night offices finished, it was time for Matins, blood began to flow from her eyes and progressed as if veins had been cut. At last, as the clergy was singing in turns the gospel hymn, which is "Blessed be the Lord God of Israel" [Luke 1:68], eye movement and sight was restored to her from above. On hearing about and seeing this, the clergy and the people who had gathered for the feast day glorified God, who had adorned the Virgin's house and feast with so great a miracle.

8.

On the feast of St. Lawrence, while a peasant girl in the region of Amiens was mixing flour in a bowl to make bread baked under ashes, she was stricken with a sudden pain in her kidneys.[12] She immediately clutched

---

blueprints in which the glass was assembled before it was soldered together and inserted into the stone tracery built to contain it.

10. The language here is technical and obscure. What is certain is that Vitalis offered himself as a serf of the Coutances cathedral and as such paid the annual tribute owed to their lords by people of servile status.

11. The feast of the Assumption is celebrated on August 15.

12. St. Lawrence was a cleric in Rome executed during a round of imperial persecutions in 258. According to legend, after being tortured on a gridiron for a long while, he said that he was done on one side and should be turned over, for which he became the patron saint of cooks and comedians. His feast is celebrated on August 10.

her hand to her back for a while, and it was twisted there and remained so as if decaying. Over the years, as directed by nature, the girl's body matured in strength and form, yet the hand remained twisted, small, and decayed. One night it was revealed to her that she should go to the church of St. Mary in Coutances where her lost hand would be restored. Not knowing what she should do, since she had already undertaken many pilgrimages and devoutly visited the dwellings of many saints, she sought the bishop of Amiens, asking him what she should do about this revelation. At his advice and instruction, she went to the church of the Blessed Virgin during Lent.[13] Prostrate on the ground, for a long while she beseeched God's mercy and that of his mother in prayers and tears. Vespers finished and the clergy leaving the church choir at suppertime, through the grace of God the woman's withered hand was restored to its former natural use.[14] She frequented the church for two weeks thereafter, that hand so restored and made like the other one that everyone thought both hands were in the same condition.

9.

In western Brittany, a rich nobleman was weighed down with such bodily weakness and illness that he could not feed himself, bring his hand to his mouth, or get out of bed. Enduring such misery for twelve years, he was advised in dreams to seek the mercy and aid of the blessed Mother of God in the church of Coutances where he would recover from all the harm to his body. Once he had told his wife what he had heard—that her husband should quickly set out on the named itinerary—she assented and promised that she would be his companion and servant on the pilgrimage. But the lord immediately forbade his wife to undertake the pilgrimage with him. Once food and other necessities for the journey had been prepared, the wife began to plead with her lord in frequent, wheedling entreaties that he allow her to travel with him, both so she could entreat the help of the Blessed Virgin with her prayers and so she could take care of his needs. At last fed up with his wife's insolence, he said, "When that white bull over in the pen comes to the church of the Blessed Virgin, then you will go with me—and not before." Once her husband had been lifted into the carriage and begun his journey,

---

13. The woman's determination was considerable: she made a roundtrip journey of almost four hundred miles, and as a peasant, she probably walked much of the way. Lent is the forty-day period before Easter.

14. In a large church or cathedral, the choir is where the clergy perform services, between the high altar and the nave, where the laity sit.

the bull soon left his accustomed herd, jumped out of the pen, and put himself at the front of those setting off. But since the bull could not be led back into the pen by threats or blows, stood firm against those around him, and led them in departure, the lord realized that this was divine will: he who had inadvisably denied his wife's devoted request and specified the departure of a brute animal should at least follow the example of the irrational beast in his own rationality. Willing and joyful, he ordered his wife to make haste and set off with him.

As the couple proceeded along with their retinue, the bull, walking ahead, took to the road. When the lord saw the church and the city from afar, he asked that he be set down immediately. He then laid himself on the ground and prayed. When he had finished his prayer, he got up, healthy and whole in all his limbs, and as his astonished wife and servants wept for joy, he proceeded at once, partly on foot and partly on horseback, and arrived at the church of the Blessed Virgin. His prayers finished and thanksgiving made in the form of offerings, a few days later the party returned home rejoicing. But the bull that had come with them as an inseparable companion and guide, so to speak, of his own accord went to the altar and stayed there. After the restoration of his bodily health, the lord left home every year, rendering to the blessed Mother of God and her church a tax on his own head.[15]

10.

Another man whose feet were turned back to his buttocks was not only crippled in his feet; nearly his whole body was balled up. Supported on hand-trestles, he reached the church. As he prayed before the steps of the altar, his feet and heels were lifted up and the structure of his body was returned to its natural state and use while he screamed in pain and a great deal of blood flowed from the ruptures.

11.

Near the basilica of the blessed Mother of God there lived in the abode of *Iurget* a weak cripple whom the abovementioned and always to be remembered Bishop Geoffrey had fed and clothed in charity for seven years.[16] This man, weak and ill in almost his entire body, never-

---

15. That is, he put himself in a sort of servile relationship with Mary and her church at Coutances like Vitalis in section 6, an act made more dramatic because it was that of a mighty man, not a peasant.

16. *Iurget* is possibly Guerney, a suburb of Coutances a few hundred yards east and a little south of the cathedral.

theless had the power of speech and talked a lot, quite charmingly. As he rested in his bed one night, heavenly medicine flowed down. First he trembled within and then, calling on God and his glorious virgin mother, he jumped to his feet from his pallet, healed. While he was still standing there, offering God prayers and thanks, it happened that a canon returning from predawn Matins passed by and asked him, as usual, how he was. The man replied that he was better than usual and by the mercy of God he could stand unimpaired on his feet. The canon, hearing of the sudden and unexpected healing of such a long and widely known illness, quickly made the sign of the holy cross in his astonishment and wonder. He hastily summoned a fellow canon as a witness to and investigator of this miracle.[17] Going together and finding the healed pauper walking around, they led him into the church and, after calling the rest of the canons together, joyfully sang a hymn of praise to the Lord.

12.

A woman was living in misery in the seaside village called Agon. Grave suffering, growing quite violently, had reduced the shape of this wretch, although once tall, into a lump. She could not work at anything, nor turn herself around. Through pleading, she was taken to Coutances by her friends so that through the merits of the blessed Mother of God she might be healed of her illness or that staying among the ill, she could at least sustain herself one way or another on the charity of the faithful in her unhappy existence. But the venerable Bishop Geoffrey, comforter of the wretched and staff of the weak, supplied her with the necessities of life for many years. She was taken into church on feast days on a bier, the apparatus on which a corpse is often carried. One day, the Friday after Pentecost, set down before the image of the Virgin, as the reverend Bishop Geoffrey and the canons stood nearby, she received complete healing from heaven. Meanwhile the afflicted one's loud and high-pitched cries were heard throughout the entire church, and people gathered in close from all sides, knowing full well that this was a mark of divine power in its usual guise. As the woman proceeded to the altar, the bishop who had long fed her and the entire clergy sang a hymn of jubilation and praise to the Lord.

---

17. Here are the ingredients of Gabriela Signori's "miracle kitchen" (see the general introduction): the miracle occurs, is narrated, confirmed, and then, in the text, recorded by the author of the collection as he saw fit.

13.

At Mont-Saint-Michel, which is called Tombe, a woman named Lamburge, miserably crippled with a severe affliction of the feet and in want of food, was a beggar.[18] After a long time, a powerful knight named William of Orval, while there as a guardian of the town, took pity on her misfortune, gave her a regular stipend, and afterward had her carried to his own house in Orval.[19] Long ago she had heard reports of the miracles in the church of Coutances, and learning that the city was nearby, she managed through pleading to be carried to the church of St. Mary. When she had stayed in it for a few days she was returned to the hoped-for bodily health through the grace of God and the merits of the Most Blessed Virgin.

14.

A knight standing in the church before the image of the glorious Virgin and admiring its beauty, that is, thinking something wicked, was excited by the thought and fell to the ground there. Shouting and roaring in distress, he began to froth at the mouth and twist his face. Those present were stricken with fear, not knowing what to do or how to help him. Theodelinus, canon, priest, and precentor of the church, ordered clergy and crowd to withdraw.[20] At length he questioned the man as he lay there, exhorting him to confess and do penance. The man confessed that he had sinned gravely in a forbidden thought concerning the beauty of the holy image. Immediately recognizing his guilt and seeking penance and absolution from the priest, on the spot he rose from the ground, healed, although his mouth remained slightly twisted for some time. From this we should infer and fear greatly that if God took such vengeance on a body for a mere wicked thought about the wood of an image of his mother, how much more wonderfully and incalculably will he do so on a soul for plunder and sacrilege in his sanctuary, indeed for wickedness and adultery and other shameless things that speak and stand in all ways against her most holy virginity.

---

18. The abbey of Mont-Saint-Michel, once called Mont Tombe, and the town around it, are on an offshore island south of Coutances. Its first religious community was established in the eighth century. According to legend, the archangel Michael instructed Bishop Aubert of the nearby city of Avranches to build an oratory there. The present church, dating largely to the eleventh and twelfth centuries, rises dramatically from the surrounding sea.

19. For a wealthy monastery like Mont-Saint-Michel, vulnerable to attack from the sea, there was a regular military presence.

20. The duties of the precentor varied from church to church, but it was an important office with responsibilities for organizing worship, often including its musical elements.

15.

In the western part of Brittany lived a woman named Rigiudua whose feet were being eaten away by putrid fire, two large joints already consumed. Since she had found no remedy whatsoever for such misery, and given the reports proclaimed, she went to the same church where through the grace of God not only was the putrid fire extinguished, but once restored to health she served God in chaste obedience and cleaned the church for many days. She went twice to Jerusalem, which was very difficult and not much done in those days.[21]

16.

Two more women suffering from the fire sat in the same church. Falling down, they begged those who entered for a small offering to sustain them. One day as the clergy was performing the evening hymns, the burning and the stench of the fire were both extinguished and by God's grace the women became well.

17.

Again in Brittany, a man born deaf and mute, although already fully grown, did not speak or hear. He was taken to Coutances by his friends and placed before the altar of the Blessed Virgin. When his family and friends had prayed for him for a while, not only was natural hearing granted to him but even understanding and an ordinary abundance of speech.

18.

A woman in Bayeux suffered from a headache through whose immensity she, long laid waste, fell into the misery of insanity. Since a variety of medicines sought and applied had done nothing, her friends, pitying her wretchedness and fearing for her shame, took her to the church of the blessed Mother of God in Bayeux. Keeping her there for several days, they entreated the mercy of the Blessed Virgin for her in prayer. But as the glorious and most powerful Virgin did not hear their prayers, but still held back the kindness of her mercy, the woman was taken to the Virgin's church in Coutances. There she received healing of her

---

21. John writes of the period before the First Crusade, during which European armies seized Jerusalem from its Muslim overlords. The victorious crusaders established a kingdom in Jerusalem and surrounding regions in 1099, which meant that pilgrimage became less complicated, although people from northern France like Rigiudua still had to travel more than two thousand miles.

senses and her body after a few days had passed. When she had returned to Bayeux cured and they had heard that she was freed from her illness in Coutances, some people, poorly assessing God's judgments, reproached her indignantly, saying, "Stupid, crazy woman, and your relatives, the most stupid of all, why did you seek the holy Virgin's church and aid elsewhere? Couldn't she whose power is everywhere have cured you here? Isn't her church here more venerable, its clergy more numerous, its cult of Mary better known? If you had waited here, perhaps likewise you would have been healed here." Blushing at these and similar rebukes, the woman suddenly relapsed. Her critics were confounded, and since she could not be cured then and there, she was taken back to Coutances. Having immediately regained her health there through the merits of the Blessed Virgin, she returned home, rejoicing and giving thanks.[22]

19.

As the aforenamed canon Theodelinus was celebrating Mass as usual at the sacred Virgin's altar, a Norman archdeacon approached him, asking that he beseech the Most Blessed Virgin's mercy, kind and inclined to hear, for a certain wretched boy who was sitting there, his mouth and face burning with the putrid fire. The suppliant priest complied at once with the archdeacon's instructions, and that very day the boy entirely escaped the burning of the growing fire.[23]

20.

The same priest, as we learned from the report of our canons, had doubts in his mind about the body and blood of the Lord.[24] One day, when the clergy was standing in the church choir and celebrating the mystery of the consecration of Christ's body and blood, Theodelinus had dipped the middle piece of the saving Host into the cup as usual. At the very moment he received the Host, it appeared to him that there was true flesh and true blood in the cup. Immediately seized with great

---

22. This story hints at rivalries between churches and their cults. Perhaps Bayeux was a well-known site of healings, but no miracle collection, if it ever existed, survives. As in section 6 here and in sections 7 and 11 of Haimo's letter, people from Bayeux and its surroundings go elsewhere for cures.

23. Like the women in sections 15 and 16, the boy may have suffered from ergotism; in any case, they had gangrene.

24. That is, Theodelinus had doubts about the doctrine of transubstantiation, the belief that during Mass, the bread and wine are turned into the body and blood of Christ while to human perception they remain bread and wine.

terror and at the same time astonished at this manifestation, he called the clergy together and tearfully revealed to God and his brothers his guilt for doubting and the manifestation of divine power. After confessing, he accepted penance. While the appearance of flesh and blood remained and all entreated and prayed to God on this account, a white dove seemed to have descended bodily from the heavens into the cup, then flown outdoors. Now looking into the cup in fear and trembling, they saw the body and blood of Christ had resumed their original appearance of bread and wine. Therefore, from that day forward the priest, strengthened in the truth of faith, devoted himself night and day to psalms and prayers and celebrated the consecration of the Lord's body and blood, receiving it with the greatest devotion, the purest worship, and in immense shedding of tears, as we saw for a long while.[25]

21.

They also bore witness that according to the faithful narration of our elders, a white dove of this sort often flew into the church. After flitting this way and that, it visibly descended to the church's well. They reported likewise that when the angelic tapers were sent, several times they descended to the well and sometimes hovered above it. Many sick people who drank the well water were cured, and for that reason it was taken to many different parts of the world. Many people fell into the well, but although it is deep, none of them came to any harm.[26]

22.

One Saturday before Easter, while according to divine will Bishop Geoffrey was examining the church's holy relics, he found among others the hair of Mary, the most blessed Mother of God, as an inscription attested. Although certain people said that in their opinion nothing of the body of the most sacred Virgin and Mother of God is to be found on earth, some thought otherwise, and thus disagreement arose between them. My uncle Walter, a priest and canon, said, "As you well know and see, for a long time now I have been gravely tormented in one

---

25. This is not a miracle worked through Mary—unless the white dove is a figure of Mary. But the New Testament represents the appearance of a dove as the descent of the Holy Spirit. Perhaps the point is simply that even a good Christian can have doubts, and miraculous events can assuage them.

26. John describes the heavenly tapers at the beginning of his collection and now adds the detail that the water from the well inside the cathedral had healing powers. Holy wells are an element of many systems of religious belief, Christian and otherwise.

eye and completely deprived of sight in it. But I trust that, according to the mercy of God and the power of his most gentle mother, if this hair is really from the body of the most powerful Virgin and my weak eye comes into contact with it and the sign of the cross made over it, it will be emptied of profound pain and restored to its original clearness." The bishop replied, "Let us first pray to the Lord, the just Judge, strong and patient, whose judgments alone are just, justified in themselves, to declare to us the truth of his justice in this judgment. That is, if this hair we are discussing is truly from the body of his most sacred mother, this eye will be healed and illuminated at the application and touch of it with our hand, however sinful and unworthy, so that we may praise his name and faithfully glory in the precious relics of the Lord's most holy mother."

Next, when they had prayed and finished their prayer, the bishop reverently picked up the most sacred hair and with the invocation of the Holy Trinity, he made the sign of the cross over the dying eye and touched it. On the spot, the relic drove all pain away as if with a death-blow. The next morning, namely Easter, the eye was rendered to such health, use, and beauty that it matched the other one. So my uncle was accustomed to recount, and I heard from his own mouth that even in his old age, that eye remained the healthier and more acute of the pair.

23.

As crowds of Normans and Britons gathered for battle, a knight from Coutances was seized by Britons. His hands, feet, and neck bound in the irons designed for each of those parts of the body, he was thrust into prison and confined without food and water until he paid the ransom demanded. While the Britons dunned him for an absolutely enormous ransom and he had no idea at all where he could raise even half of that to hand over, they plagued and taunted him with torture and torment. Seeing their cruelty and insatiable greed, because he was without any hope or possibility of redeeming himself, he turned all his hope toward God and his gentle mother, calling out to her in his torment and beseeching her with incessant prayer. One day, in the presence of the lord who had captured him as guards stood by, all the iron fetters were loosened and the prison doors opened from heaven. The knight left unharmed. Liberated from the Britons' power in this fashion, he came as a free man to the lofty Virgin's church in Coutances, still weighed down with the foot shackles and other iron restraints. Giving thanks to God and the holy Virgin there, he presented the irons at the altar to the glory and praise of the Lord and as a memorial to so great a miracle.

24.

A woman from the region of Avranches named Orielda lived in a village called *Sagenis*.[27] From youth, her knees and feet had been bent back toward her shoulders; she was balled up into a little heap, utterly feeble and seeming nearly dead. When she had endured such great harm in her body for quite some time and there was no longer any hope for her to be healed, it was announced to her in a nocturnal vision that she should prayerfully visit the cathedral of St. Mary and there she would gain release from her prison in the form of complete healing. Upon hearing this, her family and friends put her on a donkey and took her all the way to the doors of the church. Taking her down, they led her in and placed her before a crucifix. Staying there for two days, calling out with prayers and tears, on the third day she was upright, restored through God's grace to complete bodily health.

25.

A noble woman named Catherine went to a feast of St. Mary in this same church, and her retinue took various suitable lodgings in the city. One of them stayed near the church in the house of the man who guarded over the candle wax of St. Nicholas and carried it day and night to his altar, on which a crucifix had been placed.[28] His duty done, he returned home. The soldier, an enemy rather than a guest, stole the quantity of wax that could be carried away without anyone noticing. The next morning he made off with the wax as his lady was departing with all her people. As soon as he did this, divine vengeance for the theft and sacrilege struck him with inner pain and anguish that consumed him for many days. It happened that his lady was visiting him as he lay in his sick bed, asking him about the time, cause, and extent of his great affliction—for she was a knowledgeable matron—and learned through her inquiry that he had stolen church wax from his host charged with guarding it. She said, "You are justly consumed with inner pain and anguish because you stole the light of the holy church in Coutances, in particular that of St. Nicholas. Come to your senses right

---

27. It is not clear where *Sagenis* is (or was). It may be Céaux, several miles south and slightly west of Avranches, itself about twenty-five miles south of Coutances.

28. The man's responsibility appears to have been for the chapel dedicated to St. Nicolas in the cathedral.

now, go return the wax, confess, do penance, and you will be healed." He went, returned the wax, confessed, received his penance, and thus escaped the harm to his body and soul.

26.

In fact, there are countless very well-known miracles that the Lord deemed worthy to work through the grace of his glorious mother in this holy church of Coutances in the days of our bishop and father Geoffrey for the praise of his greatness and the increase of his church. They were known to our fathers and predecessors in certainty and were reported to us by them, but because many months and years have passed and we have names, reports of persons and places, and the succession of events neither in steadfast memory nor in writing, we have preferred to keep completely silent about them rather than to offend our creator—who is truly the way, truth, and life—by deviating from the truth.

27.

After the reverend bishop passed from this world, many people whom we cannot describe, stricken with various bodily ailments, were to our knowledge healed in this holy cathedral. Some were possessed by a demon, delirious, mad, or raging with suffering of this sort; others wrecked by crippled feet or hands; others still were deprived of the use of their tongues or ears. A great number were consumed by the stench and simultaneous burning of the fire. We could recount many of these miracles if either our fleeting youth had entrusted them to steadfast memory or it had once upon a time called them to mind either by frequent retelling or remembrance. What more to say? During the time of the reigns of King Louis and Henry, king of the English and duke of the Normans, the son of the elder King William, the aforementioned pitiable and horrific scourge that many call hellfire was raging anew through almost all France unbridled, to the point that hundreds and thousands of burning people—or more, or fewer—cried out in the churches. By the grace of God and the merits of St. Mary, whenever they devoutly asked for her aid in the church of Coutances, all were freed from the growing fire.[29]

---

29. The massive outbreak of disease noted here is likely the ergotism described by Hugh Farsit and known to have been widespread in France in the late 1120s. John implies that prayer in Coutances is more salutary than that elsewhere. Is he thinking of Bayeux again?

28.

Also, a boy living on a stipend from my brother, Archdeacon Richard, associated with us both before and afterward and now a grown man, was freed from the heat of that same plague as we looked on.

29.

On another Saturday, while the clergy was chanting the evening hymns, processing as usual before the crucifix in the middle of the church and standing there singing, all of a sudden someone consumed by the oft-mentioned putrid fire, sitting before the image of the Blessed Virgin, was freed through God's grace. After learning this and while they sang the *Te Deum laudamus* before God's crucifix, immediately through divine clemency another person with crippled feet stood, healed, before the image of the Virgin. And so as clergy and people together gave thanks, God's grace deemed it worthy to double their joy.

30.

I learned from the report of a priest that an old woman who lived down in the suburbs was accustomed to attend Matins. One night, arising unusually early, she went to the church, but finding its doors closed and firmly locked and bolted from inside, she knelt in prayer at the south entrance. An unusual flash of great brightness, coming through the cracks in the doors, lit up her eyes from within as she lay there. Simultaneously roused by the light's novelty and its wondrous nature, the woman immediately cast her eyes at the door joints and saw a procession of shining and glorious people inside.

31.

Through the testimony of another priest I learned that this same old woman, named Daria—the mother-in-law of Goscelin, my father's sexton—offered the canons of St. Mary a house she had in the settlement of Froide Vallée, in which the priest and Daria had lived for a long while.[30] Many of us who are still alive both saw and knew the old woman. As this priest still reports, one Saturday after Compline, whether by chance or by God's will she fell asleep in a rather remote and hidden part of the church, namely at the entry to the staircase of the west towers where she was accustomed to sit. When she had woken

---

30. Froide Vallée is very likely the text's *Frigido vico*. A sexton maintained church property and may have had other duties like bell ringing and grave digging.

up after a dream, she got up to leave, but the guardians of the church had left and the bolts and bars were all secured. Frightened, she returned to her spot. Soon, to gain the protection of prayer, she bent down in the dark night shadows. While the guardians delayed and the woman persisted in prayer, the shadows of night were overcome as the whole church suddenly shone with tremendous light, and behold! a venerable procession of matrons carrying candles proceeded from the altar of St. John.[31] Passing near the woman during a circuit around the church, the procession stood before the altar of the image of God's holy mother and just a bit afterward crossed the choir and stood again before the high altar. Three of those processing were people of venerable grandeur in their womanly likeness and costume; the candles and their flames were, so to speak, caressing and ethereal. The old woman rose from her spot to see more easily what they were doing and looked as if from the church's main door. Afterward, once they had all departed and left through what seemed to her a door, the old woman remained in darkness.

32.

One Sunday, once the nighttime hymns were ended and long before daybreak—so this same priest recounts—the same old woman was passing the night in the church and saw a taper coming down to earth from above and veering off, so to speak, toward the well. She got up, went through the doors, and saw the taper suspended, as it were, inside the well's opening, its flame showing only from outside. As she drew near to lift the taper, quickly it raised itself from the well and settled down in a candlestick before the image of the holy Virgin Mary. There it burned until day broke, and vanished, so it seemed, through the window glass.[32]

---

31. The Latin is *processio veneranda uxorum*, so literally "venerable procession of wives." This seems strange; the text may be faulty. Are these saints?

32. Here the text ends, rather abruptly. A final statement or two may have gone missing, but since no medieval manuscripts survive, it is impossible to say if there was originally much more of John's text.

Gautier of Compiègne, *The Miracles of the Blessed Virgin Mary*

Introduction

This brief and rather obscure document has received little attention from scholars. In the seventeenth century, the Jesuit Philippe Labbe edited it from two unidentified manuscripts of which I can find no trace.[1] In this edition, the author calls himself the otherwise unknown Gautier, a monk of the famed Burgundian monastery of Cluny (*Gauterius Cluniacensis monachus*). However, modern scholarship attributes the text to Gautier of Compiègne, who also wrote a satirical poem about Muhammad, the founder of Islam, portraying him as a social-climbing bogus prophet and faker of miracles.[2] Gautier (d. ca. 1160) was a monk and abbot of the monastery of Saint-Martin-en-Vallée in Chartres from 1131. The identification makes sense because Gautier says his information comes from a bishop of Chartres named Geoffrey, doubtless

---

1. Labbe, *Novae bibliothecae manuscriptorum librorum*, 650–53. Labbe includes a fifth section (653–55) that I have omitted for two reasons. First, the end of section 4 reads like a conclusion, and second, section 5 has nothing to do with Mary, instead describing a mass gathering of departed bishops led by St. Martin.

2. On the identification of Gautier as author, see Signori, *Maria zwischen Kathedrale, Kloster und Welt*, 141, and Sansterre, "Sacralité et pouvoir thaumaturgique," 69. For an edition of the Muhammad poem with English translation, see *Medieval Latin Lives of Muhammad*, ed. and trans. Yolles and Weiss, 103–78.

Geoffrey II de Lèves (r. 1116–49). Both author and bishop were operating in northwestern France.

Locating the miracles in time and space is difficult. *Dormientium*, the site of the first three, is almost certainly Dormans, a village a little over twenty miles southwest of Reims along the Marne River and about 110 miles northeast of Chartres. Dormans was the site of a women's monastery of the order of Prémontré whose origins Herman of Tournai describes in Book III of *The Miracles of St. Mary of Laon*. Sections 1 and 3 mention sisters. Labbe's edition dates the miracles to 1133, but the house of Premonstratensian sisters in Dormans was founded no earlier than 1142.[3]

I propose the following, which solves some difficulties. The year 1133 in the printed edition is in Arabic numerals, but this could be a misreading of manuscript Roman numerals. Perhaps Labbe mistook "m.c.xxxx.iii" (1143) for "m.c.xxx.iii" (1133), an easy mistake to make. Additionally, the first section describes a healing of ergotism ("holy fire") of which there was an outbreak in northern France in 1142.[4] I suggest that the three miracles set in the Premonstratensian convent of Dormans and the fourth in an unnamed house of monks are meant to have taken place in or around 1143.

Like Canon John's account, this collection is unconnected to a building campaign. The author's motivation, as he puts it in his prologue, is to write simply so simple people will revere Mary: perhaps he expected his stories to be retold in the vernacular. What unites the four sections is that rather than being centered around a relic, the miracles are set around painted images of Mary, the one in Dormans holding the infant Jesus (see section 3). Were these two- or three-dimensional images? I suspect the latter, but there is no proof either way.

The stories in sections 2 and 3 are not original to Gautier, which means that the setting in Dormans is his invention. The earliest version of section 2 appears to be in Guibert of Nogent's *In Praise of St. Mary* (translated in Appendix 3). Section 3 tells an even older tale, which dates to the late eleventh century and survives in numerous versions. Both stories appear in William of Malmesbury's *Miracles of the Blessed Virgin Mary* (ca. 1137) in a much shorter form.[5] Did Gautier read Guibert

---

3. Sansterre, "Sacralité et pouvoir thaumaturgique," 70.

4. Foscati, *Saint Anthony's Fire*, 85–86.

5. William of Malmesbury, *The Miracles of the Blessed Virgin Mary*, trans. Thomson and Winterbottom, 99 (Gautier's section 3) and 123 (Gautier's section 2). This paragraph is indebted to the translators' notes.

of Nogent? William of Malmesbury (which my proposed redating of the text would make possible)? Someone else? Again, there is no way to know. This little text is full of mysteries.

Text: Labbe, *Novae bibliothecae manuscriptorum librorum*, 650–53. It was reprinted in *PL* 173:1379–86.

The Miracles of the Blessed Virgin Mary

Prologue

To his venerable brother, a monk of Saint-Venance, who should be warmly embraced in the heart of Christ, the monk Gautier: may he bear the weight and heat of the day steadfastly to the end.[6]

Not unmindful of your request and our promise, for the edification of readers I have committed to writing the miracles of the most blessed Mother of God and ever-virgin Mary that I recounted in your presence—not in presumptuousness, but so simple people may understand things written in a simple style and through them be moved to veneration of the abovenamed and always to be named Virgin Mary. Lest anyone think these miracles should be scorned as false or worthless, you should know that I by no means saw them with my own eyes, but knew them through the venerable Geoffrey, bishop of Chartres and papal legate, as he had recounted them in a gathering of noble people. So now we will make known to you and others like you, Christ's poor to whom belongs the kingdom of heaven, what we have heard, in praise of the glorious Mother of God.

1.

In Gaul, in a village called Dormans, there is an image of the Mother of God painted with such elegance and beauty that there is nothing better.[7] The faithful of different regions come to see and venerate it, fulfilling vows and asking for Mary's help. The Mother of All Mercy showed that she was there with repeated miracles, of which we will recount a few that came to us.

When in the year 1143,[8] as our sins demanded and for the correction of many people divine providence allowed the bodies of many people to be consumed by holy fire, the church overflowed with such

---

6. See Matthew 20:12, part of Jesus's parable of the laborers in the vineyard. A landowner pays all his laborers the same wage, whether they worked all day or only an hour. One of the former complains that they should have been paid more since they had worked through a hot day. The parable is often interpreted to mean that those who come late to faith will attain the same reward as those who come early. Gautier has his dedicatee as an early adherent, a strong laborer in God's vineyard, which suggests that the unnamed monk has served a long time. Saint-Venance was a monastery just outside the old city walls of Tours. It was founded in the late fifth century and soon after dedicated to St. Venantius (d. ca. 500), a miracle-working priest and early abbot of this monastery.

7. This story is similar to the one Hugh Farsit tells in section 7 of his collection, with different emphases and details.

8. "1133" in the text. See the introduction for my proposed redating.

grace of divine favor that anyone suffering this illness who came before the face of the Blessed Virgin, immediately visited by divine grace,
felt a cooling of his fever. Therefore, this church was so filled with
sick people that the crowd of those who arrived could hardly stand
in it. It happened that the wife of a peasant subject by right to the
church, held in high regard among her people, was stricken with fear-
some and horrible vengeance on her face.[9] She was taken to the public
haven of salvation; her children and relatives led her into the church
with their hands. Groaning, she was placed face down on the ground
before the image of the most holy Virgin, called out to the Mother of
Mercy with many tears and sighs, and pleaded that she have mercy
on one so lamentable and pitiable. A community of holy virgins who
served the Queen of Virgins there hastened to her and prayed for her
as a devout servant they saw in the grip of such a miserable sort of
illness. They passed the night awake in psalms and prayers with tears
and contrition of heart, invoking the mercy of God and the aid of
the Blessed Virgin. There was a strange change of course: mercy grew
hard, as if the prayers of the virgins were being rejected. They persisted, to no effect. The woman remained wretched and still waited
for the Mother of Mercy to take pity on her. The illness raged again
and covered the poor woman's entire face as a hateful stench wafted
from it, filling the whole church. Weighed down by disgust and toil,
her husband departed; her sons and daughter were wearied by the
vigil, smell, and prayer.

The unveiled woman immodestly lifted her disfigured face in the
people's presence and now in despair after thirteen days of waiting in
prostration before the image of the Virgin, in a flood of tears and with
her pitiable face, she addressed the Mother of God, as if she were present, in words to this effect. "O Lady," she said, "I believed you were the
Mother of All Mercy, the fount of kindness, the haven of the miserable,
but I see you have turned cruel toward me and that I await your mercy
in vain. You restore to their former health all the foreigners who come,
flocking from all over, but you scorn me, your own servant. I find you
direct no intention toward me. I will therefore leave your church so

---

9. The expression "subject to the church by right" suggests that she was an ecclesiastical
serf, and she is called an *ancilla*, the usual word for a female serf, a few sentences later. Yet at
the end of the section she pledges herself to the service of the church, that is, to be a serf.
Another mystery. On the difficulties of determining peasant status in this era, see the general
introduction.

as not to further subject the others to the stench or the terror of my unheard-of ugliness." Saying this, the woman left the church. As the whole crowd of onlookers wept with her, she drew forth pitiable sounds and tearful sighs and left the village, going as slowly as she could, as the crowd marveled. The woman was made a horror to all who encountered her because she presented not a human face but the very picture of deformed monstrosity. She had no nose or lower lip, each cheek was joined to the other in the ferocity of her illness, and now a great amount of burnt blood flowed from her eyes.

At last, as night fell, the exhausted and most miserable woman reached the home of a peasant and asked him for lodging. Moved to mercy, he made up a little straw bed in a secluded part of his house and put the woman there to sleep. He admonished her to eat a little something, but she did not agree to that. As shadowy night fell, the woman seemed to have fallen asleep from exhaustion and strain. In a dream she saw God's Blessed Virgin, the Mother of the Lord, standing by in accustomed brightness, threatening and scolding her: Why had she left the church? Throwing herself at the Virgin's feet, the woman begged for mercy. The blessed Mother of God lifted the woman with her hand and commanded her to stand before her. She touched the woman's face with a gentle hand, and in an instant, all suffering driven away, she restored her to her original health in such a fashion that not even a scar or a sign of any wound remained. After blessing the woman, the glorious vision vanished. Waking up but still uncertain of her health, she called the vision to mind. She gingerly touched a hand to her face and found it whole, her illness completely driven away. Now certain about a miracle, the woman, sending forth words of praise and acknowledgment, disturbed her host's entire household with her racket. Many lamps were lit, and neighbors ran in. They saw her sitting with a radiant face that just a little while ago they had seen stinking in dreadful deformity. They asked how this had happened, and the woman told them about the vision she had seen, through which she had been cured.

The woman was brought back to the church and prostrated herself before the image of the most holy Mother of God. Wailing and on bended knee, she gave thanks to her healer, as people marveled and rejoiced with her, also calling out their praise of the Blessed Virgin. There you would have seen people running in competition to kiss the woman's face that the Mother of the Lord had shaped with her own hand. The woman gave herself to the church as a perpetual servant for the praise and glory of Jesus Christ, who lives and reigns with the Father and the Holy Spirit now and forever. Amen.[10]

2.

At another time a man of the common sort lived in the same village. Deserting his wife, he had deflowered a girl whom he kept as a mistress for his own use.[11] His wife, suffering a separation of this sort deeply and in a hostile spirit, prostrated herself daily before the Blessed Virgin, complaining about the other woman. Every day she said, "Holy Mary, Mother of God, do justice for me concerning this prostitute who is taking my husband from me through enchantment." But the sinful woman went to church daily and said the *Ave Maria* before the image of the Lord's mother.[12]

The one complained and the other paid respect until they had been doing it for a year. At dawn on Easter, the Mother of God and ever-virgin Mary appeared to the complainer and said to her, "Woman, look for someone else to do you justice concerning that common woman because I can in no way do it for you." She, as it seemed to her, replied, "O Lady, you who have power over all heavenly forces, always humble worldly pride when you please, and even in your might suppress the cruelty of demons—why, Lady, do you say that you can't do justice for me concerning that common woman who sins against your son and yourself by taking my husband from me?" The queen of virgins responded, "You speak the truth, woman: power over all things in heaven and earth was granted to me, and I do justice to demons, but that sinner remembers me daily, a greater joy than I ever had in this world. She offers me the angelic greeting, which was the joy of the redemption of the human race, and therefore I cannot allow any misfortune to befall her." Saying these words, the vision of the standing and speaking Mary disappeared.

When the woman got up in the morning, she recalled the vision and proceeded to church. She presented herself cheerfully before the image of the blessed Mother of the Lord and refrained from her usual complaint since she thought she had been deceived by enchantment and the

---

10. Labbe's edition reads *qui cum Patre, etc.* I have supplied a standard prayer ending, as I have at the end of sections 3 and 4, which also finish with *etc.*

11. See Appendix 3 for Guibert of Nogent's earlier version of this story.

12. That is, the prayer combining two greetings to Mary in Luke's gospel (1:28, 42): "Hail Mary, full of grace, the Lord is with you. Blessed are you among women." This prayer probably came into common use in the Latin Church around 1000 as the cult of Mary was expanding rapidly.

Mother of God had been induced to say these things through the malice of the mistress—which is also wicked to say. She stayed in the church in a stupor for a long while, not knowing where to turn or what to do. Afterward, she left and met the mistress we have been talking about at the door. The woman was disturbed at the sight of her and as if out of her mind exclaimed, "You wretch, how dare you enter this church? You stole my lawful husband and so seduced the Mother of God with your enchantments that she said to me last night that she delighted in your greetings to the point that she can take no vengeance on you." Addressed in this way before a crowd of men and women, the sinner replied to this insolence without malice. Merely wanting to vanish into the crowd, she threw herself into it. But the other woman, confronting her, nearly mad, and scarcely keeping her hands off her husband's mistress, screamed and chased her as the crowd held her back. Disturbed priests and clerics ran in and asked about the cause of the uproar. The woman told all (just as we have reported) and spoke of the vision that she had seen (just as we have recounted). The clerics asked the sinful woman what kind of greeting she was offering to the Blessed Virgin. She told them and they recognized the angelic greeting the archangel Gabriel offered her when he announced that the Lord was to be born of her. When the sinful woman learned that she was heard, on bent knee before the image she vowed herself to perpetual chastity and asked that she be devoted to God as the crowd listened. Following up on her pledge, she asked to be made a holy woman. Building a little cell next to the church, she shut herself in it and faithfully fulfilled her vow until she died.[13]

3.

A poor woman went into the church alone, carrying her tiny son in her arms. When she saw there was nobody else there, on bent knee before the image of the Mother of God she began to say her prayer. As if it was deemed worthy for her to be there praying in supplication, it happened that the little boy she held in her arms was chewing on a bit of bread with teeth that were still coming in. Seeing that the Blessed Virgin was holding a boy in her arms, he broke off a piece of bread and reached

---

13. It was an ordinary practice in medieval Europe for faithful individuals to live in a cell built against a church wall. The text says the sinner wanted to become a *sanctimonialem*, which often means nun, but can also refer generally to a devout woman. The language of shutting herself up (*se conclusit*) indicates the woman was a recluse (Latin *inclusa*) who led a solitary religious life.

out to the image of the Virgin's son, stammering, "Eat, baby." While he repeated this over and over, the likeness of the boy did not respond (because it had no human senses). The woman's baby began to cry because he saw another boy who did not want to eat the crust. The kindness of the Savior should never be forgotten! Speaking through the power of the Holy Spirit, the image of the boy spoke to the weeping child, saying, "I will eat with you on the third day." Upon hearing the image speaking to her son, the astonished woman, holding her son in her arms, cried out in fear. Soon the nuns arrived and asked the reason for the outcry. The trembling woman told how the image of the most holy child had spoken to her son and what it had said to him. On hearing about such a miracle, all the clergy and laity ran up and advised that the child be kept in the church for three days so they could see what would happen to him. Since this pleased everyone, the mother remained in the church with her son until the third day. When it arrived, the boy's face shone more than usual, and in that brightness, he took his last breath without pain. The Lord fulfilled what he had promised him, giving him the bread of angels with which all ranks of heavenly powers are nourished. They buried the little body of the holy child inside the church to the praise and glory of the Lord Jesus Christ with God the Father in the unity of the Holy Spirit. Amen.

4.

In a certain monastery there was an image of the Virgin depicted quite honorably. A monk who lived there lay in the church, charged with sounding the hours.[14] At the mercy of the whims of flesh, still he served the sacrosanct Virgin amid many vices. One night he entered the monastery with a prostitute he had as his own. While the other monks slept, he, abominable to God and men, sank into unlawful copulation. Because the ancient enemy was so duping him that he was totally unaware of his sin, the kindly Mother of God performed a miracle of this sort for him.[15]

There was a lake next to the church across which the very unfortunate monk crossed every night in a small boat on his way to the wretched common woman's house. When he wanted to set out, after bolting all the doors he passed before the image of the Blessed Virgin,

---

14. That is, it was his responsibility to ring a bell summoning the other monks to pre-dawn prayers.

15. The monk, then, was possessed by the devil, hence unaware of his guilt.

sought her mercy, and placed his body and soul in her care before departing through a little door. One night it happened that as he hastened to his nefarious work after seeking mercy before the image, his little boat sank in the lake. The wretched monk was submerged in the water and drowned.

There was a crowd of demons dragging his unhappy soul to the places of torment. Meeting them, the blessed Mother of God snatched the miserable soul from their punishments, saying, "O pitiful ones yet not to be pitied, why do you presume to attack the soul of this monk, who, although he was rushing off to sin, placed himself in my care?" Hearing this, the demons called out, "Let us be judged before the Lord." When they had come into God's presence, the Mother of Mercy said, "Dearest son, demons attacked this soul placed in my care and unless I had quickly repulsed them, they would have dragged him to their torments along with them. Since they sought your judgment, standing before you I pray that his soul be restored to his body. Let him thereafter live as a monk and no longer give in to demonic deceits and deceptions lest worse happen to him in death." The most kind Judge said to his mother, "Because it is not permitted me, venerable mother, to deny you anything, just as you have asked, let the monk return to his rank and do penance lest he be judged more harshly at the last day."[16] Thus the soul was dismissed from heaven and returned to the world.

While this business concerning the soul was being carried out, night had passed and the monks, not knowing that their brother was dead, looked for but could not find him. While a few of them were walking around the lake, they saw him rise from the depths and try to swim to shore. At this sight, they got in a little boat, went to meet him, and led him out. He went running toward the church, shouting, "Come with me, you who fear the Lord and venerate the Mother of Mercy." At a trot, he arrived before the image of God's mother; falling on his face in a flood of tears and deep sighs, he said that he had sinned, that he was guilty. A marveling crowd of both monks and laypeople was there, not knowing at all what they wanted for him. Finally, after protracted groans, the monk rose, and once silence fell, he disclosed everything just as we have laid it out above: how, snatched from the jaws of the devil through the Mother of Mercy, he was restored to health.

---

16. Gautier refers to the Last Judgment: see the conclusion to Hugh Farsit's miracle collection.

You would have seen the people piously weeping along with him and compassionately beating their breasts, praising the glorious Lady with hearts and voices.

We have, to the best of our ability, committed to writing things we learned about St. Mary. Let people come to her in penitence, beating guilty breasts amid inner groaning, having no doubt that if they truly repent, by the merits of this most holy Virgin they will regain the grace of her kindest son and our Lord Jesus Christ, who lives and reigns with the Father and the Holy Spirit now and forever. Amen.

APPENDIX 1

Hugh Farsit, *Otium*, Book I, 57

Introduction

In the four books of *Otium*, Hugh Farsit chose to offer something like an annual report, but in a collection of meditations, not a work of history.[1] Hugh devotes six chapters to heresy and mentions it in a seventh, but he does not identify people or places associated with heterodox beliefs, concentrating rather on heretics' denial of the efficacy of the sacraments of baptism and the Eucharist.[2] This makes I, 57 quite striking: its title and contents refer to the events in Laon in the spring of 1112. The presence of this sole excursus on current events in a text of some ninety thousand words shows how momentous the revolt was to contemporaries. Hugh wrote of quite recent events (*modo nuper*), meaning this is almost certainly the earliest record of the murder of Laon's bishop and its aftermath. I edit and translate the entire section, which offers a sample of Hugh's spirituality. In the title, Hugh refers to himself in the third person, which is not unusual in the manuscript of *Otium* consulted here.

Text: T, fol. 66r–v. I have retained the medieval orthography.

De episcopo Laudunensis trucidato anno quarto Ludovici de malis imminentibus precatur sibi finem et ut cicius macerescat anima sua amore seculi deposito

Ecclesia tua languet ubique terrarum. Modo nuper in his paschalibus sollempniis Laudunensis episcopus in medio civitatis sue seditione civium trucidatus et confossus est. Ecclesie principales succense, primores et milites civitatis combusti et confossi, parvuli trucidati. Ipsi idem qui hoc facinus patrarunt, Deo procurante, fugati et dispersi. Incendiis et bellis tota Francia vastantur et ira tua, Domine, desevit ubique fame, gladiis, et igne, quia qui aliquo anno famem evaserit gladio cadat, qui gladium effugerit igne vastetur, quasi casu in mentibus immisso, sed re vera ira Dei ubique seviente.

Inter tot mala unicum nobis esset solacium, si tibi placeret, Domine Deus, ut indulgencia data de omnibus peccatis meis, egredi iuberes de hoc corpore. Tedet nos vivere et videre contemptum ecclesie tue cuius dolor debilitat vires anime nostre. Si ergo audis preces pauperum tuorum, cicius educ nos de ergastulo carnis huius, quia facilius est nobis [fol. 66v] *tolerare mala corporea quam insultationes inimicorum Christiane fidei. Interim autem rogamus te, Domine, ut fructum pomorum tuorum ad maturitatem perducas, excluso virore terreni amoris, omnino emollita mentis duricia,*[3] *et omni acciditate in dulcorem conversa, ut opera nostra, locutio nostra, et tota cogitatio nostra omni tempore nil nisi Deum sapiant. Quod fieri non poterit nisi calore spiritus tui assiduo excitatus fuerit omnis amoris terreni humor, exinanita fuerit tota fortitudo que ex nobis esse videtur. Nunc autem quia spaciosa via est omnibus obtemperare voluptatibus arta vero et angusta omnibus contraire voluptatibus, tuo ductu necesse est procedere spiritum nostrum attenuatum a crassitudine seculari in via artata et obstructa pinguibus seculi huius. Propterea oderunt ecclesiam tuam multitudo iniquorum quia contradicit pinguibus eorum carnibus.*

Concerning the slaughter of the bishop of Laon in the fourth year [of the reign] of Louis [VI], he prays for an end of imminent evils for himself and that very soon his soul will soften after it puts aside love of the world

Everywhere on earth your church is weary. Just recently during these Easter celebrations the bishop of Laon was slaughtered and butchered in the middle of the city by a conspiracy of its citizens. The chief churches were burned, leading citizens and soldiers set afire and butchered, and children slaughtered. God also saw to it that those who perpetrated this crime were set to flight and scattered. All of France is ravaged by fires and wars, and your anger, Lord, rages everywhere in the form of famine, sword, and fire; one who in another year had escaped hunger falls by the sword, and one who had escaped the sword is ravaged by fire—as if by misfortune attacking their minds, but in fact as God's anger rages everywhere.

Amid so many evils there would be one comfort for us, if it please you, Lord God: that once your pardon for my sins has been granted, you might command me to leave this body. It disgusts me to live and see the contempt toward your church, whose grief saps the vigor of my soul. If you hear the prayers of your poor, free us very soon from the prison of this body, because it is easier for us to bear bodily ills than the insolence of the enemies of the Christian faith.[4] Meanwhile, Lord, we ask that you bring the fruit of your orchard to ripeness once the greenness of earthly love is removed, hardness of heart completely softened, and all sourness turned to sweetness, so that our works, our speech, and all our thought savor of nothing but God at all times [see Psalm 19:14]. This cannot happen except through the constant warming of your Spirit, every drop of earthly love is drained and every strength that seems to be in us is destroyed. Now because the path for all to submit to pleasure is wide but the path to resist all pleasure is small and narrow [see Matthew 7:13–14], your guidance is necessary for our spirit, worn away by the world's heaviness on a narrow path obstructed by the excesses of this world. Therefore a crowd of wicked people hates your church because it speaks against the excesses of their flesh.

Notes

1. On Hugh and his writings, see the introduction to *A Little Book of Miracles*. The *Otium* has not yet been edited. For this paragraph I have consulted T, fols. 49r–106v.

2. Hugh discusses heretics in Book I, sections 35, 42, 43, 48, and 53, and Book II, section 12; Hugh's letter to otherwise unidentified brothers in Jerusalem is mentioned in Book II, section 16. Hugh decries the heretics' refusal to eat meat that God has provided for mankind and indulges in some righteous name-calling: heretics are arrogant and stupid and animals, specifically fat bulls (*tauri pingues*). Book II, section 12 notes heretics' theft, fornication (including men sleeping with men and women with women), adultery, and blasphemy, all standard characterizations of heretics in the twelfth century. But Hugh's overriding concern is their rejection of the two most important Christian sacraments, baptism and the Eucharist.

3. Reading *duricia* for the manuscript's *duricie*.

4. Since Hugh wrote his miracle collection thirty years later, he did not get the prompt release he hopes for here.

APPENDIX 2

Herman of Tournai, *Life of St. Ildefonsus*

Introduction

Herman of Tournai probably wrote his brief *Life of St. Ildefonsus* in the late 1130s, after the author's journey to Spain. As a historical account, it is of relatively little value: it is mostly a retelling of an account attributed to Archbishop Cilixa of Toledo (r. 770–83).[1] Cilixa's version of Ildefonsus's life includes miracles not included in the most reliable source, an *Elogium* by Ildefonsus's younger contemporary and second successor, Archbishop Julian II (r. 680–90). What is certain is that Ildefonsus was born into a noble family around 607. Ordained deacon, the office below priest, in about 632, he entered the monastery of Agali, near Toledo. He was subsequently abbot of Agali before his election as archbishop of Toledo in 657. (Herman usually refers to him as "bishop," but the Toledo prelates had been archbishops since the early fourth century.) Ildefonsus served during a period of strain between the church and the Visigothic kings of Spain for ten years, dying in 667. Among his writings, the most influential was the treatise on the virginity of Mary that Bishop Bartholomew of Laon sent Herman to find (see the dedicatory letter to *The Miracles of St. Mary of Laon*). Ildefonsus's cult spread rapidly in Iberia after his death.

Cilixa and by extension Herman offer more legend than truth, but their narratives are instructive about the nature of his cult, first in Iberia, then later north of the Pyrenees. Because one of the two miracles Herman reworks from Cilixa involves Mary, the whole account (including a chase scene) is typical of the author's vivid storytelling, and there is to date no English translation, it provides a supplement to *The Miracles of St. Mary of Laon*. I have also included Herman's brief note about how the treatise on Mary's virginity, and with it the cult of Ildefonsus, came to France.

Text: *Acta sanctorum ordinis sancti Benedicti*, ed. d'Achery and Mabillon, 498–500, with reference to manuscript P, fols. 8v–10r. I have made one emendation to the printed edition based on a reading in P.

Who brought the following book from Spain?

When he went to Galicia to pray to the apostle St. James, Gottschalk, a bishop from Aquitaine, brought back from Spain a copy of the little book about the virginity of St. Mary that St. Ildefonsus, the archbishop of Toledo, wrote against the Jews as well as Jovinian and Helvidius, enemies of the Catholic faith.[2] So that the authority of Ildefonsus be known, Gottschalk also brought back his Life written by his successor to the episcopal see, Julian of Toledo, who wrote the *Prognosticon*, a very useful and eloquent book on the resurrection of the dead.[3]

Here begins the Life of St. Ildefonsus, bishop of Toledo

St. Ildefonsus was born in Toledo to a very noble family, and then out of his mother's womb reborn in holy baptism.[4] As a boy he was entrusted by his parents to St. Eugenius, the bishop of the same city, to be steeped in learning.[5] When he had seen that Ildefonsus, taught the easy beginnings of grammar, was quite capable of learning the higher arts, he sent him to St. Isidore, the bishop of Seville, whose wisdom and eloquence then perfumed all of Spain and now the entire church. This Isidore was the brother of St. Leander, the bishop of Seville, at whose request St. Gregory, the Roman pope and an outstanding teacher, wrote the thirty-six books of moral commentaries on the book of Job.[6] On the death of St. Leander, his brother Isidore, to whom the young St. Ildefonsus had been sent by St. Eugenius, succeeded him in the bishop's seat. Isidore welcomed Ildefonsus with the greatest pleasure not only for the nobility of his stock but because of the reverence and authority of the bishop who sent him and then diligently taught him dialectic, rhetoric, and the other liberal arts.[7]

Then after several years, Ildefonsus returned to St. Eugenius and adorned with the light of wisdom as well as the garlands of chastity, indeed virginity, and other virtues, he was ordained as a deacon by the bishop.[8] Having accepted this office, the very wise youth feared that if he were to remain in the world, he would, through the stimulus of youth, lose his virginity—as happens to many—and thereby dishonor the clerical order he had taken. He decided to put on the monk's habit in a monastery called Agali, built in honor of the holy martyrs Cosmas and Damian outside the gate of Toledo.[9] When he was on his way there in secret, without his parents' knowledge, his father got wind of it and followed him with his knights mounted on horseback so that he could retrieve Ildefonsus before he was made a monk.[10] Ildefonsus, looking back and seeing his father coming, in great terror hid in the hollow of a rock he happened to find near the road. By God's will his father passed him by in ignorance and on reaching the monastery began to grill the abbot and monks in a rage about what they had done with his son. When they replied that the fact was they had not seen his son, he returned home enraged.

In this way, therefore, once his duped father had passed by, the young man left the hollow and went to the monastery. When he had been made a monk with the highest degree of devotion and amid great exultation of all the brothers, he began to serve God most piously with the result that when the abbot who had made him a monk died a few years afterward, he was chosen by all to take his place. Once made abbot, he did not subject any of the monks to himself but offered himself to them all as a model of good works.[11] Why linger over many matters? When the bishop St. Eugenius had passed over to God, Ildefonsus was chosen in his place by all the clergy and people and consecrated as bishop of Toledo.

Because at that time some heretics, arguing against the virginity of Mary, the holy Mother of God, were trying to turn the people away from faith, Bishop Ildefonsus wrote—in beautiful style—three little books about the virginity of St. Mary and triumphantly overcame them using the evident testimony of holy scripture. When one day this same archbishop, along with a great gathering of the whole populace in the cathedral, was celebrating the feast of the virgin St. Leocadia, who had suffered and was buried in that same city at the command of Governor Dacian, behold! suddenly that same virgin appeared clearly and said to him, "Through the life of Ildefonsus my Lady St. Mary lives and will pay you a worthy reward for the little books you wrote about her virginity."

The archbishop, in order to have with him a testimony of this vision, asked the glorious prince Recceswinth, who was standing next to him, for his dagger. When he had taken it from the prince's hand, at once he cut a piece from St. Leocadia's garment and put it, along with the dagger, in a silver box that served as a reliquary, saying it was not worthy that anything unclean or common should be cut thereafter by the knife with which the holy garment had been cut.[12]

That same year, with the approach of the feast of the Assumption of Our Lady St. Mary, St. Ildefonsus took pains to purify himself with a three-day fast so he could celebrate the feast with a pure heart.[13] As the hour of vigils approached he set out for the church. The clergy who went before him with candlesticks so they could find the church door saw a marvelous brightness like the sun that shone throughout the entire church. Stricken with great fear, they fled. But the holy bishop entered the church without the least fear and saw Our Lady perched next to the altar in the chair on which he was accustomed to sit while preaching to the people. She was accompanied by a great throng of virgins, adorned in splendid garments heavily embroidered with red and white garlands, who stood by her and sang her praises. The bishop, on bended knee, began to worship her, saying many times the verse of the angelic greeting, "Hail Mary, full of grace, the Lord is with you. Blessed are you among women and blessed is the fruit of your womb" [Luke 1:28, 43]. He repeated the finished verse without ceasing until he came into her presence. When he had reached the chair, immediately Our Lady sweetly looked down on him with the brightest of eyes, and with both her voice and a gesture from her right hand, called him to her. She gave him, placed before her on bended knee, a precious chasuble and said, "My beloved, take this garment I have brought you, chosen just now from the treasury of my son, for the many services you have done for me many times, so you may put it on when you consecrate the body of my son as you celebrate Mass.[14] In this present life I pay this little reward for the services you have shown me, but in the future I will see to it that you are joined to my son in heaven always." After saying these words and leaving the garment to the holy bishop, Our Lady vanished along with the crowd of holy virgins and the bright light. He celebrated the feast of Our Lady with such joy, such devotion; how much more he was strengthened in her service thereafter no tongue can express nor anyone's heart easily state.

Hence Ildefonsus decided that the feast of the Conception of St. Mary, that is, when she was conceived, should be celebrated. In accordance with his decision, it was solemnly honored throughout Spain on

December 8.[15] But never thereafter did he want to sit in the chair where he saw Our Lady sitting, nor did any of his successors do so until the time of Bishop Agrannus, the first to presume to sit there. By divine judgment Agrannus was expelled from Toledo in the same year and sent into exile; in the end, too late, he repented that he had acted so foolishly.[16]

St. Ildefonsus, after thirty years as bishop, rested from the labors of the present life in a blessed death on January 23, united with St. Mary, forever virgin, in the kingdom of her son our Lord Jesus Christ, who lives and reigns with the Father and the Holy Spirit, the true God, forever and ever. Amen.[17]

Here ends the Life of St. Ildefonsus, bishop of Toledo

Notes

1. This paragraph relies on Braegelmann, *The Life and Writings of Saint Ildefonsus of Toledo*, 1–31.

2. The book in question is Ildefonsus's treatise on Mary's virginity. In manuscript P, Herman's Life of its author is between this brief account of its arrival in France and the text of the treatise.

3. The earlier manuscript Herman mentions, which dates to 950 or 951, survives: Paris, Bibliothèque nationale de France, MS lat. 2855. It contains a preface to Julian's life and the treatise on Mary's virginity copied by Gomes, a monk of the house of Albelda in northeastern Spain, a major center of learning in the tenth century. Gomes first reported what Herman repeats about how the manuscript came to be made at the behest of Gottschalk, bishop of Le Puy (r. 935–55) in southwestern France, to be taken north. Bishop Gottschalk's pilgrimage was to Santiago de Compostela. Jovinian and Helvidius were noted Christian heretics in the late fourth century; it is not clear if Ildefonsus was writing in response to older heresies, if there happened to be two men with the same names operating in Toledo in his times, or if the archbishop used them as generic names for heretics. The numerous Jews in early medieval Spain were subject to sporadic royal persecution and attempts to expel them from the kingdom. When more tolerant Muslims conquered Spain in the early eighth century, the Jews, some of whom had aided the Muslim invasion, generally welcomed the change of regime. The *Prognosticon* is among the surviving writings of Julian, who exhorted the Visigoth kings to treat Jews severely and wrote a treatise intended to convert them.

4. Toledo, for a long time a small settlement in central Spain, was an increasingly important city in the late Roman period and the Middle Ages.

5. Eugenius II was the archbishop of Toledo from 647 to 657. When he taught Ildefonsus, he was a young member of the cathedral clergy in Toledo. As in *The Miracles of St. Mary of Laon*, Herman plays fast and loose with chronology.

6. Seville is in southern Spain, about two hundred miles southwest of Toledo. Isidore (ca. 560–636) was elected bishop of Seville in 600 or 601. His most

important work is *Etymologiae*, a vast encyclopedia meant to compile a summary of universal knowledge. This compendium, organized as its title suggests by etymologies, excerpted hundreds of works from classical antiquity, many of them otherwise lost. It became the most widely used textbook in medieval Latin Christendom. Isidore succeeded his older brother Leander as bishop of Seville; both are recognized as saints. Leander was one of those who urged Pope Gregory I (r. 590–604) to write his *Moralia in Job*, a vast commentary on an important biblical book, which like Isidore's *Etymologiae* was much read in the Middle Ages. It is unlikely that Ildefonsus was Isidore's student, but Isidore's renown was such that Herman adds luster to his account of Ildefonsus by associating him with Isidore and by extension two other saints, Bishop Leander and Pope Gregory. In a few sentences, then, Herman manages to link Ildefonsus to four more saints, two of them celebrated authors.

7. The seven liberal arts as definitively established in the fifth century were grammar, rhetoric, dialectic (logic), music, arithmetic, geometry, and astronomy.

8. If Ildefonsus was ordained by a bishop, it would have been by one of Eugenius's predecessors.

9. The brothers Cosmas and Damian were martyred in Syria in the late third or early fourth century. According to Christian tradition, they were doctors from Arabia who offered medical and surgical services without charging a fee. Agali was only a few decades old when Ildefonsus became a monk there.

10. Why the father objected to his son entering a monastery is unclear. The entire episode is fiction, so logic may not matter.

11. Herman echoes the instructions in the Rule of St. Benedict that an abbot should lead by example (chap. 2) and benefit rather than rule the monks in his care (chap. 64).

12. St. Leocadia (d. ca. 304) was tortured to death by the Roman governor Dacian during the final period of persecution of Christians in the Roman Empire. Her feast day is December 9. The "glorious prince Recceswinth" was the Visigothic king who reigned from 653 to 672.

13. The editors of this text think these events took place on the eve not of the feast of the Assumption but the Annunciation, likely because Ildefonsus goes on to quote biblical passages concerning the Annunciation, which is celebrated on March 25. What Herman reports took place, in any case, the evening before a feast day.

14. Reading *tibi attuli* ("I have brought you") with P rather than the edition's *ibi attuli* ("I have brought here").

15. In fact, this feast was not celebrated in the Roman Church until well after Ildefonsus's time.

16. The editors of the text identify the otherwise unknown Agrannus as Archbishop Sisibert, who was deposed from office, excommunicated, and exiled in 693 for having conspired to assassinate King Égica.

17. The historical Ildefonsus died in early 667, having served as bishop for a little less than ten years.

Appendix 3

Guibert of Nogent, *In Praise of St. Mary,* 10 and 12

Introduction

Guibert of Nogent was a devotee of Mary, to whom his monastery was dedicated and whom he called "my sole recourse in every time of need."[1] Late in his life, Guibert wrote several short theological tracts that he envisioned as a group, one of which is *In Praise of St. Mary (De laude Sanctae Mariae)*. An expert sympathetic to Guibert remarks that this text is "particularly incoherent, a hodgepodge of thoughts and anecdotes apparently set down on parchment at different times and only collated when Guibert finally decided to circulate it."[2] *In Praise of St. Mary* probably dates to about 1119.[3] Amid biblical exegesis and theological musings stressing Mary's unique nature and character, Guibert provides earlier versions of two stories told earlier in this book: the woman of Chivy who could not be burned that Herman of Tournai recounts at the end of *The Miracles of St. Mary* (III, 27), and the feuding wife and mistress who appear in section 2 of Gautier de Compiègne's *The Miracles of the Blessed Virgin Mary.*

Whether Herman and Guibert were working from older written accounts or oral tradition of the Chivy story is unclear. The language of each is sufficiently different that a common written source seems unlikely. Since the miracle took place in the late eleventh century, Guibert may have had access to eyewitnesses that Herman, writing a generation later, probably did not. Guibert's somewhat more detailed version is interesting to compare with Herman's, starting with a key difference: Guibert calls the woman Theodeberte, but Herman says her name is Soiburge. Gautier's narrative of the wife and mistress whose stated source is the bishop of Chartres is probably based on Guibert's, but it is impossible to be certain. In this case, the later version is more developed than the earlier one.

Text: *PL* 156:564–68 and 572–74. I have not found a translation into any modern language.

10. Chivy is a village in the diocese of Laon, a full two miles distant from that town, in which a man living with his wife is known to have sired a daughter, among other children. When she had reached marriageable age and at the right time an opportunity for better fortune had arisen, she was wedded to a young man. Such affection for each parent, along with their great charity toward him, brought it about that without spending their own money, the young couple shared domestic life with them under the same roof. While the girl lived in her paternal home with her husband, her mother honored him with wonderful care for her daughter's sake; no greater love of the girl for the boy could be found except that of the father-in-law for his son-in-law. The mother outfitted the latter with a full wardrobe, busied herself with sumptuous meals, washed his face and hair, spread out soft covers when he was going to bed, was there first when he asked for a servant, occupied herself in service to her daughter in all matters except the marriage bed and, to sum it up, offered not the command of a matron but the bustle of a handmaid. Yet this care occasioned nothing impure. It was almost to the point that in spoiling him she would be drawn away from her daughter, but as mother entrusted to her daughter duties suited to her unsteady age and as she attended to the young man with every refinement, she drew forth the affection of her daughter.

Meanwhile, the cunning of the crafty devil twisted in a sinister fashion whatever was done with kind intention and through curses burned a mark of great foulness on the father-in-law, namely that the mother did this not for her child's sake but to turn her son-in-law to herself instead of her daughter. The bitterness of such a nasty rumor grew daily, and the unbearable spitefulness of such a lie shook the woman's spirit— as much because she knew she was innocent of the wicked conclusion being drawn as because she took it badly that what she was doing out of kindness was being turned into common gossip. After a while, over-come by these vexations, she suddenly began to despise the youth for whom she had once had such burning affection, fearing she could not live any longer with such notoriety if she had him before her eyes ev-ery day. So now she resolved not to end their dwelling together, which would have been enough, but to kill him. She would have been mindful of what is good if she had merely stopped her frequent attendance on him, but she turned herself into iron, preferring that the man be out of the way rather than that she suffer a filthy reputation.

Autumn weather had now arrived, and she made a deal with two boys on this condition: she promised them twenty silver pennies each if, as what happened subsequently will show, they killed him. It is said that these two were from Hainaut and had brought themselves to Laon because of grape harvest money to be had.[4] The woman approached them with the aforementioned promise while they were staying there a little while for the novelty of both wages and unaccustomed food. Cun-ning by nature and inflamed in spirit by money, they were equipped to commit the crime. Thus one day she purposely sent her husband out to do something and likewise sent her daughter somewhere else on false pretenses. When both had left home, the woman secretly opened the storehouse, led in her hired assistants, and after locking it from outside immediately planned to rouse her son-in-law to fetch wine to offer those eating their midday meal. He quickly picked up a jar and un-locked the cellar, but before he could decant the wine, he was overcome by those lying in wait and strangled on the spot. When she had learned the deed was done, the woman ordered the culprits to take the body upstairs to the bed where he was accustomed to lie with her daughter, set it down, and cover it with bedding and clothing as if he were asleep.

After a little while the head of the household came home, as did the daughter. They began to prepare the meal together, and as they busied themselves in their accustomed domestic tasks, the mother said to her daughter, "Go quickly and wake up your husband, who just now went for a nap." The young woman went to the bed and called the sleeping youth by name, then poked him when he stayed still. When he responded in no way to his wife's rebukes or pinches, she smacked her hands together and cried out to everyone that he was dead. The house-hold was roused and neighbors gathered, weeping as pitiably at his sud-den misfortune as justly lamenting that he died without confessing. As all bewailed the death in true affliction of soul, the mother, the killer, cried out to her son-in-law and indeed her daughter with feigned grief.

She lamented more calmly than the others.[5] As pitiably she described the man's good habits, charm, eloquence—the tokens of his outward nature—and added unseen qualities to these, so much more did she fear that her daring cruelties would be uncovered.

Carried away in such a fashion, the woman kept silent about the events on both sides.[6] But aware of her foul deed, she was the one to first turn against herself. Driven by regret for her useless crime, after confessing she consulted with a priest in her diocese.[7] Bound to fasting suitable for great wickedness, she concealed herself under the cover of this spiritual medicine for some time. When a long time had passed, it happened that animosity arose between her and the priest. The priest was able to have the awful disgrace hurled at the woman, which ill be-fitted his clerical status, pinning her son-in-law's death on her.[8] The youth's parents, roused as if by a frightful clap of thunder, referred the matter to the court of Ilbert, the vidame of Laon.[9] He was as tenacious in military matters as he was bold in the public administration of the diocese. Why beat around the bush? The vidame entered Chivy, arrested the woman, and demanded that the case be handed over to the law. The woman did not resist, and the sentence was to be carried out in Laon.

Next, when this same church advocate implicated some of the wom-an's kin along with her in the same disgrace, she said, "Brandish your arms against me alone and let them go free. You will know for certain that nobody is an accessory to the crime that has been exposed." At that time the bishop was Helinand, a man as clearly poorly educated as he was ill-suited to administration and especially ignorant of canon law.[10] Thus when the proposal of an ecclesiastical sentence was brought into his court and he seemed to agree with the vidame about what should be done, a schoolmaster suggested to him that it was fitting that such a crime should be punished by fire. In habitual bitterness, he had read with an eager maw that this confirmed, as it were, public opinion of the allegation. When she saw that such a harsh judgment had befallen her, long sickened by the deed she regretted and now more wretchedly despairing of this world, she was stricken with terror. The more every-thing in the present was taken from her, the more her spirit's whole vision of her future state was revealed.

Therefore, she asked the vidame's underlings that she be permitted to go to the cathedral church of our most merciful mother. Which wicked person would refuse? With a large company of people who had gathered to see a spectacle, the death of the one to be punished, she went forth in misery. In the middle of the church, she confessed her guilt to a general audience as the climax of her expiation. Then she was thrown down on the ground to beg the mercy of the mother of the world. That the woman groaned in anguish to the one who turns away from nobody in distress was made known by what happened next. An enforcer roused her and she went from prayer to punishment. The church of Saint-Just, which was just on the slope of the mountain, served as the chapel for the Bretons who lived there.[11] There the vidame's officials had at the ready a hut on whose central support they tied the woman, clothed only in a shift, by her arms and legs; they had gathered twigs and thorns from a nearby vineyard. They stuffed the hut's interior with this heap of wood and set fire to it. When the materials piled there were reduced to ash and embers, the woman was seen to stand free in their midst.

But the parents of the son-in-law she had killed, looking spitefully at her good health and thinking themselves robbed by the powerless fire, in sacrilegious hatred again gathered twigs and shrubs and remade the hearths all around her. Additionally, in raging ungodliness, they did not believe the woman who ought to have been choked by the smoke alone had been saved by a miracle and penetrated her most savagely with spears scattered in the middle of the fire. This only wounded her greatly as the fire was harmless: when this whole conflagration had died down, the woman was again free from its harm.

The vidame, stunned at such a novel spectacle, unheard of among all people and in all parts of our world, immediately shuddered at such peasant savagery and properly expressed contempt for it and for resisting a now heroic holy woman. Through his officers, he immediately ordered that she should be brought to him once the flames had subsided. When she was presented to him, he heard about the outcome from bystanders as he gazed at her. He learned that not even a bit of her hair or eyebrows had in the least been harmed (I do not mention the shift), and he was especially astonished that the fires had tested only the fetters.

He went back inside the city walls in her company, and a much larger crowd entered the city to praise her than had previously gathered when she was led to punishment. Although the vidame was able to lodge her in his own house and tend to the wounds inflicted, the blessed woman refused and said she would absolutely not go anywhere except to the one who had saved her. Therefore she turned her steps back toward the church and prostrated herself in the middle of it to give thanks to her Lady for blessings unknown in our time. It is impossible to say how many tears she shed there. We shall remain silent about the jubilant onlookers who let forth immense sobbing since the crowd of witnesses larger than the one before could nowhere restrain itself regarding the aid to so great a sinner offered as an example to all.

Then while she was sitting fixed to the ground covered only in a linen shirt, the vidame covered her with a cloak he took off his shoulders. After insatiable prayers and thanks he lifted her off the ground and took her home. Because she had been wounded by the spear attack and dirtied by smoke from the fires, he soothed her with baths and treated her as he could with poultices and soft bedding until he thought she was restored to health.[12] After three days God took care for her eternal health, for on that third day she, untroubled, put her soul into the hands of the Lady who had saved her. Plainly the woman had been able to pray to her for bodily death merited to be rewarded with a freed soul. In this, too, the most merciful heart of this blessed Lady was evident: since she had mercifully offered the woman her whole heart in the face of external danger, she did not want one who had experienced her favor to be fouled any longer by worldly life. As soon as she had cleansed her of the apparent burning carried out without harm, she led her to the heights of the ultimate freedom. The woman was called Theodeberte.

12. There is an additional miracle that can be told briefly, splendid as a moral lesson at which the ears of all sinners should perk up. According to the bishop of Arras, there was a woman who most seductively drew a married man away from his wife's side. Driven by either money or pleasure, she did not refrain from daily adultery, and the wretched man was wrapped up in foul lust. When the woman had nearly stopped remembering about the wife, nonetheless as often as she went to church, before she was about to make some prayer she would happen to see an image of our blessed Lady before her and presented her with the angelic greeting with as much reverence as she was able, saying, "Hail, full of grace, the Lord is with you" [Luke 1:28].[13]

The man's wife, accordingly, ached that adulterous caress was being preferred to her and stridently complained about her rival with the most bitter fervor. Since in fear of her husband she did not dare to act against the woman, she grumbled in public, as was not even proper, to the same extent that she raged at home, muttering rabidly. Her entire conduct toward the most blessed one was of this sort: through the power of this Lady, heavenly wrath should be invoked against the one who had cheated her of her husband and that Mary should no longer allow this common woman's filthiest kind of rivalry to go unavenged. When she thought that with her constant laments she had deeply enraged the heavenly queen against her enemy, the blessed one herself courteously appeared in her own guise in a vision. "Why," she asked, "do you seek vengeance on that woman from me? Clearly I can do nothing against her because with daily persistence she announces my joy to me. I cannot hear anything from any creature that is more pleasing to me. Do you think I should, on your behalf, be enraged against the one who, as if to remind me, calls me to pride myself on my indescribable glory?"

When after these words the woman's spirit had completely set aside her accustomed prayers, it happened that she ran across her rival one day, and as if now despairing of divine judgments, she endeavored to provoke her.[14] "Oh, you foulest of women, what suffocation of the heart you inflict. You're tearing away at my flesh with your whoring and you also proffer your presence, which I hate like poison. How happily, and oh, how justly I'd do you bodily harm, you who won't stop inflicting daily pain on my mind, ears, and eyes. When is either my bed or my home free of constant bitterness? Why do you cruelly inflict this on me in such hatred? There was only one hope remaining: that the virgin Mother of God would hurl some avenging judgment at you. But I've completely stopped asking for that since she told me herself that the 'Hail' you take good care to offer every day softens her so much that she can't do you any harm." Hearing this, the mistress shrewdly asked if it were true that the wife had heard these things from Mary. When the truth was affirmed, she said, "You should know that from now on, your husband will have nothing whatsoever to do with me that harms you, and I furthermore promise my virtue to the one who showed me such kindness for my service, small as it is." So it was brought about that thereafter the one committed herself to chastity and the other put aside her hatred, and the Lady blessed among women [see Luke 1:28] set this all in order for the salvation of each of them.

Notes

1. Guibert of Nogent, *Monodies*, 65.

2. On *In Praise of St. Mary*, see Rubenstein, *Guibert of Nogent*, 111–13, 131, 178; the quotation is from 111.

3. Huygens, *La tradition manuscrite de Guibert de Nogent*, 57.

4. Hainaut was a medieval region straddling modern-day northeastern France and southwestern Belgium and includes Herman's native city of Tournai. The boys were perhaps one hundred miles from home.

5. The text may be faulty here: the context suggests the woman played up her hysteria, so something like "She lamented no more calmly than the others" is more likely.

6. That is, about the murder and her role in it.

7. Guibert seems to mean that the murder did not stop the salacious rumors and was hence *infructuous*, "useless" or "fruitless."

8. Here is another precocious instance of lay confession. Since the contents of confessions are meant to be kept secret, the priest's action is a shocking dereliction of duty.

9. This is the same vidame Ilbert also named in Herman of Tournai's version of the story.

10. Guibert takes another swipe at Helinand, as he had in *Monodies*: see the introduction to *The Miracles of St. Mary of Laon*. Regarding canon (church) law, the Latin text reads *non nescius* ("not without knowledge"), but surely Guibert meant the opposite.

11. This church was west of the city walls at the northerm edge of the butte of Laon in what was known in the twelfth century as the Breton quarter.

12. Guibert must mean that the vidame's female servants performed these tasks. It is odd that he does not say so explicitly.

13. As in Gautier's later version, the adulterous woman often repeats the greeting of the archangel Gabriel before the announcement that she will give birth to the son of God.

14. "Accustomed prayers" translates *solitis imprecationibus*, but *imprecatio* also means curse. Guibert probably had both meanings in mind.

Guibert of Nogent, *Monodies*, Book III, 12–13 and 15

Introduction

The third book of Guibert of Nogent's *Monodies*, the most important source for the events in Laon in 1111 and 1112, also includes accounts of some of the miracles from the subsequent relic tours. Guibert states that he is not writing a complete account, using only examples that he thinks "preach," that is, that can serve as sermon exempla, stories that offer moral or doctrinal instruction. This is in keeping with his general attitude toward relics and miracles. Guibert's theological tract *On the Relics of Saints* criticizes fund-raising fakery, featuring what he sees as the foolishness of the claim that the monastery of Saint-Médard just outside Soissons had one of Christ's baby teeth. But Guibert does not condemn non-Christological relics, which he finds useful instruments of devotion, nor is he generally skeptical about miracles.

In *Monodies*, Guibert offers both more and less detailed and at times conflicting versions of events Herman recounts in *The Miracles of St. Mary of Laon* I, 5 (Buzançais); I, 10 (Angers); II, 1 (Nesle); II, 4 (on the English Channel); II, 7 (Winchester); II, 12 (Exeter); II, 10–11 (Christchurch, which Guibert does not identify and whose destruction by fire he attributes to lightning strikes rather than Herman's dragon); II, 20 (in a southwestern English town identified by neither Guibert nor Herman).

Guibert also recounts two incidents, one in Angers and the other in an unidentified town nearby, that Herman does not include. His statement in *On the Relics of Saints*—"Relic tours happen under a pretext of piety, but because saints' bodies have been ripped out of their graves and carried about in pieces here and there, a nascent wickedness unrecognizably distorts any righteous intention and an all-pervasive greed corrupts what had happened originally with great simplicity"—and his grudging opening remarks about the Laon canons' journeys show that Guibert was unenthusiastic about relic tours in general, but he took at least some of the miracles of 1112 and 1113 seriously.[1]

Monodies dates to circa 1115, only a few years after the tours. Guibert may have had access to the notes from which Herman worked or interviewed participants, likely both, since the narrative moves back and forth from first to third person. Herman did not begin to craft his much longer account of the tours until nearly a quarter century after they took place, so many eyewitnesses would have died in the interim. Guibert's versions, then, provide an important alternative record of the canons' tours in 1112 and 1113.

At the very end of his description of the events in Laon in 1111–12 and the relic tours of 1112 and 1113, Guibert offers a short version of the story of kleptomania with which Herman of Tournai concludes *The Miracles of St. Mary of Laon*. In Guibert's telling, Anselm is not the only robber of the church's treasury, but the most brazen. Herman's Anselm is a more subtle criminal.

Text: Guibert de Nogent, *Autobiographie*, ed. and trans. Labande, 378–92 and 416–22. A recent translation is Guibert of Nogent, *Monodies*, 150–54 and 164–66.

12. . . . . Meanwhile, according to the practice, such as it is, of raising money, they began to have the feretories and the relics of the saints carried around. Hence it happened that the holy Judge, who on the one hand punishes people and on the other mercifully comforts them, worked many miracles wherever they went. Carried along with a box of no particular distinction there was a magnificent phylactery containing a scrap of the virgin mother's tunic, a piece of the sponge lifted to the Savior's mouth, and a fragment of his cross. Whether there was some of Our Lady's hair I do not know. The phylactery was made of gold and gems, with verses engraved in the gold chanting the mysteries inside it.[2]

Coming into Touraine on their second journey, they reached a town called Buzançais, the outpost of a plunderer.[3] They preached a sermon to the people concerning, among other things, the disaster that had struck their church.[4] When our clerics had sensed that the lord and his townsfolk bore ill will toward our words and intended to rob them as they left the castle, the one who had the duty of public speaking was placed in a difficult position. Although he had no faith in what he promised, he nonetheless said to the people standing around, "If there is a sick person among you, let him come to the holy relics, and once he has drunk water the relics have touched, he will surely be healed." The lord and the men of his castle were pleased to hear this because they supposed they would reveal the clerics as liars from their own words. They brought the speaker a mute and deaf boy about twenty years old.

No one can say how much danger and distress bore down on the clerics at that moment. But while beseeching the Lady of all and her only son Lord Jesus with deep sighs, the anxious priest asked some question or another of the one who had drunk the holy water. He immediately replied clearly, not with an answer to the question, but with the very same words the priest had spoken. He, who had never heard anything, did not know what to say except what was said to him. Why should I linger? In a poor town, hearts were at once made more generous toward the canons. The town's lord soon offered up the only horse he had, while the largesse of the others nearly exceeded their means. They became such advocates of those whose betrayers they had wanted to be—and who were praising God for his help amid many tears—that they handed over the youth who had been healed to be a permanent attendant on the holy relics. I saw him in our church at Nogent, a dullard awkward in all expression and understanding. A faithful reporter of so great a miracle, he died not long after in the course of his duty.

In the city of Angers there was a woman who had married as a girl.[5] In her childhood she had placed a ring on a little finger that she wore day and night, irretractably, if I might put it that way.[6] Therefore, as the years passed, the young girl grew heavier, and the flesh around the ring, protruding from both sides of it, had nearly covered the metal. Hence any hope of getting it off her finger had vanished. With the arrival of the holy relics and after the sermon was finished, she had come along with other women to make an offering. When she had stretched out her hand toward the reliquary to put down the silver she had brought, the ring cracked and slipped from her hand in front of the relics. The people, especially the women, on seeing what a great favor the virgin mother had conferred on this woman—one she herself did not even dare to ask for—well, it is impossible to count the coins they gave, women in particular offering necklaces and rings. Touraine, suffused with the sweet smell of the miracles of the Lady of all, rejoiced. But Anjou boasted that it had the Mother of God at hand.

Elsewhere (in what town this took place I cannot say exactly, but it was in the same diocese) the clerics sent the relics at her urgent request to an honorable woman who had suffered a hopeless illness for a very long time. When she had venerated the relics with all her heart, she drank the holy water in which they had been bathed and recovered at once: Mary was her healer. And when she had honored God's relics with fitting offerings and the relic bearer had just stepped out of her house, a boy on horseback, pulling a carriage, blocked the middle of the lane the relic bearer was intending to cross. The cleric said to the boy, "Stay there until the relics have gone past." And when the relic bearer had gone past and the boy began to spur his horse forward to continue on his way, he struggled to no avail. The relic bearer looked back and said, "Go in the name of the Lord!" At these words, both horse and carriage went forward. See what you can do in Mary and what reverence she demands for herself!

On the third journey they happened to reach the castle of Nesle. Ralph, the lord of the castle, had in his house a young deaf and mute man who, they claimed, had knowledge of divination (doubtless from demons), and the lord was also said to love him greatly on this account. The holy relics, carried into the castle, were honored by the people with quite meager offerings. However, the young man—who knew through signs about the healing of the abovementioned deaf and mute man, who indeed seemed present to him—donated his shoes to a poor man and followed the holy relics to the monastery of Lihons, barefoot and with a remorseful heart.[7]

One day as he slept under the feretory, it came time for the midday meal, so most of the clerics left to eat while a few stayed behind to guard the relics. Then they also left the church for a short stroll. On returning they found the man lying on the ground, writhing in such torment that blood was gushing from his mouth and ears with a terrible stench. At this sight, the clerics hastened to summon their comrades who had left to eat, so they could witness the scene of such a miracle. When the man stopped convulsing, the clerics tried to see whether he could speak by asking him some question or another. He immediately replied with the same words he had heard from the questioner. All raised countless praises to God on high. Who could describe their jubilation? At last they were compelled by all sorts of pleading to return to the town of Nesle so that the people could fully make up for the paltry amounts they had offered the relics the first time, and this was done most excellently. Here, too, Our Lady—whose son, as God, completed the gifts of nature he had until then withheld—shone in glory.

13. From there, intending to seek lands overseas, on reaching the English Channel they were carried through calm seas by favorable winds on the same ship as some rich merchants.[8] And behold! they saw the ships of savage pirates, whom they greatly feared, bearing down on them from the opposite direction. The pirates' oars swept the waves as they sailed, their ships' prows parting the cresting waves. They were hardly a mile away from our people and the bearers of the relics, who along with the crew were terrified. Then one of our priests rose from their midst and lifting up the phylactery that contained the relics of the queen of heaven forbade the pirates to approach in the name of the Son and the Mother. At this command, their ships turned astern and [retreated][9] just as quickly as they had approached: hence the praise, hence the glory among those saved. The merchants, to give thanks to good Mary, offered her a great deal of money.

Therefore, successfully conveyed to England, when they reached the city of Winchester many miracles shone forth there. In Exeter, too, they occurred in equal number, the inspiration for many gifts. Let us remain silent about the usual remedies for illnesses, touching only on the unusual ones.[10] We are not writing an account of their journey—let them write it themselves—nor picking out all the events individually, but only those that preach.

Welcomed almost everywhere with fitting reverence, when the clerics had come to a certain village, the priest did not let them into the church nor the peasants into their homes. They found two uninhabited buildings there. Settling themselves and all their belongings in one, they fitted out the other for the holy relics. These most wicked people persisted in stiff resistance to divine matters and the next day, when the clerics had departed the place, behold! a thunderclap forced a terrifying lightning bolt from the clouds that upon striking destroyed the settlement and reduced all its dwellings to ash. O wondrous judgment of God! Although the two houses in which the clerics had stayed were located amid the others that were burning, they were spared, so God might give a manifest sign that those wretches suffered that fire because they had shown no reverence for the Mother of God. But the vile priest, who had increased cruelty among the barbarians he should have taught, upon collecting his possessions rejoiced that he had snatched them away from the heaven-sent fire. Planning to flee, he had gone to a river or the sea, I do not know which, planning to cross. There everything he had gathered up and endeavored to carry away was destroyed by repeated lightning strikes. Thus savage, dissolute people learned to understand the mysteries of God through their punishment.

They came to some other town where, in accordance with the holy relics' reputation and proof of their miracles, various offerings came forth. An English man standing in front of the church said to his friend, "Let's go drinking." The friend replied, "I don't have any money." The man said, "I'll get you some." "Where will you find it?" the friend asked. "I'm thinking of those clerics who are bilking fools with their lies and trickery. Obviously, I'm going to try somehow to collect some money for my own entertainment." So he said and entered the church. He approached the platform on which the relics had been placed and, pretending that he wanted to venerate them with a kiss, closing in he slurped into his gaping mouth some silver coins that had been offered. Returning to his friend he said, "Come on, let's drink together. Now I've got enough money to pay our tab." His friend asked, "Where did you get it when you didn't have it before?" "It's what I stole with my mouth from offerings to those frauds in the church," the man said. "You did a bad thing. You robbed the saints," said his friend. The man replied, "Shut up and go to the tavern over there." Why go on and on? They drank until it was almost sunset. But as evening fell, the one who had stolen money from the sacred altars mounted his horse and announced he was going home. When he had reached a nearby wood, he made a noose and hanged himself from a tree. Dying shamefully, he paid the penalty for his sacrilegious mouth.

Of the many things the mighty virgin performed among the English, let these we have mentioned suffice.

15. Before we turn to events nearby—we will mention some people from around Soissons—it must be known that the people of Laon do more abominable things than those in any other province of France. After they killed priests, a bishop, and an archdeacon,[11] most recently her own serf, a native of Laon, killed Abbess Rainsende of Saint-Jean, the cleverest of women, noble of birth, and a benefactor of the church.[12] This she suffered for faithfulness to her church. And what did that church lack in the way of sacrilege? Because the queen of all did not allow such things to go unavenged, I will proceed as fitting.

Some men called wardens, poor servants who keep careful watch over church treasures, began to steal vessels used in services and shift the blame onto their masters, the clerics (they were laymen, of course). The first theft was accomplished by several of them. In the second one, Anselm, a savage peasant and lowly native of the city, snatched away crosses, chalices, and other gold items before Matins during Christmas week. Some time later, he took a little lump of stolen gold to sell to a merchant in Soissons, revealing the sacrilege he had committed.[13] He extracted an oath from the merchant that he would not betray him. Meanwhile, the merchant heard that accomplices in this theft were being excommunicated in the parishes of Soissons; alerted to this, he went to Laon and divulged the matter to a cleric. Why go on and on? Summoned to judgment, Anselm denied the story. The merchant, after putting up guarantees to the contrary, called out Anselm for a duel, which the latter did not put off. Brought together on a Sunday through the haste of a cleric, the one who had called out the thief fell in defeat. There are two possible explanations: either the one who had revealed the theft by breaking his oath had acted badly or, what is much more likely, he had acted according to a completely illicit law. Certainly no canon agrees with this law.[14]

His victory made Anselm bolder, and he burst forth in a third sacrilege. Through some contrivance that cannot be described, he broke into the treasury and made off with a great deal of gold and gems. After this theft, he was subjected to trial by holy water. Anselm was plunged into the water with the other wardens and floated to the surface, convicted along with others who were party to the first theft. Some of them were hanged, others spared. Dragged to the gallows with the others, Anselm promised that he would talk, but once taken down he refused. Led to the gallows a second time, he swore that he would reveal what had happened. Released again, he said, "I won't do anything without a reward." They answered, "You'll be hanged." "And then you'll have nothing," he answered. Amid all this, he hurled numberless insults at the castellan Nicolas, the son of Guimar, an illustrious young man in charge of the proceedings. The bishop and Master Anselm consulted about what they should do. "It is better," they declared, "that he be given some money than that we lose an enormous amount of gold." They agreed to payment of about five hundred silver pennies. Once guarantees were made, Anselm returned much of the gold hidden in his vineyard.

Anselm had promised to leave the region, and the bishop had given him assurance of three days' grace. Because he wanted to slip away in secrecy during that time, he familiarized himself with all the ways out of the city. The appearance of wide rivers completely blocked his way out. These flowing waters visible only to him forced him to leave openly, without any profit from his theft. When the time came for him to leave, he spoke in a great rage, saying he did not want to go. As the bishop pressured him, he began to mutter like someone out of his mind that he still knew things he had put off revealing. When the bishop had learned of this from his vidame, he seized the opportunity to take back the money he had intended to give Anselm—who had sworn that he knew nothing more—and imprison him. Compelled by torture, he confessed that he had gems from a broken work of art. Leading them to the spot, he pointed them out, dangling in linen cloth under a rock. Along with all that, he had also stolen holy phylacteries; as long as he kept them he was unable to sleep because the saints terrified his savage mind until horror at his great sacrilege assailed him. Therefore he was hanged, "set beside his fathers" [Acts 13:36], who were clearly demons.

Notes

1. For the quotation from his treatise on relics, see Guibert of Nogent, *Monodies*, 214.

2. Herman of Tournai reports that the reliquary contained some of Mary's hair as noted in an engraving on it (Book II, preface). Is Guibert genuinely ignorant or skeptical about the relic's authenticity? He does not mention the cloth relics of Jesus Herman reports but says there was a relic of the cross, which Herman does not note.

3. Guibert implies there was a tour before the ones he and Herman record. Since the journey in central and western France began only six weeks after the uprising and fire in Laon, a first tour would have been local and brief. Given the recent disruption in Laon and nearby areas, it is unlikely to have been very lucrative.

4. Guibert provides a detail Herman omits: public address to explain the canons' presence.

5. The miracles recounted in this paragraph and the next are absent from Herman's narrative of the French tour.

6. Guibert liked to invent new words. *Irrectractabiliter* ("irretractably") is one of them.

7. Lihons-en-Santerre, founded at an unknown date in the early Middle Ages, was just under ten miles northwest of Nesle.

8. Oddly, Guibert refers to the English Channel as the "Mediterranean Ocean."

9. At least one word is missing from the Latin text. The meaning is clear.

10. "Remedies" translates *medicinas*; Guibert may be suggesting that the canons had some skill in secular, nonmiraculous healing that Herman of Tournai mentions.

11. Guibert refers to the events of April 1112.

12. Rainsende was murdered on August 6, 1112.

13. It seems that Anselm had already melted down some of the stolen gold.

14. Here a "canon" is an article of church law. On trial by combat and trial by water, which occurs in the next paragraph, see *The Miracles of St. Mary of Laon*, III, 28.

APPENDIX 5

Emendations to the text of Hugh Farsit, *A Little Book of Miracles of the Blessed Virgin Mary in the City of Soissons*

On the printed editions of Hugh Farsit's collection, see the end of the introduction to the translation of it. They are sufficiently flawed to make them incomprehensible at numerous points. The following handlist, derived from five manuscripts dating to the twelfth and thirteenth centuries, show the readings I have used instead of those in *PL* 179:1777–1800. The initial number in each entry identifies the *PL* column and section where the text requires emendation. The manuscripts consulted are the following:

P, folios 62r–76v; early thirteenth century; complete
P2, folios 35v–41v; late twelfth century; prologue and sections 1–3, 5–14
P3, folios 39v–48r; twelfth century but after 1143; prologue, sections 1–4, the beginning of section 5, most of section 19, sections 20–31
P4, folios 61r–72v; late thirteenth century; complete
P5, folios 51r–59v; thirteenth century; complete

1777B: reading *tabificus* with P, P3, P4, and P5, *tabeficus* with P2 for *tobificus*

1779A: reading *vincere* with P, P2, P3, P4, and P5 for *cedere*

1779B: reading *valitudo* with P2 and P3 for *valida*

1779C: reading *iunctis* with P2, P3, and P4 for *cunctis*

1779C: reading *dati* with P, P2, P3, P4, and P5 for *dari*

1779D: reading *huius* with P, P2, P3, P4, and P5 for *usus*

1780A: reading *annotati* with P2 and P3 for *advocati*

1780D: reading *movisti* with P, P4, and P5 for *novisti*

1781B: reading *horrorem* with P2, P4, and P5 for *honorem*

1781C: reading *Quid faceret* with P, P2, P4, and P5 for *Qui faceret*

1781C: reading *odio et maledictis* with P2, P4, and P5 for *odio maledictis*

1781C: inserting *fugientem* with P, P2, P4, and P5 between *frigescentem* and *fidem*

1782A: reading *inolescere* with P, P2, and P4, for *indolescere*

1782A: reading *reformatis* with P, P2, P4, and P5 for *deformi*

1782B: reading *nos* with P, P2, P4, and P5 for *dos*

1782C: reading *familiolae* with P, P4, and P5 for *familiae*

1782C: reading *adcreditato* with P and P4 for *adscreditato*

1782C: reading *utpote qui* with P, P4, and P5 for *utpote quo*

1783A: reading *auditui* with P, P2, P4, and P5 for *auditum*

1783B: reading *desertor* with P, P2, P4, and P5 for *desertus*

1783B: reading *cernitis* with P, P2, P4, and P5 for *certinis*

1783B: reading *toto anno* with P, P2, P4, and P5 for *toto animo*

1783C: reading *flagraret* with P, P2, P4, and P5 for *flagitaret*

1783D: reading *sane* with P and P2 for *satis*

1785B: reading *respectans* with P, P2, P4, and P5 for *expectans*

1785B: reading *protractam* with P and P2 for *protactam*

1785D: reading *constituta* with P, P2, P4, and P5 for *constitua*

1785D: reading *omnia nota facta* with P2, P4, and P5 for *omnia facta*

1786D: reading *viribus* with P, P2, P4, and P5 for *virtutibus*

1786D: reading *flagitantibus* with P, P2, P4, and P5 for *flagrantibus*

1787B: reading *elapsum dependentem in facie oculum* with P and P4, *elapsum in facie dependentem oculum* with P2 and P5 for *pendentem in facie oculum*

1787D: reading *integerrime* with P, P2, P4, and P5 for *integerrimae*

1788D: reading *Hac ergo* with P, P4, and P5 for *Haec ergo*

1790D: reading *discriminatae et* with P, P4, and P5 for *discriminatae at*

1791C: reading *ecclesiam piae memoriae beatae* with P, P4, and P5 for *ecclesiam beatae*

1791C: reading *aliqua* with P, P3, P4, and P5 for *Gallica*

1792A: reading *facti* with P, P3, P4, and P5 for *facit*

1792A: inserting *sed mox perterriti ob horrorem inhumanae visionis pertransibant* with P, P3, P4, and P5 between *subsistebant* and *vota*

1793D: reading *confusione* with P3 for *confessione*

1794D: inserting *iuxta* with P, P3, P4, and P5 between *locus* and *castrum*

1795B: inserting *de pane illo* with P, P3, P4, and P5 between *illo* and *a Deo*

1795C: reading *convaluit et sicut* with P, P3, P4, and P5 for *convaluit ei sicut*

1795C: full stop after *habuerimus* with P, P3, P4, and P5

1796A: reading *illuc* with P, P3, P4, and P5 for *illud*

1796A: reading *claustra* with P, P3, P4, and P5 for *claustras*

1798D: reading *iacentibus* with P, P3, P4, and P5 for *latentibus*

1798D: reading *non lucentem ingerit* with P, P3, P4, and P5 for *non lucem ingerit*

1799B: reading *millesimo centesimo xxx° ii°* (P), *millesimo centesimo trecesimo secundo* (P3), *m° c° xxx° ii°* (P4), *m° centesimo tricesimo secundo* (P5) for *1102*

1799C: reading *census* with P, P3, P4, and P5 for *caesus*

1800A: reading *vultus* with P, P3, P4, P5 for *ulterius*

1800C: reading *attendebant* with P, P3, and P4 for *ostendebant*

1800C: reading *quibus dum* with P, P3, P4, and P5 for *quibusdam*

BIBLIOGRAPHY

Manuscripts Consulted

Paris, Bibliothèque nationale de France, MS lat. 2333A
Paris, Bibliothèque nationale de France, MS lat. 2855
Paris, Bibliothèque nationale de France, MS lat. 2873
Paris, Bibliothèque nationale de France, MS lat. 12593
Paris, Bibliothèque nationale de France, MS lat. 16565
Paris, Bibliothèque nationale de France, MS lat. 17491
Troyes, Médiathèque Jacques Chirac, MS 433

Primary Sources

Actes des évêques de Laon des origines à 1151. Ed. Annie Dufour-Malbezin. Paris: CNRS, 2001.

Adgar. *Le Gracial: Miracles de la Vierge*. Ed. and trans. Jean-Louis Benoit. Turnhout: Brepols, 2020.

The Annals of Flodoard of Reims, 919–966. Ed. and trans. Steven Fanning and Bernard S. Bachrach. Toronto: University of Toronto Press, 2011.

The Book of Sainte Foy. Trans. Pamela Sheingorn. Philadelphia: University of Pennsylvania Press, 1995.

The Cartulary of Prémontré. Ed. Yvonne Seale and Heather Wacha. Toronto: University of Toronto Press, 2023.

The Chronography of Robert of Torigni. Ed. and trans. Thomas N. Bisson. 2 vols. Oxford: Oxford University Press, 2020.

Galbert of Bruges. *The Murder, Betrayal, and Slaughter of the Glorious Charles, Count of Flanders*. Trans. Jeff Rider. New Haven, CT: Yale University Press, 2013.

Gautier de Coinci. *The Miracle of Theophilus*. Ed. and trans. Jerry Root. Kalamazoo, MI: Medieval Institute Publications, 2022.

Gautier de Coinci. *Les Miracles de Nostre Dame*. Ed. V. Frederic Koenig. 4 vols. Geneva: Droz, 1966–70.

Gautier de Coincy. "Miracles of the Virgin Mary." Trans. Renate Blumenfeld-Kosinski, in *Medieval Hagiography: An Anthology*, ed. Thomas Head, 627–53. New York: Routledge, 2000.

[Gautier de Compiègne]. *De miraculis B. Virginis Mariae*. Ed. Philippe Labbe, in *Novae bibliothecae manuscriptorum librorum tomus primus-secundus*, 650–53. Paris: S. and G. Cramoisy, 1657. Reprinted in *PL* 173:1379–86.

Gothic Art 1140–c. 1450: Sources and Documents. Ed. Teresa G. Frisch. Toronto: University of Toronto Press, 1987.

Gregory of Tours. *A History of the Franks*. Trans. Lewis Thorpe. Harmondsworth: Penguin, 1974.

Guibert de Nogent. *Autobiographie*. Ed. and trans. Edmond-René Labande. Paris: Les Belles Lettres, 1981.

Guibert of Nogent. *De laude sanctae Mariae*. PL 156:537–78.

Guibert of Nogent. *Monodies and On the Relics of the Saints: The Autobiography and a Manifesto of a French Monk from the Time of the Crusades*. Trans. Joseph McAlhany and Jay Rubenstein. New York: Penguin, 2011.

[Haimo of Saint-Pierre-sur-Dives]. *Histoire des miracles qui se sont faits par l'entremise de la Sainte Vierge dans la première restauration de l'église de l'abbaye de Saint-Pierre-sur-Dive*. Trans. Léonce de Glanville. Rouen: Fleury, 1851.

[Haimo of Saint-Pierre-sur-Dives]. "Lettre de l'abbé Haimon sur la construction de l'église de Saint-Pierre-sur-Dive, en 1145." Ed. Léopold Delisle, in *Bibliothèque de l'école des chartes* 21 (1860): 113–39.

Hériman de Tournai [=Herman of Tournai]. *Les Miracles de Sainte Marie de Laon*. Ed. and trans. Alain Saint-Denis. Paris: CNRS, 2008.

[Herman of Tournai]. *Liber de restauratione ecclesie Sancti Martini Tornacensis*. Ed. R. B. C. Huygens. Turnhout: Brepols, 2010.

Herman of Tournai. *The Restoration of the Monastery of Saint Martin of Tournai*. Trans. Lynn H. Nelson. Washington, DC: Catholic University of America Press, 1996.

[Herman of Tournai]. *Vita S. Hildefonsi Toletani Episcopi*. In *Acta sanctorum ordinis sancti Benedicti in saeculorum classes distributa: Saeculum secundum quod est ab anno Christi DC ad DCC*. Ed. Luc d'Achery and Jean Mabillon, 498–500. Paris: Savreux, 1669.

Hugh Farsit. "Miracles de la Sainte Vierge arrivez en l'Eglise de l'abbaye royale de Notre-Dame de Soissons." Ed. Michel Germain, in *Histoire de l'abbaye de Notre-Dame de Soissons*, 481–504. Paris: Coignard, 1675. Reprinted as *Libellus de miraculis beatae Mariae Virginis in urbe Suessionensi* in PL 179:1777–1800.

[Ildefonsus of Toledo]. *A Translation from Latin into English of De virginitate perpetua Sanctae Mariae = The Perpetual Virginity of Holy Mary*. Trans. Malcolm Drew Donalson. Lewiston, NY: Mellen Press, 2011.

Jean Le Marchant, *Miracles de Notre-Dame de Chartres*. Ed. Pierre Kunstmann. Ottawa: L'Université d'Ottawa, 1973.

[John, son of Peter]. *Miracula ecclesiae Constantiensis*. Ed. Richard Allen, in "The Norman Episcopate, 989–1110," 1:483–502. PhD diss., University of Glasgow, 2009.

Medieval Latin Lives of Muhammad. Ed. and trans. Julien Yolles and Jessica Weiss. Cambridge, MA: Harvard University Press, 2018.

The Miracles of Our Lady of Rocamadour: Analysis and Translation. Trans. Marcus Bull. Woodbridge: Boydell, 1999.

Miracula beatae Mariae virginis in Carnotensi ecclesia facta. Ed. Antoine Thomas, in "Les miracles de Notre-Dame de Chartres," *Bibliothèque de l'école des chartes* 42 (1881): 505–50.

Norbert and Early Norbertine Spirituality. Trans. Theodore J. Antry and Carol Neel. New York: Paulist Press, 2007.

Patrologia cursus completus, Series latina. Ed. J.-P. Migne. 221 vols. Paris: J.-P. Migne, 1844–64.

The Penguin Book of Dragons. Ed. Scott G. Bruce. New York: Penguin, 2021.

The Rule of Saint Benedict. Ed. and trans. Bruce L. Venarde. Cambridge, MA: Harvard University Press, 2011.

Songs of Holy Mary of Alfonso X, the Wise: A Translation of the Cantigas de Santa Maria. Trans. Kathleen Kulp-Hill. Tempe: Arizona Center for Medieval and Renaissance Studies, 2000.

Suger. *The Deeds of Louis the Fat*. Trans. Richard C. Cusimano and John Moorhead. Washington, DC: Catholic University of America Press, 1992.

William of Malmesbury. *The Miracles of the Blessed Virgin Mary*. Trans. R. M. Thomson and M. Winterbottom. Woodbridge: Boydell, 2017.

Secondary Studies

Allen, Richard. "The Norman Episcopate, 989–1110." 2 vols. PhD diss., University of Glasgow, 2009.

Barnes, Carl F., Jr. "The Cult of Carts." In *The Dictionary of Art*, ed. Jane Turner, 8:257–59. New York: Grove, 1996.

Bartlett, Robert. *Why Can the Dead Do Such Great Things? Saints and Worshippers from the Martyrs to the Reformation*. Princeton, NJ: Princeton University Press, 2013.

Becquet, Jean. *Abbayes et prieurés de l'ancienne France*. Vol. 7, *Province ecclésiastique de Reims, diocèse actuel de Soissons*. *Revue Mabillon*, extra series, 303–4 (Ligugé: Abbaye Saint-Martin, 1986).

Berard, Christopher Michael. "King Arthur and the Canons of Laon." *Arthuriana* 26 (2016): 91–119.

Berman, Constance Hoffman. *The White Nuns: Cistercian Abbeys for Women in Medieval France*. Philadelphia: University of Pennsylvania Press, 2018.

Bisson, Thomas N. *The Crisis of the Twelfth Century: Power, Lordship, and the Origins of European Government*. Princeton, NJ: Princeton University Press, 2009.

Black, Winston. *The Middle Ages: Facts and Fictions*. Santa Barbara, CA: ABC-CLIO, 2019.

Bonde, Sheila, and Clark Maines, eds. *Saint-Jean-des-Vignes in Soissons: Approaches to Its Architecture, Archaeology and History*. Turnhout: Brepols, 2003.

Bouchard, Constance Brittain. *Negotiation and Resistance: Peasant Agency in High Medieval France*. Ithaca, NY: Cornell University Press, 2022.

Bouillie, Christian. *L'Abbaye de Saint-Pierre-sur-Dives*. Lisieux: L'Association Le Pays d'Auge, 2012.

Bourgin, Georges. *La Commune de Soissons et le groupe communal soissonnais*. Paris: Honoré Champion, 1908.

Bowers, Barbara S., and Linda Migl Keyser, eds. *The Sacred and the Secular in Medieval Healing: Sites, Objects, and Texts*. Abingdon: Routledge, 2016.

Braegelmann, Athanasius. *The Life and Writings of Saint Ildefonsus of Toledo*. Washington, DC: Catholic University of America Press, 1942.

Brown, Peter. *The Cult of the Saints: Its Rise and Function in Latin Christianity*. 2nd ed. Chicago: University of Chicago Press, 2015.

Bruce, Scott G. *Silence and Sign Language in Medieval Monasticism: The Cluniac Tradition, c. 900–1200*. Cambridge: Cambridge University Press, 2007.

Bur, Michel. *La formation du comté de Champagne, v. 950–v. 1150*. Nancy: Publications de l'Université de Nancy II, 1977.

Clark, Anne L. "Guardians of the Sacred: The Nuns of Soissons and the Slipper of the Virgin Mary." *Church History* 76 (2007): 724–49.

Clayton, Mary. *The Cult of the Virgin Mary in Anglo-Saxon England*. Cambridge: Cambridge University Press, 1990.

Colish, Marcia. "When Did the Middle Ages End? Reflections of an Intellectual Historian." In *Schooling and Society: The Ordering and Recording of Knowledge in the Western Middle Ages*, ed. Alasdair A. MacDonald and Michael W. Twomey, 213–24. Louvain: Peeters, 2004.

Constable, Giles. "Herman of Tournai and the Monastery of Saint Vincent at Valencia." In *Praise No Less Than Charity: Studies in Honor of M. Chrysogonus Waddell, Monk of Gethsemani Abbey*, ed. E. Rozanne Elder, 85–104. Kalamazoo, MI: Cistercian Publications, 2002.

Constable, Giles. "The Letter of Hugh of Soissons to the Premonstratensian Abbots." In *Cristianità ed Europa: Miscellanea di studi in onore di Luigi Prosdocimi*, ed. Cesare Alzati, 1:249–63. Rome: Herder, 1994.

Constable, Giles. *The Reformation of the Twelfth Century*. Cambridge: Cambridge University Press, 1996.

Craig, Kate M. *Mobile Saints: Relic Circulation, Devotion, and Conflict in the Central Middle Ages*. Abingdon: Routledge, 2021.

Finucane, Ronald C. *The Rescue of the Innocents: Endangered Children in Medieval Miracles*. New York: St. Martin's Press, 1997.

Foscati, Alessandra. *Saint Anthony's Fire from Antiquity to the Eighteenth Century*. Trans. Francis Gordon. Amsterdam: Amsterdam University Press, 2019.

Freeman, Charles. *Holy Bones, Holy Dust: How Relics Shaped the History of Medieval Europe*. New Haven, CT: Yale University Press, 2011.

Geary, Patrick J. *Furta Sacra: Thefts of Relics in the Central Middle Ages*. Rev. ed. Princeton, NJ: Princeton University Press, 1990.

Geary, Patrick J. *Living with the Dead in the Middle Ages*. Ithaca, NY: Cornell University Press, 1994.

Gerits, T. D. "La lettre de Hugues Farsit aux abbés prémontrés réunis à Coblence." *Revue d'ascétique et de mystique* 41 (1965): 473–83.

Germain, Michel. *Histoire de l'abbaye de Notre-Dame de Soissons*. Paris: Coignard, 1675.

Giraud, Cédric. "Écrire l'histoire d'une âme au XIIᵉ siècle: L'*Otium ad Helwidem sororem* d'Hugues de Soissons." In *Rerum gestarum scriptor: Histoire et historiographie au Moyen Age. Mélanges Michel Sot*, ed. Magali Coumert, Marie-Céline Isaïa, Klaus Krönert, and Sumi Shimahara, 649–59. Paris: Presses de l'Université Paris-Sorbonne, 2012.

d'Haenens, Albert. "Hériman." In *Nouvelle Biographie Nationale*, 1:163–71. Brussels: Académie royale des sciences, des lettres et des beaux-arts de Belgique, 1988.

Hahn, Cynthia. *The Reliquary Effect: Enshrining the Sacred Object.* London: Reaktion, 2017.

Hahn, Cynthia. *Strange Beauty: Issues in the Making and Meaning of Reliquaries, 400–circa 1204.* University Park: Pennsylvania University Press, 2012.

Hallam, Elizabeth M., and Charles West. *Capetian France, 987–1328.* 3rd ed. Abingdon: Routledge, 2020.

Huygens, R. B. C. "Herman von Tournai—Herman von Laon." *Mittellateinisches Jahrbuch* 43 (2008): 498–502.

Huygens, R. B. C. *La tradition manuscrite de Guibert de Nogent.* Steenbrugis: in Abbatia S. Petri, 1991.

Ihnat, Kati. *Mother of Mercy, Bane of the Jews: Devotion to the Virgin Mary in Anglo-Norman England.* Princeton, NJ: Princeton University Press, 2016.

Justice, Steven. "Did the Middle Ages Believe in Their Miracles?" *Representations* 103 (2008): 1–29.

Katajala-Peltomaa, Sari, Jenni Kuuliala, and Iona McCleery, eds. *A Companion to Medieval Miracle Collections.* Leiden: Brill, 2021.

Katajala-Peltomaa, Sari, Jenni Kuuliala, and Iona McCleery. "Introduction: Miracle Collections and Their Contexts." In *A Companion to Medieval Miracle Collections,* ed. Sari Katajala-Peltomaa, Jenni Kuuliala, and Iona McCleery, 1–14. Leiden: Brill, 2021.

Koopmans, Rachel. *Wonderful to Relate: Miracle Stories and Miracle Collecting in High Medieval England.* Philadelphia: University of Pennsylvania Press, 2011.

Kunkel, Thomas. *Man on Fire: The Life and Spirit of Norbert of Xanten.* De Pere, WI: St. Norbert College Press, 2019.

Kuuliala, Jenni. "Physical Disability and Bodily Difference." In *A Companion to Medieval Miracle Collections,* ed. Sari Katajala-Peltomaa, Jenni Kuuliala, and Iona McCleery, 186–205. Leiden: Brill, 2021.

Larmer, Robert A. "The Meanings of Miracle." In *The Cambridge Companion to Miracles,* ed. Graham H. Twelftree, 36–53. Cambridge: Cambridge University Press, 2011.

Mancia, Lauren. *Emotional Monasticism: Affective Piety in the Eleventh-Century Monastery of John of Fécamp.* Manchester: Manchester University Press, 2019.

McGuire, Brian Patrick. *Bernard of Clairvaux: An Inner Life.* Ithaca, NY: Cornell University Press, 2020.

Mesley, Matthew M., and Louise E. Wilson, eds. *Contextualizing Miracles in the Christian West, 1100–1500: New Historical Approaches.* Oxford: Society for the Study of Medieval Languages and Literature, 2014.

Metzler, Irina. *Disability in Medieval Europe: Thinking about Physical Impairment during the High Middle Ages, c. 1100–1400.* Abingdon: Routledge, 2006.

Murray, Alexander. "Confession Before 1215." *Transactions of the Royal Historical Society* 3 (1993): 51–81.

Niemeyer, Gerlinde. "Die miracula S. Mariae Laudunensis des Abtes Hermann von Tournai: Verfasser und Entstehungszeit." *Deutsches Archiv für Erforschung des Mittelalters* 27 (1971): 135–74.

O'Sullivan, Suzanne. *Is It All in Your Head? True Stories of Imaginary Illness.* New York: Other Press, 2015.

Ott, John S. *Bishops, Authority and Community in Northwestern Europe, c. 1050–1150*. Cambridge: Cambridge University Press, 2015.

Pigeon, E.-A. *Histoire de la cathédrale de Coutances*. Coutances: E. Salettes Fils, 1876.

Porter, Arthur Kingsley. *Medieval Architecture: Its Origins and Development*. 2 vols. New York: Baker and Taylor, 1909.

Ritchey, Sara. *Acts of Care: Recovering Women in Late Medieval Health*. Ithaca, NY: Cornell University Press, 2021.

Roberts, Edward. *Flodoard of Rheims and the Writing of History in the Tenth Century*. Cambridge: Cambridge University Press, 2019.

Rubenstein, Jay. *Guibert of Nogent: Portrait of a Medieval Mind*. New York: Routledge, 2002.

Rubin, Miri. *Mother of God: A History of the Virgin Mary*. New Haven, CT: Yale University Press, 2009.

Saint-Denis, Alain. *Apogée d'une cité: Laon et le Laonnois aux XIIᵉ et XIIIᵉ siècles*. Nancy: Presses universitaires de Nancy, 1994.

Sansterre, Jean-Marie. "Sacralité et pouvoir thaumaturgique des statues mariales (Xᵉ siècle–première moitié du XIIIᵉ siècle)." *Revue Mabillon*, n.s. 22 (=83) (2011): 53–77.

Schulze, Catherine. "Eliminating a 'Cause of Ruin'? Expulsion and Reform at the Abbey of Saint-Jean of Laon, 1128." *Revue bénédictine* 119 (2009): 164–88.

Scott, Robert A. *Miracle Cures: Saints, Pilgrimage, and the Healing Powers of Belief*. Berkeley: University of California Press, 2010.

Shoemaker, Stephen J. "Mary at the Cross, East and West: Maternal Compassion and Affective Piety in the Earliest *Life of the Virgin* and the High Middle Ages." *Journal of Theological Studies*, n.s. 62 (2011): 570–606.

Sigal, Pierre-André. *L'homme et le miracle dans la France médiévale (XIᵉ–XIIᵉ siècle)*. Paris: Cerf, 1985.

Sigal, Pierre-André. "Les voyages de reliques aux onzième et douzième siècles." In *Voyage, quête, pèlerinage dans la littérature et la civilisation médiévales*, 73–104. Aix-en-Provence: Presses universitaires de Provence, 1976.

Signori, Gabriela. *Maria zwischen Kathedrale, Kloster und Welt*. Sigmaringen: Thorbecke, 1995.

Signori, Gabriela. "The Miracle Kitchen and Its Ingredients: A Methodological and Critical Approach to Marian Shrine Wonders (10th to 13th Century)." *Hagiographica* 3 (1996): 277–303.

Tatlock, J. S. P. "The English Journey of the Laon Canons." *Speculum* 8 (1933): 454–65.

Tatlock, J. S. P. "Muriel: The Earliest English Poetess." *Proceedings of the Modern Language Association* 48 (1933): 317–21.

Twelftree, Graham H., ed. *The Cambridge Companion to Miracles*. Cambridge: Cambridge University Press, 2011.

Van Dam, Raymond. *Saints and Their Miracles in Late Antique Gaul*. Princeton, NJ: Princeton University Press, 1993.

Vauchez, André. *Sainthood in the Later Middle Ages*. Trans. Jean Birrell. Cambridge: Cambridge University Press, 1997.

Venarde, Bruce L. *Women's Monasticism and Medieval Society: Nunneries in France and England, 890–1215*. Ithaca, NY: Cornell University Press, 1997.

Vernet, A. "Les 'Loisirs' d'un chanoine de Soissons." *Bulletin de la société nationale des antiquaires de France*, 1961, 108–11.

Ward, Benedicta. *Miracles and the Medieval Mind: Theory, Record and Event, 1000–1215*. Rev. ed. Philadelphia: University of Pennsylvania Press, 1987.

Warner, Marina. *Alone of All Her Sex: The Myth and the Cult of the Virgin Mary*. New York: Knopf, 1976.

Yarrow, Simon. *The Saints: A Short History*. Oxford: Oxford University Press, 2016.

Yarrow, Simon. *Saints and Their Communities: Miracle Stories in Twelfth Century England*. Oxford: Oxford University Press, 2006.

Index

Page numbers followed by letters *m* and *t* refer to maps and tables, respectively.

www.ingramcontent.com/pod-product-compliance
Lightning Source LLC
Chambersburg PA
CBHW060608030726
47498CB00005B/1590